经贸中级汉语口语
Business Chinese Conversation
[Intermediate]

下册 II

主编：黄为之

参加编写人员：杨廷治　陈　辉　黄锡之　杨天舒

　　　　　　　杨立群　苏伯华　成伟武

北京语言大学出版社
BEIJING LANGUAGE AND CULTURE
UNIVERSITY PRESS

图书在版编目(CIP)数据

经贸中级汉语口语.下/黄为之主编.—北京：北京语言大学出版社,2011重印
ISBN 978 - 7 - 5619 - 1978 - 1

Ⅰ.经…　Ⅱ.黄…　Ⅲ.经济－汉语－口语－对外汉语教学－教材　Ⅳ.H195.4

中国版本图书馆 CIP 数据核字（2007）第 174794 号

书　　　名：经贸中级汉语口语 下册
中文编辑：唐琪佳
封面设计：03 工舍
责任印制：汪学发

出版发行：**北京语言大学出版社**
社　　址：北京市海淀区学院路 15 号　邮政编码：100083
网　　址：www.blcup.com
电　　话：发行部　82303650 /3591 /3651
　　　　　编辑部　82303647
　　　　　读者服务部　82303653 /3908
印　　刷：北京外文印刷厂
经　　销：全国新华书店

版　　次：2008 年 1 月第 1 版　2011 年 7 月第 3 次印刷
开　　本：787 毫米×1092 毫米　1 / 16　印张：21.25
字　　数：407 千字　　印数：5001—7000 册
书　　号：ISBN 978 - 7 - 5619 - 1978 - 1 / H·07200
定　　价：52.00 元

第三版前言

这次再版,主要作了四方面的修改:

一、《经贸初级汉语口语》上册,原来只有1~10课的课文配有拼音课文,现在根据外国留学生的要求,为了初学者学习口语的方便,增补了后16课的拼音课文;下册每课练习最后一题的小故事,对初学者也有一定的难度,这次修改也一并删去了。

二、世界发展很快,与时俱进,修改一些陈旧的信息是必要的,如改"对外经济贸易合作部"为"商务部",改"欧洲共同体"为"欧洲联盟",改"关贸总协定"为"世贸组织";欧元流通以后,法国法郎、德国马克等已不再流通,也作了相应修改;书中引用的各种数据,有许多变化,凡是能查到的,都修改征引了最新资料;等等。

三、修改了部分课文、注释和练习,以反映社会生活和经济生活的巨大变化。

四、修订了一些打字排版的错误和书写不规范之处。

这次修订一定还有不尽如人意的地方,欢迎专家、同行、外国朋友和留学生指正。

对外经济贸易大学
黄为之
2006年5月

Preface to the Third Edition

The major changes of this edition include the following four parts:

Firstly, as only texts in the first 10 lessons of *Business Chinese Conversation* (*Elementary*) were supplied with *pinyin* in the previous editions, *pinyin* texts of the other 16 lessons have been added for the convenience of foreign Chinese beginners. Short stories in the last exercise of each lesson in Book Two are deleted to decrease the difficulty for beginners.

Secondly, changing old terms is necessary along with the development of the world. For example, "Ministry of Foreign Trade and Economic Cooperation" has been changed into "Ministry of Commerce", "European Communities" into "European Union" and "General Agreement on Tariffs and Trade" into "World Trade Organization". As francs and marks are taken out of circulation, they are replaced by euros.

Thirdly, some of the notes, exercises and texts have been revised so as to mirror the great changes in social and economic lives.

Fourthly, some typos and nonstandard writings have been corrected.

We realize that this edition is not free of errors and shortcomings, and suggestions from experts, fellow teachers, foreign friends and students are welcome.

Huang Weizhi
University of International
Business and Economics
May, 2006

再 版 前 言

　　《经贸中级汉语口语》1992 年出版后，受到社会各界的热烈欢迎，被各院校和自学者广泛采用。出版至今，中国的经济贸易形势发生了很大变化，有许多新的内容、新的语言需要学习；在教学实践中，我们也积累了经验，听取了各方面的意见，觉得对这本口语教材，现在进行修订、再版，是适时的。

　　2001 年新版《经贸中级汉语口语》，在保持初版体例和优点的基础上，作了全面修改。全书从原来的 20 课增加到 40 课，由一册分为上、下册，原有的内容作了调整，增加了经贸领域出现的新话题、新词语。上册以货物贸易为主要内容，以贸易洽谈为中心，增加了"信用管理"、"网上贸易"等新的国际贸易运作方式；下册以"大经贸"为主要内容，从"全方位开放格局"的角度，展现经济贸易的各个领域，专业内容和专业语言，更加适应当代中国和国际经济贸易实务。我们相信，这个新版本，会在更高的水准上满足教师和学习者的需要。

　　2001 年新版《经贸中级汉语口语》的英语翻译是黄震华教授。

对外经济贸易大学

黄为之

2000 年 2 月

Preface to the Second Edition

Since its publication in 1992, *Business Chinese* (*Intermediate*) has been well-received by people from all walks of life and adopted as textbook by many universities, schools and autodidacts. Since its publication, China's situation of economy and trade has undergone great changes, providing many new contents and expressions worth learning. We have also accumulated considerable experiences in our teaching practice and listened to suggestions and comments from different sources. We feel now it is the right time to revise the book and publish the revised edition.

While maintaining the format and the merits of the first edition, the revised 2001 edition of *Business Chinese* (*Intermediate*) is the outcome of a comprehensive revision. The book has been extended from 20 lessons to 40 lessons, and is now divided into two books. The original contents have been adjusted, with new topics and expressions in the realm of economy and trade added. Book One mainly deals with trade in goods, with business negotiation as its center, with new modes of business operation such as "credit management" and "E-Commerce" added. Book Two takes "broadly based economy and trade" as the main content. From the angle of "the layout of all-round opening", it unfolds the various fields of economy and trade and their specific substance and language, thus being better suited to the contemporary economic and trade practice at home and abroad. We believe that this new edition will, at a higher level, meet the needs of teachers and learners.

The English translation of *Business Chinese* (*Intermediate*) is done by Professor Huang Zhenhua.

Huang Weizhi
University of International
Business and Economics
February, 2000

原 版 前 言

伴随中国对外开放的进程,外国人同中国的经济合作与贸易往来,出现了空前未有的高涨热潮。这种高涨的"经贸热",使大有燎原之势的"世界汉语热"变得更加红火炽热。世界各国的贸易客商,想在华做生意,恨不能三日、五日,十天、半月就学好汉语。为了适应这种"经贸热",满足外国朋友学习经贸汉语的要求,我编写了这本教材。

这本《经贸中级汉语口语》,是供具有初级汉语水平的外国朋友使用的专业汉语教材,共20课,1 016个生词。内容涉及外国人在中国做生意的各个方面,从建立联系渠道,到洽谈的各个环节,乃至近十年来,在中国大地上兴起的"三资"企业、经济特区、开放城市、乡镇企业、农贸集市以及中国的改革开放政策,等等。这些内容,反映了中国实行改革开放以来,对外经济贸易方面的新形势,新课题,新词语。每一课由课文、生词、练习三部分组成。课文都用对话体,是标准的普通话;生词有汉语拼音和英文注释;练习分A、B两大组。A组是重点词语的例解和练习;B组以灵活运用新课文的语言知识为主,适当重现旧课文的语言知识。在B组还有一篇短文,内容风趣,语言生动,为学员提供了当今中国广泛的风俗民情;外国友人在中国做生意,稔熟这些风俗民情也是必不可少的。考虑到经贸中级汉语专业性强,语言难度大,我们特别把20课课文全部译成英文,附在全书之后,这样可减少学习中的困难,帮助外国朋友更准确地理解和运用汉语。书后附有生词总表。

现在常用的对外汉语教材,每一课都由包括"注释"或"词语例释"在内的四部分组成,本书没有完全采用这种体例,省去了"注释"或"例释"部分。我是这样考虑的:凡是需要学生掌握的,就不仅要让学生弄懂,更要让学生会用;所以在"注释"或"例释"之后,应该紧紧伴随适量而有效的练习;如果不要学生掌握,只为理解生词或课文,则只需查查字典或课上点明即可,不需有详尽烦琐的"注释"、"例释",这样,学生可省去许多精力。

对外经济贸易大学对外贸易理论教授孙玉宗先生审阅全部课文,保证了本书经贸专业知识的科学性;由对外经济贸易大学外贸英语系主任黄震华教授负责全书的英文注释和翻译,黄教授在英译过程中,还对本书的内容提过许多宝贵的修改意见;英籍专家 Angela O'Connell 女士校阅过全部英文译文;对外经济贸易大学校长孙维炎教授最后审定了全书。国家对外汉语教学领导小组办公室诸位领导同志,给本书的编写、出版给予了指导和帮助;我校校领导、出版社和外事处的同志们,都给这本书的出版以大力支持。在此,一并表示由衷的感谢。

对外经济贸易大学
黄为之
1991 年 5 月

Preface to the First Edition

Along with China's opening to the outside world, there has emerged an unprecedented upsurge among foreigners in developing economic cooperation and trade contacts with China. This growing "craze in economy and trade" has added to the "world's desire to learn Chinese", which has spread like a prairie fire. In order to do business in China, many businessmen from all over the world wish that they could learn Chinese in no time. Faced with this "craze in economy and trade", we have compiled this textbook so as to meet the desire of foreign friends to learn business Chinese.

Business Chinese (Intermediate), is a Chinese textbook designed for those who have already acquired elementary Chinese for professional purpose. It consists of 20 texts, with 1016 new words and expressions in all. Its contents cover all aspects that concern a foreigner doing business in China, from the channels of establishing relations to all sections in business negotiations. It also introduces such phenomena as the three types of foreign-invested enterprises, special economic zones, open cities, township enterprises, farmers' markets, and China's reform and opening-up policy, which have emerged in China during the past 10 years and more. These contents reflect the new situation, topics and expressions used in foreign economic relations and trade since China's reform and opening to the outside world. Each lesson comprises a text, new words and exercises, three parts in all. All the texts are in dialogue form, written in standard Chinese. The new words and expressions are introduced with *pinyin* and English explanations. Exercises fall into sections A and B. Section A consists of exemplifications and exercises on key words and expressions, while Section B is mainly for the purpose of flexible practice of the linguistic knowledge learned from the new lesson, and also for review of what was learned in previous lessons. Also included in Section B is a short article which is lively and humorous. These short articles provide the learners with broad knowledge about present customs and conditions of the Chinese people. Getting familiar with these customs and conditions of the Chinese people is also indispensable for foreign friends to do business in China. Considering that a textbook of business Chinese at the intermediate level is rather specialized with considerable difficulty of language, we have translated all the 20 Chinese texts into English and attached them to the back of the book. We hope that this will help to reduce the difficulty in learning, and to develop a more accurate understanding of, and a higher level of proficiency in, the Chinese language. A vocabulary list is provided at the back of the book.

The usual format of a Chinese textbook for foreign learners is that each lesson consists of four parts including a part called notes or exemplifications. We have not exactly followed this format in this book, but have omitted the notes and exemplifications. Our reasons are as follows: For the points that the learners should have a good command of, a mere understanding about them is inadequate. We must ensure that the learners can use them competently. Therefore, the notes or exemplifications must be followed by considerable amount of effective exercises. However, for those points that the learners do not have to master, the learners only need to look them up in the dictionary for the sake of understanding the text or the new words, or a brief mentioning in class will be sufficient. There is no need to include detailed notes and exemplifications for these points, and thus a large amount of the learners' energy can be saved.

Professor Sun Yuzong, a professor of foreign trade theories at our University, went over the manuscript so as to ensure that the knowledge embodied in this book about foreign economic relations and trade is correct. Professor Huang Zhenhua, Dean of the Faculty of International Business Communications of our University, did the English translation for all the texts and explanations. In the course of translation, he also gave many valuable suggestions and amendments to the contents of the book. Ms Angela O'Connell, a British expert working at our University, went over the English translation. And Professor Sun Weiyan, President of our University, finalized the manuscript of the whole book. Leading members from the National Office for Teaching Chinese as a Foreign Language have provided concrete guidance and financial support for the compilation and publication of the present book. Leading members from our University, and comrades from our University Press and Foreign Affairs Office have also given substantial support to this book. I hereby extend my heartfelt thanks to all those who have made contributions to the compilation and publication of the present book.

Huang Weizhi
University of International
Business and Economics
May, 1991

使 用 说 明

　　对外汉语教学有许多特点。就学习者来说,他们来自不同国家,不同民族,有不同经历和不同文化背景,在学习汉语时,会明显表现出各自的特殊性和彼此的差异性;就教师来说,每一个教师,都有自己的教学个性和教学经历,教学风格和教学方法。鉴于此,不可能有一个整齐划一的教法与学法,我们这里的"使用说明",仅仅是一个建议,供使用这套《经贸汉语口语》的教师和学习者参考。事实上,许多问题已经在这套书各册的前言中说到了,这里就不再重复,现在只作如下几点补充说明。

　　这套《经贸汉语口语》虽然是从零学起,但它"采用了低起点,大容量,高密度,分阶段而又大步推进的强化训练教学法"。从上面一段话,我们知道,这套书涉及的内容很广,又有相当的难度,一个学期大致要学完一册书,因此,预习和复习,就显得特别重要,尤其是预习,学生更要多花些时间,多下些工夫。像课文中的生词和语法点,书中已有简明扼要的注释,学生可以自学习得,教师只需讲解其中的难点,做些熟巧练习;每一篇课文,应要求学生在预习时,通过学习生词和参看课文的英语翻译,能比较顺畅地阅读下来并基本理解,教师可通过师生互相问答,检验学生阅读与理解的程度,讲解其中的疑难问题;课文中有关文化知识的注释及课文后的一篇短文,也要以自学为主。有些练习,也当作如是处理。不要把有限的课堂时间耗费在课文及相关材料的阅读上,要以课文和这些材料为"谈资",开展生动活泼的谈话;"大容量",要求许多东西在课下消化;"高密度",则要求合理有效地利用时间,强化口语训练。总之,教师与学习者,都要有一个牢固意识,这是一部口语教材,练习口语,习得一口流利的汉语,是这套教材的终极目的。

　　与上述问题相关的,是在教与学的过程中,如何抓住重点。以这套书的《中级口语》和《高级口语》为例,每一课都是生词量大,内容多,篇幅也相对长,企图在一个教学单元时间里(4~6课时),把课文中出现的全部生词和全部内容都学会、都掌握,一般来说,几乎是不可能的。要善于根据课文题目的提示,找出每一课的关键词、重点句和核心内容,学会和掌握这些关键词、重点句和核心内容即可,其余的,在以后的重现中会逐渐习得和熟悉。教材在编写过程中,十分重视新知识的重现率和温故而知新的学习渐进性,老师和学习者都不需担心顾此失彼。

《初级口语》上、下册一共 50 课,每课 4 课时,一周 6 课时;《中级口语》上、下册一共 40 课,每课 4~6 课时,一周 6 课时;《高级口语》上、下册一共 32 课,每课 4 课时,一周 4 课时。如果条件允许,尽可能多安排一些课外实践活动。如《初级口语》,每一个话题都有"课内"和"课外"两篇课文,在学习"课外"一篇课文前,一定要学生走出去,学生在社会上会得到许多新鲜的东西,"课外"课文就变活了;学习《中级口语》时,可以组织去观摩正式谈判,或观看正式谈判录像,也可以到市场演练货物贸易谈判,有做生意经历的学生还可以现身说法;学习《高级口语》时,可围绕一个文化专题组织一些参观、访问和座谈活动。社会实践方式是多种多样的,这里只是举例而已,目的是要把死的文字材料变成活的知识,变成学生可以自由表达的口语能力。

对外经济贸易大学
黄为之
2006 年 10 月

Users' Guide

Teaching Chinese as a foreign language has its own characteristics. The learners are from different countries of different ethnic groups with different life experiences and cultural backgrounds and display their own characteristics in learning Chinese, while the teachers too have their own teaching styles, methods and experiences. Considering this diversity, we do not want to offer a standardized teaching and learning method to use this series of Chinese textbooks. However, we'd like to offer some suggestions for teachers and learners. Since some questions have been discussed in the Preface, we only address several additional points here.

Business Chinese Conversation adopts the teaching method for intensive training characterized by low threshold, large volume of content, high density, and staged and quick progressing in teaching. With a wide range of topics, the content of certain difficulty and the curriculum requirement to finish one volume within a term, it attaches particular importance to the preview and review. Especially for preview students should spend more time and efforts on new words and grammar points and try to learn on their own with the aid of explanations and English translation of the texts. They should read through the texts and gain basic understanding before class. Then in class the teacher can use "questions and answers" to examine their reading comprehension, and will only need to explain the difficult points. The notes on cultural knowledge and the short essays at the end of the lesson should also be learned by students themselves. Some of the exercises should also be handled this way. Don't waste class hours on reading the texts and related materials, which should instead be the "lead" to lively dialogues among the students. "Large volume of content" indicates that lots of content have to be digested after class; "high density" requires effective use of time and intensive training of speaking. All in all, teachers and learners together should be aware that this is a series of textbooks for practicing speaking with the ultimate goal to enable learners to speak fluent Chinese.

Closely related to these questions is the question of how to grasp the key points during teaching and learning. Take the *Intermediate* and *Advanced* of this series for example. In each lesson there are a large number of new words, rich content, and texts of longer length. The attempt to master all the new words and content within a teaching unit (4 ~6 class hours) is almost impossible. Therefore, students should be able to focus on key words, important sentences and core content of each lesson according to the hint of its title. As for the rest, they will achieve the mastery of them in their later reappearance. During the compilation, we put a lot of emphasis on the reoccurring rate of new knowledge and the progressiveness of learning, so the teachers and learners can rest assured of our arrangement.

Altogether the two volumes of *Business Chinese Conversation* (*Elementary*) have 50 lessons, with four class hours for each lesson and six class hours each week. The two volumes of *Business Chinese Conversation* (*Intermediate*) have 40 lessons, with four to six class hours for each lesson and six class hours each week. And the two volumes of *Business Chinese Conversation* (*Advanced*) have 32 lessons, with four class hours for each lesson and four class hours each week. If possible, please arrange extracurricular activities as many as possible. For example, in *Business Chinese Conversation* (*Elementary*), there are usually one text for "in-class learning" and the other for "after-class learning" under each topic. Before learning the latter one, ask the students to go outside, and they can bring in lots of fresh stuff which will enliven the learning. While teaching the *Intermediate*, the teacher can arrange students to watch a real negotiation or one on the video; students can go to practice trade negotiation themselves; and those with experience in doing business can also talk about their own stories about negotiation. While teaching the *Advanced* a variety of social activities like visits, seminars, etc. are also encouraged. Our purpose is to turn the "dead" language materials into "live" knowledge, and enhance the students' ability to express themselves freely in Chinese.

Huang Weizhi
University of International
Business and Economics
October, 2006

目录

Contents

| 第二十一课 Lesson 21 | 对外贸易的开放格局 Opening Pattern of China's Foreign Trade | 1 |

| 第二十二课 Lesson 22 | 技术贸易 Technology Trade | 10 |

| 第二十三课 Lesson 23 | 服务贸易 Service Trade | 19 |

| 第二十四课 Lesson 24 | 工程承包与劳务合作 Project Contracting and Labor Cooperation | 29 |

| 第二十五课 Lesson 25 | 加工贸易 Processing Trade | 39 |

| 第二十六课 Lesson 26 | 零售业的开放 Opening of Retail Trade | 50 |

| 第二十七课 Lesson 27 | 3 月 15 日 Fifteenth of March | 60 |

第二十八课 | **Lesson 28** 金融服务业 Financial Services 70

第二十九课 | **Lesson 29** 资本市场 Capital Market 82

第三十课 | **Lesson 30** 证券和股票市场 Markets of Securities and Stocks 92

第三十一课 | **Lesson 31** 商业保险市场 Market of Commercial Insurance 104

第三十二课 | **Lesson 32** 环保产业市场 Market of Environmental Protection Industry 115

第三十三课 | **Lesson 33** 信息产业市场 Market of Information Industry 127

第三十四课 | **Lesson 34** 知识产权与许可贸易 Intellectual Property Rights and Franchise Trade 139

第三十五课 | **Lesson 35** 倾销与反倾销 Dumping and Antidumping 149

第三十六课 | **Lesson 36** 农业产业化与贸易机会 Industrialization of Agriculture and Trade Opportunities 160

第三十七课 | **Lesson 37** 乡镇企业 Village and Township Enterprises 170

第三十八课
Lesson 38
外商投资企业
Foreign-Invested Enterprises
181

第三十九课
Lesson 39
开放城市和经济特区
Open Cities and Special Economic Zones
194

第四十课
Lesson 40
跨国经营与全球经济一体化
Transnational Operation and Integration
of the World Economy
206

英译课文
English Translations of the Texts
217

生词总表
Vocabulary List
300

21 对外贸易的开放格局

Opening Pattern of China's Foreign Trade

一、中国对外贸易的现状和未来

亨　特：爱德华先生，我介绍一下，这是我的中国朋友江奇先生，在商务部工作。

江　奇：很高兴认识您，爱德华先生！

爱德华：我也很高兴认识您，江先生！

亨　特：江先生，爱德华先生这次来中国作商业旅行，我们公司负责为他安排一切事务。今天是他的第一项日程安排，就把你给请来了。

爱德华：江先生，在20世纪最后一次全球金融危机中，中国的经济不仅没有衰退，反而取得了辉煌成就，实在了不起，所以我来中国作这次商业旅行，要亲眼看看中国。

亨　特：爱德华先生的公司是一家大型跨国公司，在这种大好形势下，他们决定要进一步扩大同中国的合作。

江　奇：这很好啊，我们热烈欢迎！

爱德华：我注意到，这些年，中国的对外贸易取得了长足进步。

江　奇：是的，现在中国的对外贸易排名第三，仅次于美国和德国。

亨　特：中国的经济建设成就和发展蓝图，向世界展示出无限的经济贸易合作机会！

爱德华：是的，是的，所以我们不愿失去机会！

江　奇：那么，爱德华先生有什么打算呢？

爱德华：啊，我得更深入了解中国未来的发展方向。

江　奇:爱德华先生是不是还心存疑虑?

爱德华:那倒也不是。许多外国公司在中国的成功,已经让我羡慕
　　　　不已!

亨　特:爱德华先生是想更清楚知道中国未来有什么新举措。

江　奇:噢,以更加开放的姿态迎接未来! 积极参与世界和区域的
　　　　经济技术合作,大力发展双边和多边贸易关系,加快实现
　　　　市场多元化。

亨　特:这符合全球经济一体化的潮流。

爱德华:世界变得越来越小了,各国人民都需要互相交流,取长补
　　　　短,共同发展。

江　奇:中国人民愿意为此作出更大的贡献。

二、"大经贸"战略

爱德华:江先生,我对您提到的"全方位开放",十分感兴趣,您能说
　　　　得再具体一点儿吗?

江　奇:您可能知道,改革开放以前,中国的对外贸易,基本上是单
　　　　一的货物进出口贸易。

亨　特:好像贸易额也不大。

江　奇:那时我们在世界贸易中的排名是第32位。

爱德华:噢,这与中国这样的大国极不相称。

江　奇:更重要的是极大地阻碍了中国同世界各国的交流与合作,
　　　　束缚了我国国民经济的发展。

爱德华:所以现在要搞"全方位开放"?

江　奇:是的。我们首先是要彻底转变观念,搞大经贸!

爱德华:多大?

江　奇:啊,我们所说的大经贸,是指货物进出口贸易、技术进出口
　　　　贸易和国际服务贸易。

爱德华:这就意味着,中国将从单一货物贸易转向同世界各国全方

位的交流与合作。

亨　特：不是"将从"，中国已经这样做了，而且这几年的发展很快。

爱德华：这样全方位开放，对我们这样的大型跨国集团公司，有巨大的吸引力。

江　奇：这只是贸易领域的开放，我们所说的"全方位开放"，还包括地域的开放，积极、有效地引进与利用外资，在"引进来"的同时，也"走出去"，大力开拓国内和国际两个市场，实现双向交流与合作。

爱德华：这是名副其实的全方位开放！请问，中国对外国人都开放了哪些地域？

江　奇：中国开放的地域，已经从经济特区、沿海开放城市，扩大到了沿边、沿江、省会城市等内陆地区。

亨　特：中国现在正在积极引导外资向中国的中、西部发展。

江　奇：总之，我们已经形成了一个全方位、多层次、多渠道的对外开放格局。

爱德华：这太令人兴奋了！

亨　特：中国有句话，叫"海阔凭鱼跃，天高任鸟飞"，爱德华先生，就看你的了！

爱德华：你们就看好吧！

生　词

1. 格局	géjú	pattern，structure	
2. 现状	xiànzhuàng	present situation	
3. 未来	wèilái	future	
4. 事务	shìwù	work，routine，general affairs	
5. 衰退	shuāituì	decline；recession	
6. 反而	fǎn'ér	on the contrary；instead	
7. 辉煌	huīhuáng	magnificent	

8. 成就	chéngjiù	achievement
9. 长足	chángzú	leaps and bounds
10. 蓝图	lántú	blue print
11. 疑虑	yílǜ	doubt, misgiving
12. 羡慕不已	xiànmù bùyǐ	admire immensely
13. 举措	jǔcuò	move, act
14. 姿态	zītài	posture, pose
15. 迎接	yíngjiē	welcome, usher in
16. 取长补短	qǔ cháng bǔ duǎn	overcome one's own weak points by learning from other's strong points
17. 贡献	gòngxiàn	contribution
18. 相称	xiāngchèn	match, suit, be worthy of
19. 阻碍	zǔ'ài	hinder, block
20. 束缚	shùfù	bind up, restrict
21. 转变	zhuǎnbiàn	change
22. 观念	guānniàn	idea, concept
23. 意味着	yìwèizhe	mean
24. 领域	lǐngyù	domain, realm
25. 地域	dìyù	region, district
26. 引进	yǐnjìn	introduce from elsewhere
27. 双向	shuāngxiàng	two-way
28. 名副其实	míng fù qí shí	the name matches the reality
29. 经济特区	jīngjì tèqū	special economic zone
30. 沿海	yánhǎi	coastal
31. 沿边（境）	yán biān(jìng)	along the border
32. 沿江	yánjiāng	along the river
33. 省会	shěnghuì	provincial capital
34. 内陆	nèilù	inland
35. 引导	yǐndǎo	guide, lead
36. 海阔凭鱼跃，天高任鸟飞	hǎi kuò píng yú yuè, tiān gāo rèn niǎo fēi	the sea is wide enough for all fish to leap and the sky is high enough for all birds to fly

 练 习

A

反而

表示在前文提到的情况下,通常应当产生某种结果,可是实际上产生了相反的结果,在句子中起转折作用,语气也比较强。"反而"常与"不但"、"不仅"等配搭使用,这时"不但"等后面多是否定格式。

On the contrary; instead. It indicates that the circumstances mentioned above should normally bring about a certain result, but actually an opposite result was produced. It plays the role of transition, and the tone is fairly strong. 反而 often collocates with 不但 or 不仅 (not only). In such cases, the part following 不但 is more often than not in the negative form.

一、熟读下列各句,体会"反而"的意义和用法。

1. 他的贡献最大,得到的反而最少。
   contribution *gongxian*
2. 他经历了这次不幸,反而变得更坚强了。
   strong on soul *strong-willing* *grasp/bankrupt* *jianqiang* *unlucky*
3. 在激烈的市场竞争中,这个企业不但没有垮掉,反而更加发展壮大了。
   jilie *fierce* *kuadiao*
4. 积极引进外资,不仅没有影响民族工业的发展,反而增强了民族工业发展的活力。
   Active *jiji* *jin* *not only* *minzu* *zengqiang* *power, strength, vitality*

二、请用"反而"完成下列句子。

1. 你怎么越说我 反而 越不 dong
2. 越有经验的人 反而 越 zuo mar .
3. 老板在外经商,多年没回家看望老母亲了,这次回家 反而 gens mei shijia 陪他 kan .
4. 高新技术不断开发,世界变得越来越小了,但人们之间的 gnangxi yue lai yue yuan .
5. 吃惯了山珍海味 反而 jvede 示 好 吃
   guan

意味着

yi wei zhe

意思是"含有某种意思、可以理解为……"它前面的主语多为动词、动名

shhuianyu

词或小句,它的后面必带动词、动名词或小句做宾语。

Mean; signify; imply. Its meaning is "having a certain meaning; can be understood as...". The subject that precedes it is normally a verb, a gerund or a clause, and it always takes a verb, a gerund or a clause as its object.

一、熟读下列各句,体会"意味着"的意义和用法。

1. 电子商务的出现,意味着传统贸易方式的结束。

2. 信息产业的繁荣,意味着一个新时代的开始。

3. 彻底转变观念,这就意味着要抛弃落后的旧思想,接受先进的新思想。

4. 我们之间虽然发生了一些不愉快的事情,但这决不意味着我们双方已经没有合作的基础了。

二、请用"意味着"完成下列句子。

1. 欧元(euro)的出现,_____。

2. 合同经双方签字后,_____。

3. 双方有合作的意向,_____。

4. 中国现在提出要搞大经贸,_____。

5. 货物一旦投保_____。

看好吧

课文里的"就看你的了"和"你们就看好吧",是口语中常能听到的对话。"看你的",意思是"我要观察你究竟会怎么做,会有什么结果",表示出某种希望与期待的心情。而"你就看好吧"则是一种肯定的回答,表示一定能做好、有好的结果。

就看你的了 and 你们就看好吧, as used in the text, are expressions frequently used in spoken Chinese. 看你的 means "I'll watch how you are going to do it and what the result will be", expressing a hope or an expectation. 你就看好吧, on the other hand, is an affirmative reply, expressing the certainty of achieving a good result.

一、熟读下列各句,体会"看好吧"的意义和用法。

1. A:这事儿就拜托你了。

   B:没问题,你就看好吧!

2. A:你能把这事办成吗?

   B:这有什么难? 你就看好吧!

二、请用"看你的"或"看好吧"完成下列对话。

1. A:你是中国通,你在中国有许多贸易伙伴,希望你能为我公司牵线搭桥。

B:＿＿＿＿＿＿＿＿＿＿＿＿＿＿＿＿＿＿＿＿＿＿。

2. A:这次全球金融危机,对我国进出口贸易造成很大压力,我们与贵公司是多年的贸易伙伴,请多多关照。

B:＿＿＿＿＿＿＿＿＿＿＿＿＿＿＿＿＿＿＿＿＿＿。

3. A:我公司希望进一步开拓国外市场,你能提供我们需要的信息吗?

B:＿＿＿＿＿＿＿＿＿＿＿＿＿＿＿＿＿＿＿＿＿＿。

4. A:中国全方位开放后,你公司有什么举措?

B:＿＿＿＿＿＿＿＿＿＿＿＿＿＿＿＿＿＿＿＿＿＿。

B

一、请用下列词语组成短语。

转变　观念　开放　领域　双向
阻碍　姿态　合作　交流　积极
引导　格局　束缚　发展　开拓

二、请用括号里的词语完成下列句子。

1. 改革开放以来,中国经济＿＿＿＿＿＿＿＿＿＿＿＿＿＿＿＿。(辉煌成就)

2. 改革开放以前,中国的对外贸易和它在世界贸易中的排名＿＿＿＿＿＿＿
＿＿＿＿＿＿＿＿＿＿＿＿＿＿＿＿＿＿＿＿＿。(相称)

3. 众多外国公司在中国的成功,吸引了更多外商来华投资,现在中国政府
＿＿＿＿＿＿＿＿＿＿＿＿＿＿＿＿＿＿＿＿＿。(积极引导)

4. 改革开放以来中国的经济成就和发展蓝图,向世界＿＿＿＿＿＿＿＿＿
＿＿＿＿＿＿＿＿＿＿＿＿＿＿＿＿＿＿＿＿＿。(合作机会)

5. 中国将以更加开放的姿态迎接未来＿＿＿＿＿＿＿＿＿＿＿＿＿＿＿＿
＿＿＿＿＿＿＿＿＿＿＿＿＿＿＿＿＿＿。(经济一体化潮流)

三、熟读下列短语,并选择适当的短语填空。

羡慕不已	名副其实	海阔凭鱼跃,天高任鸟飞
取长补短	长足进步	机不可失,时不再来

1. 中国改革开放以来,经济发展,市场繁荣,人民生活水平普遍提高,对外

贸易_____，令世界各国朋友欢欣鼓舞。

2. 随着高新科技的发展，世界变得越来越小了，各国人民都需要互相交流，_____。

3. 中国对外商来说是一个很有吸引力的市场，中国政府为外商和来华投资者提供了许多优惠政策，他们在中国做生意，真是_____。

4. 近几年中国纺织工业朝着精加工、深加工方向发展，采用高新技术对传统的纺织工艺进行了大力改造，产品质量产生了根本变化，开发了一批_____的名优产品，深受国内外顾客欢迎。

5. 这是一次难得的机会，希望你好好想想，_____哟。

6. 贵公司在激烈的竞争中不断开拓市场，发展新产品，几年来使公司利润翻了几番，令同行们_____。

四、想一想，谈一谈。

1. 在 20 世纪最后一次全球的金融危机中，你对中国经济在亚洲及世界经济中的地位和影响怎么看？

2. 你知道中国面对未来有什么新举措吗？

3. "全方位开放"是什么意思？为什么全方位开放对大型跨国集团公司有巨大吸引力？

4. 中国已经并正在形成什么样的对外开放格局？你能对此谈谈自己的看法和认识吗？

五、阅读下面的短文，然后回答问题。

姜太公"下海"

姜太公，西周初年(公元前 11 世纪)人，80 岁时遇周文王，拜为丞相。但他在遇文王以前，曾四次经商，四次惨遭失败。

第一次是产品定位失误，没人买他的竹制漏勺。

第二次，他挑了一担面粉进城去卖，面粉自然是有人买的，不料他选错了销售地点。他把一担面粉放在闹市中，突然一匹惊马奔来，踢翻了面粉，一阵风起，升起团团粉尘，他又一次血本无归。

第三次，他的一位朋友，见他两次做生意都赔了老本，很同情他，就把自己的一家酒店让给他经营一天。酒店临近练兵场，不愁赚不了钱。谁知他信息不灵，这天练兵场不练兵，结果门庭冷落，无人光顾。天气炎热，他准备的美酒佳肴，全都变了味儿。

第四次，他决定贩卖牲口，心想，这总是风吹不走、天热也不会变质的货。

当时,久旱无雨,政府下令严禁贩卖、屠宰牲口。结果,他因为不了解政府的政策、法令,牲口被没收,他本人也险些进了监狱。

1. 姜太公是什么时候的人？你知道他的一些故事吗？
2. 姜太公四次经商,四次都失败了,原因是什么？
3. 你认为,做生意应该重视哪些因素？为什么？
4. 你知道"姜太公经商"一类的例子吗？请说说。

技术贸易 22

Technology Trade

一、技术贸易业务

爱德华：江先生，今天我想向你请教一些有关技术贸易的问题。

江　奇：别客气，我们共同探讨吧！

爱德华：您能简要介绍一下贵国的技术贸易情况吗？

江　奇：我国的技术贸易，在改革开放前，在对外贸易中的比重很小。

亨　特：所以，有一种意见认为，中国那时的对外贸易还是单一的进出口贸易。

江　奇：这种意见不无道理。

爱德华：那么，中国的技术贸易是改革开放以后才大力发展起来的啰。

江　奇：是这样。特别是我国的技术出口贸易，从二十世纪八十年代才真正开始。经过二十多年的发展，我国的技术贸易出口已经扩大到一百多个国家和地区。

爱德华：发展得太快了！

江　奇：我国技术贸易起点低，与发达国家的差距大，所以发展的潜力也大。

爱德华：但是，不管怎么说，这毕竟是一个了不起的进步！

江　奇：最近几年，我国大力调整出口产品结构，逐步实现了从资源密集型向劳动密集型、再向技术密集型的转变，我们在国际市场上已经具备某些技术贸易优势。

亨　特：我知道，中国的技术贸易，无论是软件贸易还是硬件贸易，都具有竞争力。

爱德华：请再说一遍，这句话的中文意思我不懂。

亨　特：噢，软件贸易是指知识的买卖，而硬件贸易是指成套机器设备的买卖。

江　奇：具体地讲，包括许可证交易、技术咨询和专业人员培训、工程设计、设备安装和调试、成套设备交易和专利技术、专有技术的转让。

爱德华：在这些方面，中国都有自己的优势？

江　奇：是的。我国向美国、日本、德国及其他一些发展中国家出口过杂交水稻等多项软件技术；我国的机电、石油化工、水泥、建材、通讯、船舶、航空航天行业的成套设备和知识贸易，也已经具有相当规模。

亨　特：中国长期以来靠出口农产品、原材料和低附加值产品的时代已经结束了。

爱德华：我听到这些非常高兴，我相信，我们在技术贸易与合作方面将成为最亲密的伙伴！

二、技术贸易的合同谈判

爱德华：江先生，您知道，技术贸易是一种有偿的技术转让。在技术贸易谈判中，合同价格常常是一个十分棘手的问题。

江　奇：是的。技术贸易是一种知识、智慧和精神的转让，这种无形资产怎么估价，谈判双方确实难以达成共识。

亨　特：一般货物买卖，有相对稳定的市场行情，有同类商品的比较，价格比较好确定。知识产品，往往不具有实体性，怎么定价？

江　奇：这在很大程度上取决于转让方和受让方双方的意愿，随意性很大。

爱德华：江先生，一项专利技术，从开发到投产、使用，是一个艰巨的过程,需要投入大量劳动和资金,技术转让费应该是这种投入的合理补偿。

江　奇:但是,具有不同条件、利用不同研制手段开发的技术,投入成本存在着很大差异,这很难成为谈判的基础。

爱德华:江先生,您所说的"不同条件、不同手段",那也是有先期投入才获得的,不是天上掉下来的,也应当获得补偿。

江　奇:除了受让方要求开发的专项技术,其他作为转让的技术,都是拥有者在自身的产品生产过程中实现的,技术开发的费用已经计入生产成本,并且已经在产品销售时分摊或回收。

亨　特:江先生的意思是不是说,这类技术应该无偿转让?

江　奇:当然不是。我只是说,这样来计算技术转让费,不可能成为谈判的基础。

爱德华:那么,江先生有何高见呢?

江　奇:啊,说不上是什么高见。我认为比较合理而又容易操作的方法是,由技术转让方和受让方共同分享使用该项技术后所取得的额外利润。

爱德华:这固然不失为一种计算方法。但是,要核查额外利润,十分烦琐,实施起来也很困难。

江　奇:所以比较通行的做法是,以使用该项技术生产的产品销售额作为计算技术转让费的基础。

爱德华:好,我们双方将来在技术贸易谈判中,可以深入研究这种方式。

亨　特:作为技术贸易合同所必需的其他条款,中国还有什么特殊做法吗?

江　奇:当然,还有一些问题,我们也十分关注。

爱德华:比如说……

江　奇:比如说关键性词语定义条款,许可证协议范围条款,技术的改进与发展、技术情报与保密、技术服务与协助等条款。

亨　特:嗯,这些条款,技术转让双方在法律、解释方面都可能出现分歧。

爱德华:只要双方有诚意,这些可能出现的分歧可以消除。

江　奇:我们有诚意,也有足够的耐心。

爱德华:那太好了,我期待着一次成功的合作!

 生 词

1. 探讨 (v)	tàntǎo	discuss, probe into
2. 简要 (n)	jiǎnyào	concise, brief
3. 比重	bǐzhòng	proportion
4. 潜力	qiánlì	potential
5. 毕竟 (adv)	bìjìng	after all
6. 结构	jiégòu	structure
7. 逐步 (adv)	zhúbù	gradually; step by step
8. 密集 (adj)	mìjí	intensive
9. 软件	ruǎnjiàn	software
10. 硬件	yìngjiàn	hardware
11. 许可证	xǔkězhèng	license
12. 培训 (n,v)	péixùn	training
13. 工程	gōngchéng	project, engineering
14. 设计 (n,v)	shèjì	design
15. 调试 (v)	tiáoshì	~~commissioning~~ adjust & try
16. 转让 (v)	zhuǎnràng	transfer
17. 杂交 (adj)	zájiāo	cross breeding
18. 水稻	shuǐdào	paddy, rice
19. 水泥	shuǐní	cement
20. 建材	jiàncái	building materials
21. 航空	hángkōng	aviation
22. 航天	hángtiān	aeronautics
23. 结束 (v)	jiéshù	end, finish
24. 亲密 (adj)	qīnmì	close
25. 棘手 (adj)	jíshǒu	knotty -very, very difficult
26. 智慧 (n)	zhìhuì	wisdom

27. 共识	(n)	gòngshí	common understanding	*to reach (dacheng)*
28. 实体		shítǐ	substance, entity	*industrial company*
29. 意愿	(n)	yìyuàn	desire, will	
30. 随意性	(n)	suíyìxìng	randomness	*, do something randomly*
31. 艰巨	(adj.)	jiānjù	formidable, arduous	*(for a job)*
32. 差异		chāyì	difference	
33. 先期		xiānqī	earlier stage; in advance	
34. 拥有		yōngyǒu	possess	
35. 分摊	(n)(v)	fēntān	apportion	*share/divide up burden*
36. 回收	(n)(v)	huíshōu	retrieve, recover	
37. 分享	(v)	fēnxiǎng	share	
38. 额外	(adj.)	éwài	extra, additional	*opportunity, $*
39. 固然	(adv.)	gùrán...*danshi*	admittedly; no doubt	*(pattern)*
40. 核查	(v)	héchá	check, examine and verify	
41. 烦琐	(adj.)	fánsuǒ	tedious, troublesome	
42. 定义	(n)	dìngyì	definition	
43. 情报	(n)	qíngbào	intelligence	*(company)*
44. 保密	(w)	bǎomì	maintain secrecy	
45. 分歧	(n)	fēnqí	divergence	*(eg viewpoints)*
46. 消除	(v)	xiāochú	eliminate, remove	
47. 期待	(v)	qīdài	expect	*(bis, important things)*

练 习

A

毕竟

　　副词，①强调事物的状态、性质、特点，意思是"不管怎么说，都是那样"或"即使出现了新情况，原来的状况也不会改变"。②强调某种事情、现象到最后还是发生了、出现了，句中或句尾总有表示新情况出现的语气词"了"。

　　After all(adverb); in the final analysis. 1)It is used to emphasize that the state, nature and characteristics of something are just like that no matter what happens. Even when some new circumstances occur, the original state will not change. 2) It is used to emphasize that a certain thing or phenomenon still occurs or takes place eventually. For this usage, the modal particle 了 is used in the middle or the end of the sentence to signify the occurrence of the new situation.

一、熟读下列各句,体会"毕竟"的意义和用法。

1. 中国的综合国力确实增强了,但毕竟还是发展中国家。
2. 我们不会满足现状,我们的生活水平毕竟还很低。
3. 专利技术是一笔无形资产,但它毕竟并不等于可以直接购买商品的现金。
4. 市场竞争毕竟是残酷、激烈的,我们必须有危机感。
5. 他虽然很不情愿,毕竟还是答应了我的要求。
6. 工程进展虽然很不顺利,现在毕竟也完成了。
7. 货款毕竟收回来了,你还着什么急?
8. 他毕竟承认了错误,你就原谅了他吧!

二、请用"毕竟"和下面的短语造句。

1. 某些技术贸易的优势
2. 双方达成共识
3. 成功的合作
4. 最亲密的伙伴
5. 与发达国家的差距
6. 市场潜力

说不上

①根据熟悉程度而能说,能说清楚,叫"说得上";不能说,不能说清楚,叫"说不上"。②够得上某种程度,叫"说得上";够不上某种程度,叫"说不上"。它后边必带动词、形容词做宾语。

Cannot say; cannot tell. 1) Depending on the extent of familiarity with the matter, if you can say it or explain it clearly, it is called 说得上; if you cannot say it or explain it clearly, it is called 说不上. 2) 说得上 indicates that a certain extent is reached, while 说不上 means vice versa. It must take a verb or an adjective as its object.

一、熟读下列各句,体会"说得上"、"说不上"的意义和用法。

1. 他同经理是多年的老朋友,能说得上话。

2. 他们俩说不上两句话就要吵起来。

3. 这种产品的质量,说不上好,也说不上坏。

4. 我们公司一年到底有多少营业额,我可说不上。

5. 我们见过两次面,还说不上熟悉。

6. 他工作很努力,可说不上出色。

7. 要论这家企业的设备,可说得上是一流的。

8. 这个设计,说不上有什么新意。

二、请用"说得上"或"说不上"完成下列句子。

1. 你别看她只是一个小小的秘书,可她在总经理那儿_____。

2. 这些年来他俩的关系_____,_____。

3. 开发这项专利技术,从投产到使用需要一个过程,要投入多少劳动和资金_____。

4. 由于区域性差异,人们的生活习惯和文化都不同,老外_____中国特色的不多,中国人_____自己国家的风俗人情的也不少。

5. 怎么计算技术转让费更合理,又容易操作,双方反复协商_____花了多少时间与精力。

固然

①表示确认某一事实,然后转入下文,又提出一种新情况,前后两小句意思矛盾。后一小句常用"但是、可是、却"等词配合。②表示确认某一事实,接着说同时也应该承认另一事实,前后意思不矛盾,只是突出后一个意思。多用"也"配合。

Though of course; admittedly. 1) It is used to acknowledge a certain fact, to be followed by a transition, introducing a new situation. The two clauses are contradictory to each other. The second clause is often linked by such words as 但是,可是 or 却 (but). 2) It is used to acknowledge a certain fact, to be followed by a statement that another thing also needs to be recognized. There is no contradiction between the two clauses, but the emphasis is laid on the latter. The word 也 (also) is often used with it.

一、熟读下列各句,体会"固然"的意义和用法。

1. 你的工作固然很忙,可也不能不管老婆、孩子。

2. 大夫固然可以治病,可糊涂大夫也会治死人。

3. 你的设计固然很好,但是成本太高了。

4. 从国外引进先进技术固然很重要,如果因此产生依赖心理,不开发自己的智力资源就不好了。

5. 钱固然重要,可是有一个健康的身体也许更重要。

6. 你的建议固然很好,比尔的也不错。

7. 企业固然需要技术,可更需要人才。

8. 我在以前那家公司的工资固然很高,可我现在的工资也不低。

二、请用"固然"和下列短语完成句子。

1. 一流设备重要　　人才开发

2. 用优惠政策吸引外商　　人才开发

3. 日程安排很紧　　失去机会

4. 了解今天中国改革开放的形势很重要　　未来发展方向

5. 中国技术贸易起点低　　发展潜力

B

一、请用下列词语组成短语。

探讨　结构　棘手　技术　消除

调整　问题　转让　合作　分歧

差距　培训　逐步　期待　结束

二、完成下列句子。

1. 最近几年,中国大力调整了_____,逐步实现了从_____向_____、再向_____的转变。

2. 软件贸易是指_____,硬件贸易是指_____。

3. 改革开放以来,中国结束了长期靠出口_____的时代。

4. 中国的技术贸易是改革开放以后才大力发展起来的,起点低,_____,所以_____。

5. 技术贸易是一种_____,在技术贸易谈判中,_____常常是一个十分棘手的问题。

6. 计算技术转让费比较通行的做法是_____。

三、想一想,谈一谈。

1. 中国的技术出口贸易从什么时候开始? 业绩如何?

2. 为什么说中国技术贸易的发展潜力很大？你怎么看？

3. 中国在国际市场上已经具备某些技术贸易优势，对此你怎么看？

4. 为什么在技术贸易谈判中，合作价格是一个棘手问题？

5. 怎样计算技术转让费比较容易达成共识，从而使转让方和受让方有谈判的基础？

四、阅读下面的短文，然后回答问题。

卖鸡与卖蛋

谁都知道，是鸡生蛋，蛋孵鸡。那么，是先有鸡呢，还是先有蛋？这好像就很难说清了。

一天，一个美国朋友杰米问我："嗨，张先生，你说是卖鸡合算，还是卖蛋合算？"我想了想，笑着说："当然是卖蛋合算。""为什么？""这还不明摆着？一只鸡一年下蛋按160只计算，差不多是20斤，每斤2.50元，是五十多元。两年就是一百多元。一只鸡当肉卖呢？充其量卖二十多块钱。我的朋友，这么简单的问题，你们美国人难道也弄不明白？"杰米笑笑说："过去，我们美国的许多人也不明白，现在明白了。还是卖鸡合算。""什么？卖鸡比卖蛋合算？"我不禁大吃一惊，他的答案太出乎我的意料了。

杰米立即解释说："一项新技术，创造了一种新产品，是卖这项新技术合算呢，还是卖这项新技术创造的新产品合算呢？现在的事实证明，是卖这项新技术合算。"我立即反驳说："不对。你如果是拥有一项专利技术或专有技术，你的产品就是独一无二的，你就可以垄断市场，这种产品带来的利润肯定要远远超过卖技术。等到一定时候，再用赚来的钱开发新技术，造成新的一轮垄断，价值就更不可估量。""在一定时候可能是这样，但在高科技如此发达和迅速传播的今天，垄断是不可能持久的。电脑行业曾经是我们美国垄断了的，可没有几年，这种垄断就被韩国打破了。当今世界，技术贸易和知识产权贸易成交额已占世界总贸易额的一半以上。这足以说明出售技术比出售产品更合算。"

我一时语塞了。这又是一个鸡生蛋与蛋孵鸡的难题。

1. 你认为卖鸡合算，还是卖蛋合算？为什么？

2. 你认为卖技术和卖技术产品，哪一种合算？为什么？

3. "我"与杰米的讨论有结论吗？是什么结论？

23 服务贸易

Service Trade

一、新领域，新产业

爱德华：江先生，今天我想了解一下贵国服务贸易业的情况。

江　奇：噢，很好。这也是我感兴趣的话题。

爱德华：我知道，贵国在海运和旅游业方面有很大的优势，但许多服务业，如电信、金融、保险等服务业，对贵国来说，恐怕还是崭新领域、崭新课题。

江　奇：你说得对，但也不完全对。

爱德华：这是什么意思？

江　奇：海运和旅游是我国的优势产业，而我们国家的电信、金融、保险等服务业，国际竞争力确实还很低。这点你说得很对。

爱德华：那么，我说得不对的，是什么呢？

江　奇：我们国家的国际服务贸易也正在走向高级化，所有现代服务贸易，对我们来说，非但不是什么新鲜话题，而且我国的现代服务贸易近几年也有了长足发展。

爱德华：现在，在经济发达国家，国际服务贸易占了全球服务进出口贸易总额的75%，服务贸易已经成为国家经济的支柱产业，成为保持国际收支平衡的重要手段。贵国的状况又怎么样呢？

江　奇：我们知道，在服务业方面，我们同经济发达国家还有不小差距。我们国家服务业出口还只占贸易总额的9%，明显低于19%的世界平均水平。我们的服务贸易，也还存在近

100亿美元的逆差。

爱德华：当然，这可以理解，凡事都有一个过程嘛。

亨　特：其实，中国是一个非常重视商业服务的国家，在中国到处都可以看到"顾客至上，服务第一"的标语。

江　奇：是这样。不过，传统的服务业，多是以家庭和个人服务为主要形式，而现在的国际服务贸易，是建立在现代科技发展与产业升级基础上的新兴产业。

爱德华：你说得很对。根据《服务贸易总协定》定义，服务贸易涵盖了几乎所有除直接货物交易之外的一切领域。

江　奇：是这样，如电信、金融、保险、建筑、计算机和信息服务、特权使用和许可、专业服务等等，而且像卫星导航、电子商务、电子银行、电子货币等等，不仅大大提高了服务效率和质量，服务的增值率也大幅度攀升。

亨　特：服务贸易，已经成为各国经济新的增长点，带动全球经济发展的新的引擎。

江　奇：我们接受了服务贸易这个概念，我国政府已经把服务贸易和服务贸易对外开放，列为我们的基本国策。我们正在创建一个在国际贸易中有竞争力的崭新产业。

爱德华：啊，听起来令人兴奋！中国政府都有什么举措呢？

江　奇：我们是不是休息一下再谈？

二、新挑战，新机遇

江　奇：爱德华先生刚才问中国有什么举措，我可以告诉你，中国正在有计划、有步骤地开放服务贸易市场。

爱德华：愿闻其详。

江　奇：我国国内的服务业发展很快，我国国际服务贸易范围也正在逐步扩大。

亨　特：中国在服务贸易的许多方面都有优势，比如货物追加服务

（运输、国际结算）、国际旅游服务、对外工程承包和劳务合作等等。

江　奇:啊,只能说我们正在缩小这方面的差距。

亨　特:中国服务贸易的年增长率在 16% 以上,不仅高于国民经济的增长速度,也高于世界服务贸易同期增长水平。江先生太自谦了!

江　奇:不是谦虚,我们在传统服务贸易行业还有很大潜力,而更多的新兴行业还刚刚起步,甚至有些行业我们还是空白。

爱德华:这不是你们的问题。世界服务贸易以高新技术为基础,科学技术日新月异,就不断从制造业中分离出服务业来,创造出崭新的服务业,谁都会有空白。

江　奇:正因为这样,我们才有更强烈的危机感!

亨　特:可是,用中国的一句时髦话说,挑战与机遇并存!

江　奇:来自这方面的挑战十分严峻。你们知道,20 世纪末,世贸组织签署了电讯和信息技术服务两个文件。

爱德华:是的,这意味着签署上述文件的国家占有信息技术产品和电讯的 90% 以上的市场。

江　奇:而这一领域的服务贸易自由化,必然要求制定一个全球统一的计算机标准和通讯标准。你能设想中国不跻身其中吗? 中国能有什么选择?

亨　特:还是用你们中国人的说法,迎接挑战,抓住发展机遇!

江　奇:我们只有这种选择。在世贸组织的谈判中,我们对其他一些领域,如金融、保险、商业零售等几十个部门都有承诺。

爱德华:就是说,贵国承诺将开放这些领域的服务贸易?

江　奇:事实上我们已经这样做了。我国已经有合资的外贸公司;外国银行在中国开设分行,获准经营人民币业务;外资零售业连锁店已经开张;旅游、航空、会计、法律咨询等等领域,都已迈开了服务贸易的开放步伐。

爱德华:啊,这对我们也是一个大好机遇,我们希望中国能充分实现服务贸易自由化!

江　奇:服务贸易的管制与保护,主要依靠国内政策和法规,不像货物贸易可以依靠关税和其他边境措施,所以在国民待遇、市场准入、透明度以及统计数据和信息收集等方面,都还有许多工作要做,我国的服务贸易对外开放,只能是循序渐进的。

爱德华:我们可以理解。

 生 词

1. 话题	huàtí	topic
2. 崭新	zhǎnxīn	brand new
3. 非但	fēidàn	not only
4. 支柱	zhīzhù	pillar
5. 产业	chǎnyè	industry
6. 平衡	pínghéng	balance
7. 逆差	nìchā	deficit
8. 至上	zhìshàng	supreme, the highest
9. 标语	biāoyǔ	slogan
10. 升级	shēngjí	upgrade
11. 涵盖	hángài	cover
12. 建筑	jiànzhù	building, architecture
13. 卫星	wèixīng	satellite
14. 导航	dǎoháng	navigate
15. 效率	xiàolǜ	efficiency
16. 攀升	pānshēng	climb to a higher point
17. 带动	dàidòng	bring along, spur on
18. 引擎	yǐnqíng	engine
19. 列为	lièwéi	list, add to a list
20. 步骤	bùzhòu	step
21. 愿闻其详	yuàn wén qí xiáng	I'd like to hear the details.
22. 追加	zhuījiā	supplementing
23. 结算	jiésuàn	settle accounts

24. 承包	chéngbāo	contract
25. 劳务	láowù	labor services
26. 缩小	suōxiǎo	reduce, shrink
27. 谦虚	qiānxū	modest
28. 起步	qǐbù	start, move
29. 空白	kòngbái	blank
30. 日新月异	rì xīn yuè yì	change with each passing day
31. 分离	fēnlí	separate
32. 挑战	tiǎozhàn	challenge
33. 自由化	zìyóuhuà	liberalization
34. 制定	zhìdìng	formulate, draw up
35. 设想	shèxiǎng	imagine
36. 跻身	jīshēn	ascend, mount
37. 抓住	zhuāzhù	grasp
38. 获准	huòzhǔn	obtain approval
39. 会计	kuàijì	accounting, accountant
40. 迈开	màikāi	step, stride
41. 步伐	bùfá	step, pace
42. 管制	guǎnzhì	control
43. 依靠	yīkào	rely on
44. 边境	biānjìng	border
45. 市场准入	shìchǎng zhǔn rù	market access
46. 透明度	tòumíngdù	transparency
47. 收集	shōují	collect
48. 循序渐进	xúnxù jiànjìn	proceed in an orderly and step-by-step way

专　名　Proper Noun

| 世贸组织 | Shìmào Zǔzhī | the World Trade Organization (WTO) |
| (世界贸易组织) | (Shìjiè Màoyì Zǔzhī) | |

 练 习

A

非但

连词,与"不但"相同,表示递进关系,用前一层意思衬托后面更进一层的意思。经常与"并且"、"而且"等连用,连接复句的两个分句。

Not only. It is a conjunction. Same as 不但, it expresses a progressive relationship, using what is expressed in the first clause to set off a further meaning in the latter. It is often used together with 并且 or 而且(but also)to link up the two clauses in the sentence.

一、熟读下列各句,体会"非但"的意义和用法。
　　1.非但我不知道,而且我们大家都不知道。
　　2.非但顾客不满意,我们自己也不满意。
　　3.这种进口水果非但贵,而且也不好吃。
　　4.服务贸易非但能弥补逆差,而且可以变逆差为顺差。

二、请把下列短语用"非但"和相应的连词组成递进复句。
　　1.他没能说服我们　　被我们说服
　　2.我们接受了服务贸易这个崭新的概念
　　　我国政府已经把服务贸易对外开放列为我们的基本国策
　　3.他投资于环境保护没赚钱　　赔了本
　　4.服务贸易离不开科技　　以高新技术为基础
　　5.服务贸易越来越受到重视　　已经成为各国经济新的增长点
　　6.两年没见,她没有老　　更年轻、更精神

至上

"至",副词,这是一个古文言词,意思与"最"相同,但使用范围比"最"狭窄得多,它只能修饰单音节词。

Supreme;the highest. 至 is an adverb, a word in classical Chinese. Its meaning is the same as 最（extreme, most）, but is used in a much narrower scope. It can only be used to modify a monosyllabic word.

一、熟读下列各句，体会"至"的用法。
1. 他得到一条信息，如获至宝，高兴得一夜没睡。
2. 有不少人信奉"爱情至上"，你觉得怎么样？
3. 有人说，市场不同情眼泪，是一句至理名言。
4. 他们俩共同经历了不少风风雨雨，已经成为至交。

二、熟读下列词语，体会它们的意义和用法。
至亲　至爱　至宝　至高
至上　至理　至诚　至交
至极　至大　至少/多

三、选用上面的词语完成下列句子。
1. 在几千年的中国封建社会，皇帝拥有＿＿＿＿＿＿＿＿＿＿无上的权力。
2. ＿＿＿＿＿＿＿＿＿＿骨肉都不能相见，你怎么能不感到孤独呢？
3. 在激烈竞争的市场中，有些商人奉行利润＿＿＿＿＿＿＿＿＿＿，不顾信誉，这是不对的，终有一天他会自食苦果。
4. 母亲节你不能看望母亲，或送去一份礼物，＿＿＿＿＿＿＿＿＿＿应该打个电话或写封信表示你的祝愿和爱。
5. 他的公司获得了巨大成功，他多年的辛苦努力得到了补偿，他高兴＿＿＿＿＿＿＿＿＿＿，掉下了眼泪。

来自

①"自"，介词，它和介词宾语构成的词组，表示处所、时间的起点。②"自"用在"来"、"出"、"发"、"寄"等动词后做补语，表示处所。

Coming from. 1）自 is a preposition. The prepositional phrase it forms with its object expresses the starting point of a time or place. 2）It indicates the locality when it is used after such verbs as 来（come），出（indicating an outward direction），发（send out），or 寄（post, mail）as complement.

一、熟读下列词组，体会它们的意义和用法。
来自　　出自　　寄自　　选自
引自　　译自　　抄自　　发自

1. 这件包裹寄自上海。
2. 这是一位来自英国的留学生。
3. 我的这些话都是发自内心的。
4. 这篇经济论文,译自美国今年第三期的《幸福杂志》。

二、请用下列短语造句。
1. 自小/幼
2. 自古
3. 来自
4. 引自

B

一、请用下列词语组成短语。

崭新　　产业　　缩小　　机遇
迈开　　迎接　　支柱　　领域
差距　　挑战　　抓住　　步伐

二、请用括号里的词语完成下列句子。
1. 在许多发达国家,服务贸易_____。(支柱产业)
2. 不是自谦,改革开放至今,中国的服务贸易还刚刚起步,_____
_____。(迎接挑战)
3. 中国已经迈开了服务贸易的开放步伐,相信_____
_____。(大好机遇)
4. 服务贸易以高新技术为基础,科学技术日新月异,为_____
_____。(崭新天地)
5. 中国服务贸易起步晚,与发达国家比差距大,但在许多方面都有优势,
_____。(迈开步伐)

三、熟读下列短语,并选择适当的短语填空。

日新月异　　跻身其中　　循序渐进
愿闻其详　　挑战与机遇并存

1. 中国的经济建设成就和发展蓝图,向世界展示出无限的经济贸易合作机会。许多外国公司在中国的成功,让我公司羡慕不已,_____。

2. 在 20 世纪最后一次全球金融危机中,中国经济不仅没有衰退,反而取得了辉煌成就,实在了不起。中国政府采取了哪些举措,_____。

3. 中国的技术贸易,无论是软件贸易还是硬件贸易,都有自己的优势,_____。

4. 中国已经迈开了服务贸易的开放步伐,但还有许多工作要做,_____。

5. 改革开放以后,中国的变化很大,尤其是高新科学技术真是_____,这给中国的经济发展提供了巨大的动力。

四、想一想,谈一谈。

1. 为什么服务贸易越来越受到重视?

2. 你认为中国的服务贸易在哪些方面有优势? 它同发达国家比有哪些差距?

3. 服务贸易为什么比货物贸易难操作?

4. 你认为中国的服务贸易面临着怎样的形势?

5. 服务贸易涉及哪些领域?

五、阅读下面的短文,然后回答问题。

如此服务

现在时兴旅行结婚,我同小李结婚,也想赶赶这个时髦,度一个难忘的蜜月。我们来到一座风景秀丽的城市,住进一家三星级的宾馆。我为了给小李一个惊喜,就趁小李洗澡的时候给一家花店打了一个电话。"喂,花店吗? 请给我送一瓶花儿来,是我送给新娘子的,花儿要最新鲜的,还要配一个精美的花瓶。噢,顺便说一句,当然是越便宜越好,价钱不要超过 50 元,我不是大款。"花店接了这笔生意,当然是又高兴又为难,但他们还是想出了一个办法。在电话那边说:"您看这样行不行? ……""嗯……这不好吧! ……也只好这样了。"不久,门铃响了,花店送花儿来了。"亲爱的,过来,我给你买了一件礼物。"我一手接过礼物,一手付钱给送花儿人。"你真好!"说着,小李抱着我热烈地吻我。"砰!"礼物掉在了地上。"啊,真糟糕! 对不起,亲爱的!"小李连忙打开精美的外包装,只见一个长方形的盒子。她掀开盒盖,里面是两件包装物,她拿起一件拆开。"啊,鲜花,好漂亮!"又一个热烈的吻! 她拿起了另一件,拆了一层又一层,里面露出无数小包装。我一见,不禁在心里叫起来:"我的天!"小李没有注意我的表情,小心拆开一个小包,里面是一块破碎的玻璃片,再拆一包,还是一块玻璃碎片。小李拆完所有的小包装,竟然全是碎玻璃片。小李惊呆了!

1. 花店给新郎出了一个什么主意？
2. 新郎看见无数小包装后，为什么在心里惊叫起来？
3. 新娘得到这份礼物后，会怎么想？
4. 题目为什么叫"如此服务"？

24 工程承包与劳务合作

Project Contracting and Labor Cooperation

一、商机无限

爱德华：我真幸运，有机会参加这次国际盛会。

江　奇：这次国际工程承包研讨会，二十多个国家和几百家企业的有关人士，济济一堂，对许多问题作了深入探讨，真是受益匪浅！

亨　特：工程承包和劳务合作，是一项综合性服务贸易，涉及面很广，确实是一个很有发展前途的产业！

江　奇：是的，它不仅可以直接输出劳务人员，赚取外汇，而且可以带动大量商品、技术和成套设备出口。

爱德华：嗯，更重要的是高智能服务的出口！

江　奇：重心从商品输出向资本、智能和技术输出倾斜，正是当今国际贸易发展的一大趋势，工程承包与劳务合作的空前活跃是其显著特点。

亨　特：这里商机无限！

江　奇：但也是机遇与挑战并存。

爱德华：我注意到了，发展中国家的介入，正在改变国际工程承包和劳务合作市场的格局。

亨　特：它们的劳动力低廉，在劳动密集型项目竞争中，特别是在那些不需要很高技术的发展中国家，他们有优势。

爱德华：噢，与其说是优势，不如说是对发达国家承包商已经构成不小威胁，导致工程承包利润率大幅度下降。

江　奇：但是，发达国家在资金、技术方面仍然占据着绝对优势。

爱德华：当然，这也是事实。所以，他们大多只负责工程设计、咨询、技术指导、监督、监理和设备供应，而乐得把土木工程和相关的劳务分包出去。

亨　特：因为这种高智能服务的利润率，通常要比一般劳务高出数十倍，其至数百倍。

江　奇：特别是现在，综合性、高技术、超大型项目日益增多。发展中国家同发达国家在竞争中的不平等和差距就更加明显了。

亨　特：是这样，像机场、港口、工业城、核电站、高速公路、大型水库等工程，承包金额往往在几十个亿以上。

江　奇：目前，发达国家承包商垄断这些项目的局面，基本上没有改变。但是，垄断正在被打破，在激烈竞争中，发展中国家与发达国家正在形成新的分工与合作格局。

亨　特：我想，这是一个可喜的变化。

爱德华：发达国家和发展中国家可以充分发挥各自的优势嘛！

江　奇：爱德华先生，你不怕有人抢了你的生意？

爱德华：哈，哈，有饭大家吃，有生意大家做嘛！

二、工程承包和劳务合作市场

爱德华：江先生，你能谈谈中国的工程承包和劳务合作吗？

江　奇：我国的对外工程承包和劳务合作发展很快，正在从过去以派遣施工人员为主向派遣技术人员、从事高智能服务为主转变。我国在建筑、远洋运输、卫星发射、计算机软件等方面都有相当的竞争力。

爱德华：啊，了不起！那么，中国的劳务市场呢？

江　奇：中国有劳动力资源最充足、最活跃的劳务市场。

亨　特：我认为，中国工程技术人员和劳工的素质是世界上最优秀的，他们敬业，能力强，技术熟练，在中国的外国企业都乐于聘用他们。

爱德华：外国的承包商在中国也能寻找到商机吗？

江　奇：同货物交易市场一样,中国的工程承包市场也可以说是无限广阔。

亨　特：举世瞩目的黄河小浪底水利工程,就是由德国、法国和意大利三国承包的,还有众多国家高级技术和管理人员参加设计与施工,承包金额高达11亿美元。

爱德华：啊,这是一笔好生意!

江　奇：中国国门已经敞开,中国承包商正走向世界,外国承包商在中国也是大有用武之地。优势互补,有来有往嘛!

亨　特：据我所知,单就建筑业来说,美国、法国、日本、韩国、马来西亚等世界上著名的建筑公司在中国都有承包项目。

江　奇：我们国家基础建设薄弱,地域辽阔,许多关乎国家经济持续发展的重大工程项目,亟待上马。

亨　特：许多项目,中国都向国际公开招标,国外竞标者如云。

江　奇：竞争非常激烈!

爱德华：我们不怕公开、公平的竞争!

亨　特：工程招标中,发包单位"暗箱操作"或违规操作的现象不少。

爱德华：承包人在投标中的不正当行为,承包后分包和层层转包中违规、违法,也是常见的事。

江　奇：所有这些,在以后的实施过程中,都可能导致不堪设想的后果和隐患。所以,我们第一是反对,第二是坚决取缔。

爱德华：我希望中国能有很好的竞争环境。

亨　特：北京最近就有一个大型工程招标项目,爱德华先生有没有兴趣去竞标?

爱德华：啊,我倒愿意去凑凑热闹,看看那儿的竞标场面。

 生 词

1. 人士	rénshì	personage, public figure
2. 济济一堂	jǐjǐ yì táng	gather together under the same roof
3. 受益匪浅	shòuyì fěi qiǎn	benefit a great deal
4. 前途	qiántú	future, prospect
5. 智能	zhìnéng	intellectual power
6. 重心	zhòngxīn	centre of gravity, core
7. 倾斜	qīngxié	tilt, incline, slant
8. 介入	jièrù	intervene, get involved
9. 构成	gòuchéng	constitute, make up
10. 威胁	wēixié	threat
11. 导致	dǎozhì	lead to, result in
12. 下降	xiàjiàng	decent, come down
13. 占据	zhànjù	occupy
14. 指导	zhǐdǎo	guide, direct
15. 监理	jiānlǐ	supervise
16. 供应	gōngyìng	supply
17. 乐得	lèdé	be only too glad to
18. 分包	fēnbāo	subcontract
19. 核电站	hédiànzhàn	nuclear power plant
20. 水库	shuǐkù	reservoir
21. 打破	dǎpò	break, smash
22. 可喜	kěxǐ	gratifying, heartening
23. 发挥	fāhuī	bring into play
24. 派遣	pàiqiǎn	send, dispatch
25. 施工	shīgōng	carry out construction
26. 从事	cóngshì	go in for; be engaged in
27. 发射	fāshè	launch
28. 素质	sùzhì	quality, character
29. 优秀	yōuxiù	excellent, outstanding
30. 敬业	jìngyè	love one's work

31. 熟练	shúliàn	skilled, proficient
32. 聘用	pìnyòng	employ
33. 广阔	guǎngkuò	broad, vast
34. 举世瞩目	jǔshì zhǔmù	attract worldwide attention
35. 水利	shuǐlì	water conservancy
36. 敞开	chǎngkāi	open wide
37. 用武之地	yòngwǔ zhī dì	scope to display one's abilities
38. 薄弱	bóruò	weak
39. 辽阔	liáokuò	vast, extensive
40. 关乎	guānhū	related to
41. 亟待	jídài	wait anxiously
42. 上马	shàngmǎ	start, mount a horse
43. 招标	zhāobiāo	invite tenders
44. 竞标	jìngbiāo	compete in bidding
45. 发包	fābāo	give out a contract for a project
46. 暗箱	ànxiāng	black box
47. 投标	tóubiāo	submit a tender, enter a bid
48. 正当	zhèngdàng	proper, legitimate
49. 转包	zhuǎnbāo	transfer the contract
50. 不堪	bùkān	be unable to; extreme; cannot bear
51. 隐患	yǐnhuàn	hidden danger
52. 反对	fǎnduì	oppose; be against
53. 坚决	jiānjué	resolutely
54. 取缔	qǔdì	ban, suppress
55. 凑	còu	join in, move close to, happen by chance, gather together
56. 场面	chǎngmiàn	scene, occasion

 练习

A

与其

连词,与"不如"、"宁可"、"宁愿"等相配搭使用,表示在比较以后作出选择,在说话人看来,"与其"带起的前一项是应该舍弃的,而应选择后一项。"不如"的前面还可以加"还、倒、真"等副词。"与其说……不如说……"是一种固定用法,表示对情况的判断,在说话人看来,后一种说法更正确,应该选择后一种。

Rather than. It is a conjunction, used together with 不如,宁可, or 宁愿(it would be better to; would rather) to indicate a choice made after comparison. In the speaker's opinion, the former item introduced by 与其 should be given up, and the latter one is the correct choice. 不如 can be preceded by such adverbs as 还(even more), 倒(indicating contrast), or 真(indeed). 与其说……不如说……is a set expression to indicate a judgment. In the speaker's opinion, the latter is more correct and should be the right choice.

一、熟读下列各句,体会"与其"的意义和用法。

1. 与其多而滥,不如少而精。
2. 与其买三件处理的,我宁可买一件高档的。
3. 与其坐等天上掉馅儿饼,倒不如老老实实找点儿工作做。
4. 在激烈竞争中,与其维持现状,我宁愿去冒冒风险。
5. 这次事故的责任,与其说是某一个人的,倒不如说是大家的。
6. 与其说是我们的竞争对手太强大,还不如说是我们自己太软弱。

二、请用"与其……不如/宁可/宁愿"把下列短语组成句子。

1. 学汉语
   一个人老在房间里做练习
   多交几个中国朋友练习听和说
2. 对子女
   教会他生存技能

留下百万资产

3. 在激烈的市场竞争中

担心、害怕有人抢了你的生意

作好市场调研,抓住信息,不断开创新产品

4. 面对机遇与挑战

积极争取

消极等待

5. 为了经济发展

保护自然环境,稳步开发,合理利用

破坏自然环境,打破平衡,开发资源

乐得

动词,表示某种情况正合自己的心意,很高兴那种情况存在,或很高兴去做某事。在句中做谓语,它后边必带动词、形容词词组做宾语。没有否定式和疑问式。

Be only too glad to. It is a verb indicating that a certain situation is to one's liking, and so he is pleased about the existence of that situation or is glad to do something. It is used as the predicate, taking a verb or an adjective phrase as its object. It does not have a negative or interrogative form.

一、熟读下列各句,体会"乐得"的意义和用法。

1. 他不在我身边,我乐得清静。

2. 不上班也好,我乐得在家休息。

3. 朋友劝他不要介入这场经济纠纷,他也乐得坐山观虎斗。

4. 既然这笔生意赚不了什么钱,我们乐得做个人情,让给别人算了。

二、请用"乐得"和括号里的词语完成下列句子。

1. 国际工程承包和劳务合作市场的格局正在改变,发达国家和发展中国家 _____。(优势互补,充分)

2. 中国有劳动力资源最充足、最活跃的劳务市场,_____ _____。(建厂办企业,聘用)

3. 中国基础建设相对地说比较薄弱,地域辽阔,许多与国家经济持续发展有关的重大项目,_____。(公开招标,竞标)

4. 中国国门已经敞开,外国承包商在中国_____

_____。（用武之地,利用）

5.工程承包和劳务合作确实是一个很有发展前途的产业,发达国家_____
_____。（绝对优势,分包）

就……来说

"就",介词,经常跟"看、说、来看、来说"等配搭使用,指出观察、思考、分析、讨论、说明、评述等活动的对象或范围。

As to;talking about;so far as...is concerned.就 is a preposition here,which is often used together with 看(see),说(speak),来看(seeing from;concerning),来说(talking about)to point out the object or scope of observation,reflection,analysis,discussion,explanation or comment.

一、熟读下列各句,体会"就……来说"等的意义和用法。
　1.这场棋赛,就现在来看,小刘略占上风。
　2.就我个人来说,这点儿损失算不了什么。
　3.就公司目前的经营状况来看,我们还不具备与跨国集团竞争的实力。
　4.就市场来说,我们只看到它的繁荣一面,没觉察它潜在的危机。

二、请用"就"和下列短语造句。
　1.投资环境　　亟待改善
　2.中国目前工程技术人员和劳工的素质　　强有力的竞争对手
　3.对市场的调研和分析　　投资风险
　4.当今国际承包和劳务合作市场的格局　　发展中国家
　5.中国服务贸易　　崭新的领域

B

一、请用下列词语组成短语。
　威胁　项目　构成　取缔　垄断　坚决
　优势　招标　发挥　承包　打破　投标

二、请用括号里的词语完成下列句子。
　1.中国地域辽阔,基础建设薄弱,许多关乎国家经济持续发展的重大工程
　　项目_____。（竞标者如云）
　2.不法承包商在投标中的不正当行为,承包后分包和层层转包,使工程质

量不能保证,_____。(不堪设想)

3. 中国敞开了国门,中国承包商走向世界,外国承包商在中国_____
_____。(用武之地)

4. 中国的工程承包市场同货物交易市场一样,也可以说_____
_____。(无限广阔)

5. 在国际工程承包和劳务合作市场,发达国家的垄断局面正在被打破,在
激烈的竞争中_____。(可喜变化)

三、熟读下列词语,并选择适当的词语填空。

> 受益匪浅　　空前活跃　　凑凑热闹　　举世瞩目
> 济济一堂　　呕待上马　　乐于聘用

1. 高素质的工程技术人员和劳工,因为他们技术熟练、能力强、又敬业,老
板们都_____。

2. _____的长江三峡水利工程是关乎中国国计民生的大
工程,工程完工后长江两岸,尤其长江中、下游的水患可根除,为此_____
_____。

3. 在世界环境保护研讨会上,各国专家和有关人士_____,
就环境保护和改善的许多问题进行了深入的探讨和研究。

4. 改革开放后中国的对外贸易取得了长足进步,近年来以更加开放的姿
态积极参与世界和区域的经济技术交流和合作,双边和多边贸易
_____。

5. 我这次来中国作商业旅行,目的是亲眼看看中国,所到之地无不受到热
烈欢迎,_____,这大大增强了我来中国投资的信心。

6. 我不是运动员,报名参加1 000米赛跑,只是_____,
重在参与嘛。

四、想一想,谈一谈。

1. 当今国际贸易发展的趋势是什么? 对此你怎么看?

2. 当今国际工程承包和劳务合作出现了什么样的局面,为什么?

3. 你对中国的工程承包和劳务合作怎么看?

4. 你听说过"豆腐渣"工程吗? 你知道为什么会出现"豆腐渣"工程吗?
对此你是什么态度?

五、阅读下面的短文,然后回答问题。

点子公司

现在,有各种各样的咨询公司。所谓咨询公司,就是在作了大量调查研究以后,为委托者出个好的"点子",即经营管理的思路、谋略、技巧、招数,以便在买方市场条件下出奇制胜,拓宽市场,提高效益。所以有的咨询公司干脆就叫"点子公司"。但在市场格局基本形成、竞争日益激烈的今天,"点子"并不好出。

汽车公司为买主送来订购的新车,开到车库门口,却进不去。买主从车库里拿出一把锤子,抢起铁锤就敲打车厢顶篷。买主的老朋友走过来:"嗨,你干什么?""车库的门太矮,汽车进不去!"买主说。"傻瓜,你把汽车轮子卸掉,不就进去了吗?"这是"聪明人"为"傻瓜"出的"馊点子"。

现在,不少旅客对大饭店的服务不满意,说那儿是"门难进,脸难看,话难听"。一家饭店经理上"点子公司",请他们出点子。在谈妥劳务费后,"点子公司"给这家饭店提出三条改进措施:"一、扩建饭店大门;二、服务员上班必须化妆;三、在接待客人时,服务员用手势或其他形体语言代替说话。"这是幽默大师给神经麻木者的一点儿小刺激。

那么,有没有能真正收到奇效的好点子呢,应该是不乏其例。

1. 你读了两个小故事后,有什么感想?
2. 请你谈一两个对提高企业效益产生了奇效的"好点子"。
3. "点子公司"怎样为委托人提供劳务服务? 怎样收取劳务费?
4. 你有在"点子公司"工作的经历吗? 请谈谈。

25 加工贸易

Processing Trade

一、加工贸易的几种形式

爱德华：江先生，我很想了解贵国的一些加工贸易情况。

江　奇：爱德华先生对加工贸易感兴趣？

亨　特：哈，岂只是感兴趣，可以说是情有独钟！这是他这次中国
　　　　之行的一个主要目的。

江　奇：那好啊，在这方面我们有很多合作机会。

爱德华：我希望是这样。那么，贵国的加工贸易状况如何呢？

江　奇：加工贸易是服务贸易的重要形式之一，在我国的对外贸易
　　　　中，加工贸易已经占了半壁江山。

爱德华：这是什么意思？

江　奇：我是说，我们的加工贸易进出口总值，已经占全国商品进
　　　　出口总值一半儿以上。

爱德华：啊，这对中外双方都有好处。

亨　特：在我们那里，工资高，能耗高，因而产品成本高，相对削弱
　　　　了市场竞争能力。

爱德华：所以，世界上许多大型企业，都在境外建立加工基地。

江　奇：是这样，最典型的例子恐怕要算耐克公司，享誉全球的耐
　　　　克鞋，没有一双不是在国外生产的。

亨　特：这是可以效法的榜样。加工贸易给双方都带来了丰厚的
　　　　利润。

爱德华：坦率地说，中国有广大的劳动力市场，有技术熟练的工人，

工资又低,是世界上最理想的加工贸易场所。

江　奇:发展加工贸易,可以增加就业机会,学习到先进的生产技术和管理经验,还可以带动一些辅助材料的销售,我们何乐而不为!

爱德华:那么,请问江先生,中国的加工贸易都有什么形式呢?

江　奇:主要有三种形式,即来料加工、进料加工和来件装配。

爱德华:你方的义务是什么?

江　奇:根据双方签订的合同,把外方提供的原料或辅料加工成成品,交给外方,销往国外。

爱德华:你方怎么收费呢?

江　奇:来料加工和进料加工要收取加工费。来件装配,要收取加工费和装配费,也就是工缴费。

亨　特:如果要求你方提供生产辅料或装配元件和零部件呢?

爱德华:外方当然还要付相应的价款。

江　奇:这应该是不言而喻的。

爱德华:江先生,如果进料加工商品因故不能或者不能全部出境外销,可以转为内销吗?

江　奇:可以。但应按原进口料件向海关补交税款,如属于许可证管理商品,还需要向海关交验进口货物许可证。

爱德华:这是一项相当灵活的政策!

二、加工贸易监管

爱德华:江先生,世界上许多国家对加工贸易都实行区域管理,贵国也是这样吗?

江　奇:不是,我们实行的是开放式,遍地开花儿式。中国的加工贸易政策和管理模式,是世界上最宽松的。

亨　特:爱德华先生,这就是说,你在中国到处都能找到加工贸易的合作伙伴。

爱德华：这也就是说，我有充分的选择自由。

江　奇：欧美国家对加工贸易实行税收保全机制，对料件进口和成品出口实行先征税后退税或银行担保，而我们只要求办理登记与核销手续，也不实行银行保证金台账制度。

爱德华：啊，这很吸引人！

亨　特：中国对加工贸易品种和数量的限制也比较少。

江　奇：目前，我们只对少数几种商品如羊毛、棉花等实行总量控制。

爱德华：中国的这些宽松政策，对发展加工贸易十分有利。

江　奇：总之，我们国家在加工贸易方面，有许多优惠政策，为外商营造了一个很好的环境。

爱德华：是这样。不过，我听了这些介绍，倒产生了一个疑问，你们不担心加工贸易失控吗？

亨　特：哈，不法商人总是有的，他们做梦都想钻政策的空子。

江　奇：一些守法的商人，也希望对加工贸易的管理松之又松，宽之又宽。

爱德华：可凡事都有个限度，市场经济中也有一只无形的手嘛，没有这只手，市场不就乱套了？

江　奇：所以，我们实行优惠的、宽松的开放政策，但同时也严格监管。

爱德华：理应如此。贵国是怎么管的呢？

江　奇：比如对深加工结转问题，我们坚持先向海关办理有关手续后转厂。

亨　特：加工料件属于海关监管货物，先办后转，海关才能实施有效控制。

江　奇：可有些企业要求先转后办，而且不经海关许可就擅自行事。我们在稽查中一律以违规论处。

爱德华：还有别的问题吗？

亨　特：据我所知，因为中国不实行区域管理，问题出得最多的是料件进境不进厂，成品出厂不出境。

爱德华：这不是偷税漏税、走私贩私行为吗？

江　奇：还有高报单耗骗取核销，倒卖保税料件和成品等等。这些都违背了加工贸易的基本原则。

亨　特：中国的态度很坚决,强化海关监管,严厉打击走私。

江　奇：对那些违法案件,我们根据《海关法》有关追溯期和处罚的
　　　　规定,进行坚决处理。

爱德华：这些做法,可以在宽松政策的条件下,保证正常的经济秩
　　　　序,一定会得到拥护和尊重。

江　奇：所以,我国的加工贸易才有了飞速发展和巨大成绩。

生　词

1. 加工	jiāgōng	processing
2. 岂	qǐ	(adverb used to ask a rhetorical question)
3. 情有独钟	qíng yǒu dú zhōng	the only thing one is in love with
4. 江山	jiāngshān	rivers and mountains, country
5. 工资	gōngzī	wage, salary
6. 能耗	nénghào	energy consumption
7. 削弱	xuēruò	weaken
8. 基地	jīdì	base
9. 典型	diǎnxíng	typical
10. 效法	xiàofǎ	follow the example of
11. 榜样	bǎngyàng	role model
12. 丰厚	fēnghòu	rich and generous
13. 就业	jiùyè	employment
14. 辅助	fǔzhù	auxiliary
15. 何乐而不为	hé lè ér bù wéi	why not do it
16. 装配	zhuāngpèi	assembly
17. 工缴费	gōngjiǎofèi	processing and assembling fees
18. 元件	yuánjiàn	component, part
19. 零部件	língbùjiàn	parts, component
20. 因故	yīngù	for one reason or another
21. 外销	wàixiāo	sell abroad

22. 内销	nèixiāo	for domestic sale
23. 遍地	biàndì	all over the place
24. 保全	bǎoquán	preserve
25. 机制	jīzhì	mechanism
26. 核销	héxiāo	cancel after verification
27. 台账	táizhàng	a guarantee account set up at the bank counter
28. 营造	yíngzào	construct, build
29. 失控	shīkòng	get out of control
30. 钻	zuān	go into, exploit
31. 空子	kòngzi	loophole, opening, opportunity
32. 限度	xiàndù	limit
33. 乱套	luàntào	muddle things up
34. 结转	jiézhuǎn	completion and transfer
35. 擅自	shànzì	do something without authorization
36. 稽查	jīchá	check
37. 偷税	tōushuì	evade taxes
38. 漏税	lòushuì	evade payment of a tax
39. 走私	zǒusī	smuggle
40. 贩私	fànsī	traffic in smuggled goods
41. 倒卖	dǎomài	resell at a profit, scalp
42. 违背	wéibèi	violate
43. 强化	qiánghuà	strengthen
44. 严厉	yánlì	severe
45. 打击	dǎjī	hit, strike
46. 追溯	zhuīsù	trace back
47. 处罚	chǔfá	punish, penalize
48. 秩序	zhìxù	order
49. 拥护	yōnghù	support

专 名 Proper Noun

| 耐克公司 | Nàikè Gōngsī | Nike Corporation |

 **练习**

A

岂

古汉语虚词,意思相当于"难道",只用在反问句中来加强语气。用在肯定形式的反问句中,是强调表示否定的语气,经常放在"是、有、能、敢"等词前面,意思相当于"哪里"或"怎么";用在否定形式的反问句中,是强调表示肯定的语气,经常放在"不、不是、非"等词的前面,意思相当于"那"。

(Used to ask a rhetorical question). It is a function word in classical Chinese. Its meaning is similar to that of 难道, only used to give force to a rhetorical question. When it is used in a rhetorical question in the positive form, it is to emphasize the tone of negation and often precedes such words as 是(be),有(have),能(be able to), or 敢(dare), with a meaning equivalent to that of 哪里 or 怎么(how). When it is used in a rhetorical question in the negative form, it is to emphasize the tone of affirmation and often precedes such words as 不,不是, or 非(not), with a meaning equivalent to that of 那(that).

一、熟读下列各句,分别指出它们强调的是肯定语气还是否定语气,表达的是什么意思。

1. 老板的心思岂是我们这些小职员能了解的。

2. 他们如此无理,我岂能不管?

3. 你非要他去做这事,岂不是为难他吗?

4. 你提出这样无知的问题,岂不笑掉人的大牙!

5. 走私贩私而不受到严厉打击,岂非怪事?

二、请用"岂"完成下列句子。

1. 双方签订的合同_____。

2. 技术贸易是一种知识、智慧和精神的转让,对这种无形资产的估价,

_____。

3. 执法人自己犯法_____。

4. 一方面说保护消费者合法权益,一方面又出售不合格产品,_____

_____。

5. 这个老外对中国饺子_____。

之一

"之",古汉语虚词,可做代词,也可做助词。做代词时,大致相当于宾语位置上的"他、它",如"求之不得"、"当之无愧"、"听之任之"、"久而久之"等。课文中"宽之又宽"的"之"字用法也属此类。

做助词时,大致相当于现代汉语的结构助词"的"。如"成功之日"、"新婚之夜"、"职工之家"等,用现代汉语说就是"成功的那一天"、"新婚的夜晚"、"职工的家"。但在有些格式中"之"不能改用"的",如"之一、之二"、"……分之……",还有课文中"……之行"即属此类。

One out of...之 is a function word in classical Chinese. It can be used either as a pronoun or a particle. When it is used as a pronoun, it is more or less equivalent to "him" or "it" functioning as an object, e.g., 求之不得(all one could wish for), 当之无愧(be worthy of), 听之任之(let matters drift), 久而久之(in the course of time), etc. 之 as in 宽之又宽(lenient to the maximum) in the text is also such a case.

When it is used as a particle, it is more or less equivalent to the structural particle 的('s; of) in modern Chinese, as in 成功之日(the day of success), 新婚之夜(the first night of marriage), 职工之家(home of the staff), etc. But in certain collocations, 之 cannot be changed into 的, as in 之一(one of), 之二(two of), ……分之……(...out of...), etc. ……之行(one's trip to...) as in the text also falls into this category.

一、熟读下列各句,说明句中"之"的意义和用法。
　　1. 我们为你这次中国之行安排了丰富节目。
　　2. 财务总监的那个位置,他做梦都想取而代之。
　　3. 全体职工精诚团结之日,就是我们公司成功之日。
　　4. 这些事情,我们切不可操之过急。
　　5. 对人的处理,我们应该慎之又慎。

二、请用"之"完成下列句子。
　　1. 中国人口占世界人口_____。
　　2. 多同中国朋友交流是了解中国的_____。
　　3. 中国的加工贸易主要有三种形式,来料加工只是_____。
　　4. 一日三餐,三餐_____,我对晚餐最重视。
　　5. 千里_____始于足下。

何乐而不为

"何",古汉语疑问副词,意思相当于"怎么、为什么"或"哪里"。"何不",意思是"为什么不"。"何乐而不为"是"何不"的一个扩展形式,"为"是古汉语动词,意思是"做"。"何乐而不为",意思是"为什么不愿意去做"或"为什么不乐意去做"。

Why one would be only too glad to do it. 何 is an interrogative adverb in classical Chinese, with its meaning similar to 怎么(how), 为什么(why), or 哪里(where). 何不 means "why not". 何乐而不为 is an extended form of 何不. 为 is a verb in classical Chinese, meaning 做(do). So 何乐而不为 means "why should one not be willing to do it", or "why should one not be glad to do it".

一、熟读下列各句,体会疑问副词"何"的意义和用法。

1. 这个问题,何不请教一下内行?
2. 这个想法很好,你为何不去大胆试试?
3. 此事对我们双方都有好处,我们何乐而不为?
4. 现在,要抓住一个就业机会,谈何容易?

二、请用"何不"或"何乐而不为"完成下列句子。

1. 趁这次来中国作商业旅行的机会_____。
2. 中国有广大的劳动力市场,有技术熟练的工人,工资又低,中国政府对加工贸易有许多优惠政策,是当今世界上最理想的加工贸易场所,

   _____。
3. 这次商品展销会上不仅提供新产品说明、资料,厂家还为感兴趣的外商安排了参观、访问_____。
4. 全球经济一体化是时代潮流,各国人民都需要互相交流,取长补短,

   _____。
5. 中国的对外贸易取得了长足进步,举世瞩目,许多外国公司在中国取得成功,这是不争的事实,先生如果还有疑虑,_____。

以违规论处

"以",介词,表示动作、行为的方式,相当于"按、根据"。"以"组成的介词结构在句中做状语。"以……论处"意思是"按照……来衡量;评定而给予处理、处罚"。

Be punished for a breach of rules and regulations. 以 is a preposition, indicating the manner of an act or behavior, equivalent to 按（according to）, or 根据（on the basis of）. The prepositional structure formed with 以 functions as an adverbial in the sentence. 以……论处 means "to measure, judge and then deal with or punish in the light of...".

一、熟读下列各句,体会"以……论……"的意义和用法,然后说说它是什么意思。

1. 如果他再不来上班,就以自动离职论处。
2. 倒卖进料加工贸易的料件,一律以走私贩私论处。
3. 我下次再酒后开车,甘愿以违犯交规论罚。
4. 究竟以什么论罪,要视案件性质和情节而定。

二、请用下列短语造句。

1. 以违反合同论处
2. 以责任事故论处
3. 以坚决取缔论处
4. 以承包的工程质量不合格论罚
5. 以擅自离开工作岗位论罚

B

一、请用下列词语组成短语。

削弱　监管　限度　机制　违背　处理　实施
效法　失控　拥护　强化　规定　乱套　装配

二、请用括号里的词语完成下列句子。

1. 为了降低产品成本,许多大型企业,跨国公司,_____
_____。（加工基地）

2. 外商在中国到处都能找到加工贸易的合作伙伴,中国政府为外商营造了_____。（宽松环境）

3. 一些不法商人总想偷税漏税,做梦都想挣大钱,_____
_____。（钻政策的空子）

4. 加工贸易给双方都带来丰厚的利润,一些守法商人也希望_____
_____。（松之又松,宽之又宽）

5. 中国政府对外商既提供优惠、宽松的开放政策,但为了保证正常的经济秩序_____。（严格监管）

6.享誉全球的耐克鞋,没有一双不是在国外生产的,＿＿＿＿＿＿＿＿＿＿＿

＿＿＿＿＿＿＿＿＿＿＿＿＿＿＿＿＿＿＿＿＿＿＿＿＿。(效法的榜样)

三、熟读下列词语,并选择适当的词语填空。

> 半壁江山　　情有独钟　　何乐而不为
> 遍地开花　　一只无形的手

1.加工贸易是中国服务贸易的重要形式之一,在中国对外贸易中,加工贸易的进出口总值,已经占全国商品进出口总值＿＿＿＿＿＿＿＿＿＿＿＿。

2.我对中国的手工艺品、手织地毯＿＿＿＿＿＿＿＿＿＿＿＿。

3.在市场经济中,商品价格＿＿＿＿＿＿＿＿＿＿＿＿。

4.享誉世界的中餐在各国都有中餐馆,真可谓＿＿＿＿＿＿＿＿＿＿＿＿。

5.太太的业余爱好是对她过时的衣服进行加工处理,这既省了我为她买时装的钱,又提高了她的欣赏水平,还常令她的女伴羡慕不已,＿＿＿＿＿

＿＿＿＿＿＿＿＿＿＿＿＿。

四、想一想,谈一谈。

1.中国的加工贸易在对外贸易中占有什么地位? 为什么外企、外商对中国的加工贸易情有独钟?

2.中国的加工贸易都有什么形式? 中方怎么收取加工费?

3.进料加工商品,如因故不能外销或不能全部外销,可以转内销吗?

4.举例说明中国加工贸易优惠、宽松的政策。

5.发展加工贸易有哪些好处?

6.你对中国加工贸易怎么看? 中国加工贸易不实行区域管理带来哪些弊端? 如何防止和克服?

五、阅读下面的短文,然后回答问题。

太 生 动 了

某绣花厂接受了某运动衫厂一批订货,在双方正式签订合同后,就开始了生产。因为数量大,工期短,绣花厂就把其中一部分加工业务转包给了另一家绣花厂。到期,某绣花厂把全部绣好的衣片交给运动衫厂,运动衫厂当时验收,对绣花质量表示满意,并口头答应20天后,付给绣花厂加工费。

但是,20天后,绣花厂去收加工费时,运动衫厂说要再等几日。以后几次催收,都无结果。突然有一天,绣花厂得到法院传票,运动衫厂以绣花质量有问题为由,拒付加工费,并要求赔偿经济损失 10 万元。

法院受理了此案。在法庭辩论中,被告律师说在交货时,原告当场验收,对质量表示满意,没有提出异议,按照我国法律,如果产品外观、质量、规格、花色等不符合合同规定,应在 10 天内提出书面异议,超过这个期限,就应视为所交产品符合合同规定。因此,原告拒付加工费是违约行为。但原告称,运动员穿了这些绣花衣后,对质量问题反映很大。法官问:"什么问题?"原告律师说:"绣花图案太生动了!"法官说:"这不是很好吗?""是很好,运动员出了汗,用运动衫一擦,运动衫上的喜鹊都飞到脸上去了!"听众席上立即响起了一阵笑声。

经过法庭辩论,法院作出了判决。

1. 绣花厂的产品质量有没有问题?是什么问题?
2. 运动衫厂拒付加工费是不是违约行为?为什么?
3. 你认为,法院会作出什么样的判决?为什么?

零售业的开放

26

Opening of Retail Trade

一、逛 市 场

亨　特：爱德华先生,我们从东城跑到西城,从南城跑到北城,已经参观了七八个大商场了,是不是该休息了?

爱德华：听说好运购物中心生意很红火,我们也去看看。

亨　特：北京一万平米以上的超大型商场近两百多家,如果都想去看看,跑得过来吗?

爱德华：我保证,这是参观的最后一家。

亨　特：你真是个工作狂! 晚上你请客,让我们好好儿放松放松!

爱德华：没问题,走!

亨　特：看,这就是好运购物中心,很普通!

爱德华：你刚才不是说,这是一家超市连锁店吗?

亨　特：是,跟国外连锁店、仓储店的格局差不多,不像走进赛特、王府井、东方广场、国贸中心,仿佛是徜徉在世界一流豪华商场里。

爱德华：可我还想去感受一下另一种业态的商场。

亨　特：所以你要来好运看这种普普通通的超市?

爱德华：普通正是这类商场的特点,它的服务对象是普通群众,商品全,价格低。看,这外面还有一个很大的停车场,有购货小推车,看来也很方便,是普通人购物的地方。

亨　特：你还没进门,就对它赞不绝口了。进去吧!

爱德华：好。啊,货区好宽敞,顾客真不少!

亨　特：你要不要买点儿东西，看看他们的管理水平？

爱德华：那倒不用，我们是干这一行的。你看，开架售货，电子结算，售货员少，货架补充及时，这就说明物流畅通，管理科学，商场运作已经上了档次。

亨　特：这真叫外行看热闹，内行看门道。那么，现在我们是不是可以回去了？

爱德华：不，我还想找他们的总经理谈谈。今天参观一天，关于中国的零售业，我有许多问题要问。

亨　特：哦？也好，省得再花时间去向别人请教了。

二、"解禁"后的零售业

丁一波：对不起，今天总经理不在，我能为你们效劳吗？

亨　特：我们是不速之客，没有预约就贸然闯进来了。

爱德华：是我们失礼了！

丁一波：不用客气，我能为你们做些什么呢？

爱德华：我们今天逛了一天商场，有些问题想向你请教。

丁一波：请教，不敢当，尽我所知吧！

爱德华：你能谈谈贵国零售业的发展情况吗？

丁一波：我国的零售业同世界零售业一样，也已经走了三大步。

亨　特：就是说，已经从百货商店、超级市场走向了连锁经营。

丁一波：是的。我们已经实现了从业种向业态零售业的转变。

亨　特：早期的零售业，都是按商品大类来设置商店的，如菜店、布店、粮油店、日用杂货店等等。

爱德华：按业种划分零售企业，是商品经济不发达、卖方市场形态下的产物。

丁一波：改革开放以前，我国的零售业，就是属于这一类。现在的情况就大不同了。

爱德华：我已经注意到了。我们今天就参观了不同类型的商场。

丁一波：所谓业态，就是根据不同层面的消费者、消费群体来切分市场，设置零售企业和商店。于是，除了超大型豪华百货商城外，又有了普通的、仓储式的超市，连锁店，便民店，十元店，主食厨房等等各种业态的商店。

亨　特：所以我们今天看到了零售业的一片繁荣景象。

爱德华：贵国零售业今天这种巨大变化是怎么出现的呢？

亨　特：当然是实行改革开放的结果。

丁一波：是这样。在改革开放初期，我国零售业可以说还是一片禁区，是不允许外资进入的。

爱德华：丁先生是说，你们已经对外开放了零售业？

丁一波：是的，现在已经解禁，并且正在逐步扩大零售业的开放范围。

爱德华：能说得具体一点儿吗？

丁一波：有国务院批准的合资零售企业，有地方自行审批的合资零售企业，也有通过租赁、房地产商招商、宾馆附设专卖店等形式经营的外资零售企业。

亨　特：我知道，像美国沃尔玛、法国家乐福、德国麦德龙、荷兰万客隆等世界超大型跨国连锁公司都进入了中国。

丁一波：他们以雄厚的资金做后盾，以低价位的进入策略挤占中国零售业市场，对我国零售商业形成了巨大冲击。

爱德华：你们这样开放国内零售业市场，不担心吗？

丁一波：噢，我们把它看成是一种竞争，一种激励！

爱德华：我想冒昧地提一个问题。据说，北京现有一万平米以上超大型豪华商场近两百多家，还有同样规模、同样数目的商场在建设中，中国有这么高的消费需求和消费能力吗？

亨　特：据有关资料，消费能力只有东京和纽约1/8的北京，高档商厦却分别是这两座城市的8倍。

爱德华：如果受世界金融危机影响，内需不旺，零售市场的竞争会是什么局面呢？

丁一波：这个问题问得很好。根本问题是要不断扩大内需，内需旺盛，大家都好过日子，零售商们彼此跳楼大甩卖似的恶性竞争，也就不会有了，是不是？

爱德华：看来，你对你们开放零售业充满了信心。

丁一波：我们一方面加强宏观控制，鼓励吸收国际上著名商业集团进入国内市场，同时提高我国零售企业与外国企业的抗衡能力，共同开拓中国的零售业市场，前景还容怀疑吗？

 生 词

1. 工作狂	gōngzuò kuáng	workaholic
2. 放松	fàngsōng	relax, loosen
3. 仓储	cāngchǔ	keep in a storehouse
4. 仿佛	fǎngfú	seemingly; as if
5. 徜徉	chángyáng	roam leisurely
6. 豪华	háohuá	luxurious
7. 业态	yètài	business status
8. 推车	tuīchē	cart
9. 赞不绝口	zàn bù jué kǒu	be profuse in praise
10. 宽敞	kuānchang	spacious
11. 开架	kāijià	open-shelf
12. 畅通	chàngtōng	unimpeded, unblocked
13. 档次	dàngcì	grade
14. 外行	wàiháng	layman
15. 内行	nèiháng	expert
16. 门道	méndao	way to do something, knack
17. 解禁	jiějìn	lift a ban
18. 不速之客	bú sù zhī kè	unexpected guest
19. 预约	yùyuē	make an appointment
20. 贸然	màorán	rashly
21. 业种	yèzhǒng	kind of business
22. 设置	shèzhì	establish
23. 杂货	záhuò	sundry goods, groceries
24. 形态	xíngtài	form, pattern

25. 产物	chǎnwù	product, outcome
26. 类型	lèixíng	type
27. 层面	céngmiàn	stratum
28. 群体	qúntǐ	group
29. 切分	qiēfēn	divide
30. 禁区	jìnqū	forbidden zone
31. 批准	pīzhǔn	approve
32. 自行	zìxíng	by oneself, of oneself
33. 审批	shěnpī	examine and approve
34. 租赁	zūlìn	lease
35. 附设	fùshè	have as an affiliated unit
36. 后盾	hòudùn	backing
37. 价位	jiàwèi	price level
38. 挤占	jǐzhàn	squeeze into and occupy
39. 激励	jīlì	encourage, urge
40. 冒昧	màomèi	venture, take the liberty
41. 建设	jiànshè	construction; build
42. 内需	nèixū	domestic demand
43. 旺盛	wàngshèng	vigorous, exuberant
44. 恶性	èxìng	vicious
45. 鼓励	gǔlì	encourage
46. 吸收	xīshōu	absorb
47. 抗衡	kànghéng	contend with, match

专 名 Proper Nouns

1. 沃尔玛	Wò'ěrmǎ	Walmart
2. 家乐福	Jiālèfú	Carrefour
3. 麦德龙	Màidélóng	Metro
4. 万客隆	Wànkèlóng	Makro

 练 习

A

过来

我们学习过趋向动词"过来"、"过去"。"过来"表示从一地向说话人所在地来，"过去"则是离开或经过说话人所在地向另一地点去。例如："他向我走过来了。""汽车从我身边开过去了。"

课文里的"过来"是表示能不能周到、圆满地做完某事，说这话时常涉及时间、数量等因素。中间加"得"或"不"构成或肯定、或否定的形式。受事一般都放在前边。

Come over. We already learned the directional verbs 过来 and 过去. 过来 indicates motion towards the speaker, while 过去 indicates motion away from the speaker. For instance: 他向我走过来了, 汽车从我身边开过去了.

过来 in the text indicates whether one could or could not finish doing something satisfactorily, often involving such factors as time, quantity, etc. 得 or 不 is inserted in the middle to form a positive or negative form. The receiver of the action is normally placed in the front.

一、熟读下列各句,体会各种"过来"的意义和用法。

　　1.这个展览会上的新奇玩意儿太多了,实在看不过来!

　　2.这个自助餐馆好吃的东西这么多,你吃得过来吗?

　　3.超级市场失窃现象时有发生,再多保安人员也看不过来。

　　4.不就是这么点儿事吗? 我一个人也干得过来!

　　5.现在的人际关系太复杂了,都要照顾周全,我照顾得过来吗?

二、请用下列短语造句。

　　1.核查不过来

　　2.安排不过来

　　3.处罚不过来

　　4.接待得过来

　　5.忙得过来

仿佛

①动词,意思是差不多,单独做谓语,前面可加"相"字。②副词,意思是好像、似乎,表示一种不十分肯定的感觉和判断,句末可加"似的"、"一样"、"一般"等加强语气。但"仿佛"与"似乎"有时不能互换。"仿佛"还可以表示比拟,即用一个事物比另一个事物,而"似乎"不能这么用;"似乎"也不能与"似的"、"一样"、"一般"连用。

Seemingly;be alike. 1) When used as a verb, it means "about the same". It is used independently as the predicate, and can be preceded by 相(mutually). 2) It can also be used as an adverb, meaning "seemingly;as if". It expresses a not so certain kind of feeling or judgment. At the end of the sentence, such words as 似的(similar)、一样 or 一般(same)can be added for emphasis. But sometimes 仿佛 and 似乎 are not interchangeable. 仿佛 can also be used metaphorically, using one thing as an analogy for another, and 似乎 cannot. What's more, 似乎 cannot be used together with 似的、一样 or 一般.

一、熟读下列各句,分别指出句中"仿佛"的意义和用法。

1. 他仿佛是一个大老板,神气得很!
2. 他们俩的年纪相仿佛。
3. 看他那样子,仿佛十分痛苦。
4. 几年没见他,他仿佛变了一个人似的。
5. 这方面的业务,他仿佛很精通。
6. 看见这份市场调查报告,总裁仿佛看见了成功的希望。

二、请用"仿佛"完成下列句子。

1. 太太进了仓储店见什么都想买,＿＿＿＿＿＿＿＿＿＿。
2. 欧美人看汉字＿＿＿＿＿＿＿＿＿。
3. 爱德华先生是位中国通,请他谈中国改革开放后的变化＿＿＿＿＿＿＿
＿＿＿＿＿＿。
4. 爱德华先生的汉语水平＿＿＿＿＿＿＿＿＿＿。
5. 老板五十开外的人了,可他的精力＿＿＿＿＿＿＿＿＿＿。

省得

连词,表示避免发生某种不希望的情况,多用于后一小句的开头。多用于口语。

So as to avoid. It is a conjunction, expressing avoidance of certain circumstances that are not wished for. It is normally placed at the beginning of the second clause. It is often used in spoken language.

一、熟读下列各句,体会"省得"的意义和用法。

1. 这事儿我自己去办,省得麻烦别人。

2. 你如果有事儿,请先打个电话来,省得你白跑。

3. 出外旅行就多带点儿钱,省得到时候着急。

4. 凡事都应该想得周全一点儿,省得将来后悔。

二、请用"省得"完成下列句子。

1. 合同签字前要反复协商、审核,_____。

2. 外商、外企到中国投资前先要作好市场调查,_____。

3. 购买空调前要好好咨询,并请专业人员安装、调试,_____。

4. 出去旅行要作好充分准备,_____。

5. 技术转让双方在法律、解释方面都可能出现分歧,必须一一磋商,寻求解决的途径,_____。

贸然/冒昧

"贸然",副词,表示动作、行为轻率,欠考虑。修饰动词成分,在句中做状语。"冒昧"是形容词,形容一个人不顾地位、能力、场合、言行是否合适。多用作谦辞。在句中可以做状语,也可以做定语、宾语。

Rashly, take the liberty. 贸然 is an adverb, indicating a rash or hasty act or action without careful consideration. It modifies the verb and functions as an adverbial in the sentence. 冒昧 is an adjective, describing a person who disregards the appropriateness of position, ability, situation, words and deeds. It is often used as a self-depreciatory expression. It can function as an adverbial, attributive or object in a sentence.

一、熟读下列各句,体会"贸然"、"冒昧"的意义和用法。

1. 我贸然造访,你不介意吧?

2. 我冒昧地来打扰你,实在抱歉!

3. 你没有调查清楚就贸然下结论,是不是太轻率了?

4. 你的冒昧言行,只能说明你没有教养。

5. 请恕我冒昧,我有点儿急事要请教,不得不打断你们的谈话。

6. 现在的形势十分严峻,切不可贸然行事!

二、请用"贸然"或"冒昧"填空。

1. 你说话这么_____，说明你还不老练。

2. 商场如战场，_____作出决定，只能自取失败。

3. 在许多国家事先不打电话预约，不能拜访，即使老朋友也不例外，否则被认为太_____，不礼貌。

4. 总经理知道自己说话有影响力，所以他从不_____赞成或反对什么。

5. 我知道我这样做很_____，但我实在不得已。

6. 爱德华先生，我_____地向您提个问题，在您碰到疑难问题时，您首先找谁？

B

一、请用下列词语组成短语。

允许　租赁　抗衡　鼓励　机制　贸然

设置　吸收　旺盛　激励　内需　审批

二、请用括号里的词语完成下列句子。

1. 在改革开放初期，中国的零售业是不允许外资进入的，_____
_____。（一片禁区）

2. 改革开放前，中国的零售业按业种划分，这是商品经济下，卖方市场形态的产物_____。（情况大不同）

3. 北京一万平米以上的超大型豪华商场两百多家，宽敞的货区，琳琅满目的商品，文明礼貌的服务，徜徉其间，仿佛_____
_____。（世界一流）

4. 世界超大型跨国连锁公司都进入了中国，他们_____
_____。（巨大冲击）

5. 不断扩大内需是解决零售商们_____。（恶性竞争）

三、熟读下列短语，并各造一个句子。

1. 赞不绝口

2. 外行看热闹，内行看门道

3. 不速之客

四、想一想,谈一谈。

1. 连锁店、仓储店用什么跟一流豪华商场竞争?

2. 中国的零售业改革开放以来已走了哪三大步? 实现了什么转变?

3. 世界超大型跨国连锁公司纷纷进入中国零售业市场,请列举2~3例。他们凭借什么挤占中国零售业市场?

4. 中国政府为什么开放零售业市场,并对开放零售业市场充满信心?

五、阅读下面的短文,然后回答问题。

商 业 诚 信

　　我喜欢去超级市场买东西,那儿店堂宽敞明亮,洁净舒适,商品丰富,开架售货,可以任意挑选,在那儿买东西是一种享受。今天又有一家超市开业,我就兴冲冲地去了。"啊,好漂亮呀!"我们现在的豪华商场真是一个赛一个。我在商场里悠闲愉快地漫步着,一边像观赏风景,一边观察有没有我所需要的东西。果然,我看见了一种皮革转椅,正是我书房里所需要的。一看价钱,一千挂零,也不贵,我当即就买了一把。回到家,我粗略地看了一下说明书,就把椅子组装起来了。试了试,坐着还真舒服。可是,三个星期以后,我觉得椅子有点儿高,我想调低一点儿,可怎么也不行。我决定去商场换一把。我想把椅子拆了,重新包装好,到商场去换。但椅子怎么也不能完全拆下来,我只好提着没有拆完的椅子和包装箱去了商场。在货物退换柜台,我说:"小姐,我想换一把椅子。"小姐问:"你还有购物小票吗?""有。"小姐接过我的购物小票,看了看,就把椅子收进了柜台,把钱如数退给了我。我说:"你不检查检查,看看少没少什么?"小姐笑了笑说:"不用。"我又说:"对不起,椅子我没有拆完,也没有包装好。""没有关系。""那太谢谢你了!"小姐说:"不谢,欢迎您下次再来!"我高高兴兴离开了柜台,可我喜欢那把椅子,退了又有些遗憾。我不禁又走到卖椅子的地方,那种椅子还有得卖,而且还降价了,只卖八百多块了。我站了好半天,最终还是决定再买一把回去。我对自己说,这次好好儿看看说明书,一定要把椅子安装好。

1. 顾客买的商品,没有保持完好,甚至没有包装好,可以退回商场吗?

2. 商场的小姐为什么不检查顾客退回的商品?

3. 商家需要商业诚信,顾客也需要商业诚信吗? 从这个故事能得出怎样的结论?

3月15日 27

Fifteenth of March

一、谁 的 节 日

亨　特：爱德华先生，今天是什么日子？

爱德华：什么日子？一个平平常常的日子啊！

亨　特：不，这是一个很特殊的日子。你说今天是几月几号？

爱德华：3月15。嗯，想起来了，今天是国际消费者权益日。

亨　特：这就对了，你看这大街两边，到处都插着彩旗，挂着横幅标语，还有敲锣打鼓、唱歌跳舞的呢！

爱德华：真的，像过节一样，这可比我们国家过"3·15"热闹多了。

亨　特：可最早是肯尼迪总统倡导的。

爱德华：我记得。1962年3月15日，他在发表国情咨文时，首次提出消费者有获得安全保障、自由选择、获悉资料和发表意见四项基本权利。

亨　特：后来，他又补充了一条，就是消费者有获得赔偿的权利。

爱德华：1983年，国际消费者联盟组织就把每年的3月15日定为国际消费者日了。

亨　特：看样子，中国比哪个国家都更重视这个节日。

爱德华：你是从哪儿看出来的？

亨　特：中国每年到了这一天，都要大张旗鼓宣传消费者的权益，中央和地方的电视台都要搞一台"3·15"专题晚会，大街上到处都在搞"3·15"咨询。可以说，"3·15"已经成了中国全民的节日。

爱德华:没想到,中国会这么重视消费者的权益!

亨　特:中国当局还制定了一部《消费者权益保护法》,现在执行得很坚决。

爱德华:怎么个坚决法？你说来听听。

亨　特:啊,我给你举一个例子吧。商店里是不是常有假冒伪劣产品出售？

爱德华:是的,哪个国家都有不法商人。

亨　特:中国就有"打假"专业户,专门到商店购买假冒伪劣产品,然后到消费者协会投诉,甚至上诉法庭。

爱德华:他这样做的目的是什么？

亨　特:教训那些不法商人,维护消费者的权益啊!

爱德华:他能达到自己的目的吗？

亨　特:他手中有武器——《消费者权益保护法》,他总能得到中国有关方面的支持。大家管这种人叫"打假英雄"。

爱德华:听起来很新鲜!

亨　特:看,那家商场门前正在搞"3·15"现场咨询,我们过去同那里的人聊聊,会听到更多的新鲜事儿。

爱德华:好,我们过去看看!

二、街头"3·15"咨询

爱德华:小姐,你是来现场咨询的?

芳　芳:是的,我在一家商店买了一件打折的衣服,拿回家后发现有质量问题,我要求商店退货,可商家说打折商品概不退换。

爱德华:衣服很贵吗?

芳　芳:不贵,所以我妈说,算了,谁让你贪便宜!

爱德华:你不听你妈的话,还是上这儿来了?

芳　芳:是。我偏要同商家较较这个真儿,讨个公道。

爱德华:你已经咨询过了吗?有什么说法?

芳　芳：国家质量技术监督局的一位先生告诉我,打折商品不是处理商品,同其他商品一样,按照产品质量法的规定,出现质量问题,应当负责修理、更换、退货,而且售后服务一样也不能少。

爱德华：啊,太好了。小姐,祝贺你讨回了公道!

芳　芳：谢谢! 不过,我还得回去找商家。

爱德华：这回商家该没话说了!

芳　芳：也不一定,他们总有托辞和办法对付你。

亨　特：那你怎么办?

芳　芳：无非是多搭上些时间和精力。他们要是不理睬我,我就先找新闻媒体给它曝曝光。

亨　特：商家要是不怕呢?

芳　芳：再不行,我就找消协,或者上法院告它。

爱德华：噢,小姐,我十分钦佩你这种不达目的誓不罢休的精神!

芳　芳：谢谢! 我得走了,再见!

爱德华：先生,您是市消协的,我可以咨询一些问题吗?

吴开继：欢迎! 您想问什么问题?

爱德华：你们"3·15"每年都作这样的现场咨询吗?

吴开继：每年都作,但每年都有不同的主题。

爱德华：今年"3·15"活动的主题是什么?

亨　特：是横幅上写的"安全健康消费"吗?

吴开继：对,"安全健康消费"。

爱德华：这方面存在很大问题吗?

吴开继：消费中,人们在人身、健康和财产等方面受到损害的事时有发生。

爱德华：能说一两个例子吗?

吴开继：比如说女士买化妆品,使用后严重感染;买家用燃气热水器,造成煤气中毒甚至死亡;在超市购物,被非法搜身,人格尊严和身心健康受到伤害;等等。

爱德华：啊,这些问题很严重,难道消费者不知道怎么保护自己,还需要你们这样宣传吗?

吴开继:大多数人都能主动寻求法律保护,但也有不少人对赔偿请
　　　　求权、产品安全使用期等相关法律法规不了解,受到损害
　　　　后不知道寻求保护。

爱德华:我发现,中国抽烟的人很多,有烟民控告烟草商吗?

吴开继:还没有这样的案例。据有关权威部门统计,消费者在消费
　　　　中受到损害后去投诉的现在仅占受害者的10%。

亨　特:噢,这个比例太小了。

吴开继:有的消费者明知是商家的责任,甚至被商家无理刁难,受了
　　　　窝囊气,但对投诉缺乏信心,也只好忍气吞声,自认倒霉。

爱德华:那么,除了像你们现在这样搞宣传活动外,消费中的纠纷
　　　　和投诉实际解决得怎么样呢?

吴开继:绝大多数投诉都得到了圆满、妥善解决,我们一年要为消
　　　　费者挽回经济损失一二十亿。

亨　特:成绩真不小。

吴开继:有些方面的投诉一直居高不下;也有些纠纷,因为取证不足,
　　　　长期悬而未决。我们还要继续加强宣传和执法的力度。

生 词

1. 平常	píngcháng	ordinary
2. 权益	quányì	rights and interests
3. 插	chā	stick in, insert
4. 彩旗	cǎiqí	colored flags
5. 横幅	héngfú	banner, streamer
6. 敲锣打鼓	qiāo luó dǎ gǔ	beat the drums and the gongs
7. 倡导	chàngdǎo	initiate, advocate
8. 国情咨文	guóqíng zīwén	State-of-the-Union address
9. 获悉	huòxī	learn (of a event)
10. 大张旗鼓	dà zhāng qí gǔ	on a grand scale, in a big way
11. 晚会	wǎnhuì	evening party

12. 当局	dāngjú	authorities
13. 打假	dǎjiǎ	combating shoddy goods
14. 专业户	zhuānyèhù	specialized household
15. 武器	wǔqì	weapon
16. 英雄	yīngxióng	hero
17. 打折	dǎzhé	discount
18. 贪(图)	tān(tú)	seek , covet
19. 偏	piān	willfully , insistently
20. 较真	jiàozhēn	serious , earnest
21. 说法	shuōfǎ	way of saying a thing , statement
22. 托辞	tuōcí	excuse
23. 搭上	dāshàng	throw in more , add
24. 理睬	lǐcǎi	pay attention to
25. 新闻	xīnwén	news
26. 媒体	méitǐ	media
27. 曝光	bàoguāng	exposure
28. 钦佩	qīnpèi	admire
29. 誓不罢休	shì bú bà xiū	swear not to stop
30. 主题	zhǔtí	theme
31. 人身	rénshēn	person ; personal
32. 感染	gǎnrǎn	infect
33. 燃气热水器	ránqì rèshuǐqì	gas water heater
34. 煤气	méiqì	coal gas
35. 中毒	zhòngdú	be poisoned
36. 搜身	sōushēn	make a body search
37. 人格	réngé	personality , moral quality
38. 尊严	zūnyán	dignity
39. 寻求	xúnqiú	seek
40. 控告	kònggào	charge , accuse
41. 权威	quánwēi	authority
42. 刁难	diāonàn	create difficulties
43. 窝囊气	wōnangqì	(be subjected to) petty annoyances
44. 缺乏	quēfá	lack
45. 忍气吞声	rěn qì tūn shēng	swallow an insult

46. 妥善	tuǒshàn	appropriate
47. 挽回	wǎnhuí	retrieve
48. 居高不下	jū gāo bú xià	stay high without coming down
49. 取证	qǔzhèng	collect evidence
50. 悬而未决	xuán ér wèi jué	unresolved
51. 执法	zhífǎ	enforce the law
52. 力度	lìdù	strength

专 名 Proper Nouns

1. 肯尼迪	Kěnnídí	Kennedy
2. 国际消费者联盟组织	Guójì Xiāofèizhě Liánméng Zǔzhī	International Organization of Consumers Unions

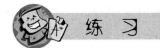

管……叫……

"管",介词,构成"管……叫……"的格式,用来称说人或事物,只用于口语。

Call somebody.... 管 is a preposition, used to form the pattern of 管……叫…… It is used to call somebody or something. It is colloquial.

一、熟读下列各句,体会"管……叫……"的意义和用法。

1. 四川人管白薯叫"红苕"。

2. 他们管我叫老板,其实我也是打工的。

3. 他特别聪明,常有好主意,大家管他叫"小诸葛"。

4. 在别人面前说到自己的妻子,中国人有许多说法。旧时,管妻子叫"内子"、"贱内";现在,有管妻子叫"爱人"的,城市里有管妻子叫"我那口子"的,农村里很多男人管妻子叫"孩子他妈"。

二、完成下列句子。

1. 中国人管计算机叫_____。

2. 改革开放后出现了许多新词语。人们管离开行政、事业单位从事贸易活动叫_____。管先富起来的有钱人叫_____。管非法倒换外币的活动叫_____。

3. 北京电视台"今晚我们相识"栏目为未婚男女牵线搭桥,人们管这个栏目及主持人叫_____。

4. 中国人幽默风趣。他们用汉字的谐音,管怕妻子的先生叫_____,管被娇惯的独生子女叫_____。

偏/偏偏

副词。①表示出乎意料,所发生的事与某种愿望、要求或常理相反。②表示行为主体的强烈意志,决心要做某事,比用"倒、却、反而"等语气更坚决。③表示范围,意思是"只有"、"仅仅",同时含有出乎意料和不满意的口气。

偏 or 偏偏 is an adverb. 1) It means "contrary to expectations". What happened is contrary to a certain wish, requirement or norm. 2) It expresses the strong will or determination of the subject to do something. It is stronger in tone than 倒、却, or 反而. 3) It indicates the scope, meaning "only" or "alone". It implies at the same time a tone of dissatisfaction or out of expectation.

一、熟读下列各句,分别指出各句中"偏"或"偏偏"的意义和用法。

1. 一场精彩足球赛正要开始,偏偏下起大雨来了!

2. 这种处理品,我不叫你买,你偏要买,怎么样,白花钱了吧?

3. 开会的人都到了,偏偏会议主持人还没到。

4. 政府不准出售假冒伪劣产品,而一些不法商人偏要制假卖假。

5. 大家都涨了工资,偏偏不给我涨工资,为什么?

6. 他的孩子都在上学,正是需要钱的时候,他偏偏失业了!

7. 政府正在大张旗鼓打假,一些人偏要顶风作案。

8. 我们扩大了生产规模,偏偏遇上内需不旺,产品滞销。

二、请用"偏"或"偏偏"和下列短语造句。

1. 挽回经济损失

2. 碰上堵车

3. 市场行情不稳定

4. 对加工贸易感兴趣

5. 普通超市

6. 资金周转不灵

无非

副词,常用在判断句里加强肯定语气,表示所说的事物不会超出说话人设定的范围,因此常组成"无非……之流"、"无非……之类"的格式。有时还含有轻蔑的意味。

Nothing but. It is an adverb, often used in a sentence that contains the link verb 是 (be), stressing that the things mentioned would not go beyond the scope set by the speaker. Therefore it often forms such patterns as 无非……之流 or 无非……之类. Sometimes it implies a sense of contempt.

一、熟读下列各句,仔细体会"无非"的意义和用法。

1. 学外语有什么难,无非是少睡点儿觉,多下点儿工夫。

2. 打假英雄的行为,无非是想教训不法商人,维护消费者的利益。

3. 这些人无非是酒囊饭袋之流。

4. 这笔生意我决定做了,无非是赔点儿钱。

5. 这个商店卖的无非是油盐酱醋之类,没什么值钱的东西。

二、请用"无非"和括号里的词语完成下列句子。

1. 维护消费者的合法权益,_____。(坚决执法)

2. 消费者买了不合格商品跟商家较真儿,目的_____
_____。(讨个公道)

3. 大张旗鼓宣传消费者权益,目的_____
_____。(寻求法律保护)

4. 有些消费者在消费中受到损害却不肯投诉,_____
_____。(缺乏信心)

5. 一些不法商人知法犯法,_____。(贪图钱财)

B

一、请用下列词语组成短语。

媒体　　商品　　获悉　　力度　　执法

打折　　曝光　　宣传　　资料　　倡导

二、熟读下列词语,并选择适当的词语填空。

> 忍气吞声　　敲锣打鼓　　誓不罢休
> 悬而未决　　大张旗鼓　　居高不下
> 无理刁难　　受窝囊气　　自认倒霉

1. 自古以来中国人民一碰到高兴的、值得庆贺的事儿便_____庆祝。

2. 为了保护人类的生存环境,增强人们的环保意识,每到世界环保日,中国政府都要_____宣传。

3. 令人痛心的是,由于各种各样的原因,艾滋病感染的人数,多年来_____。

4. 改革开放后,商家纷纷提供良好的售后服务,现在拒不更换货物的事儿很少见到了,_____顾客的事儿也没有了。

5. 一不小心,买了路边无证摊贩的水果,缺斤短两是常事儿,你找他评理,他会不认账,你只好_____。

6. 老外初来北京,不会汉语,不熟悉北京,乘坐出租汽车难免_____。

7. 市场上老年保健食品、营养品、女士化妆品相对地说存在问题较大。一来名目繁多,标准难统一;二来取证困难。一旦名不副实,你只有_____。

8. 这个项目,双方已经进行了长达半年的耐心谈判,许多问题仍然_____。

9. 总经理来华不久便对自己说,我不学好汉语_____。

三、想一想,谈一谈。

1. 国际消费者权益日是谁倡导的,它的内容有哪些?

2. 作为消费者,你的权益受到损害时,你会怎么做?

3. 你认为中国的消费者消费保护意识怎么样? 中国政府为保护消费者权益做了哪些工作?

4. 贵国如何保护消费者权益?

四、阅读下面的短文,然后回答问题。

熊掌风波

一天,女大学生小王和小黄,带了150元钱,到一家个体餐厅吃饭。殷勤的服务员递过菜谱,小王一看,轻声叫起来:"哎,熊掌,20元一份!"小黄也惊喜道:"常听人说熊掌是多么名贵的菜肴,这么便宜,我们来两盘!"她们又要了两听饮料、两碗米饭。高高兴兴吃完,"买单!"服务小姐递过账单:"一共是4 025元!""什么?4 025?""是,熊掌一盘2 000元,饮料和米饭25元。""熊掌不是20元一盘吗?""20元?二位小姐,请看清楚了!"小王拿起菜单再看,果然是2 000元一盘,只是后边的两个零写得小一点儿。她们这下可傻了眼,只好留下学生证,回学校东挪西借,第二天才凑足钱,还了账。

一位律师听说了这事,就去找到两个女学生,让她们去饭店要回付款收据,然后请工商局的人一起去了个体饭店。工商局的人对老板说:"你们经营熊掌,违反了国家《野生动物保护法》,罚款20 000元!"这时,该个体老板傻眼了,"我哪有那么多钱!我以后再也不卖熊掌了不行吗?""不行,没钱交罚款,那就吊销营业执照,关门!""同志,我老实交代,我根本就没有卖什么熊掌,那全是牛蹄筋。"律师说:"一盘牛蹄筋10元钱,你们把多收的钱退给学生,另外赔偿精神损失费1 000元。""好,我退,我退!"说完,当即把5 000元交给学生。这时,工商局的人又说:"你违法经营,又坑害顾客,按规定,罚款2 000元,限你明天交到工商局。"

1. 女大学生为什么会看错菜价?
2. 律师怎样保护了两个女大学生的利益?
3. 个体老板是怎么经营饭店的?结果如何?
4. 你有过类似的经历吗?是怎么处理的?

金融服务业 28

Financial Services

一、北京金融街巡礼

亨　特：出租车！

司　机：请上车！二位先生去哪儿？

亨　特：去金融街！你知道北京金融街吗？

司　机：怎么能不知道？我常拉外国朋友去那儿,他们说,那是中国的"华尔街"。

爱德华：哦？中国的"华尔街"？

司　机：我不知道美国的华尔街是什么样,可我知道我们这条金融街真是气派得很呢！那里的大楼一座比一座高,一座比一座漂亮！

爱德华：你感到很自豪？

司　机：那当然,这是北京的一道亮丽风景线嘛！

亨　特：那你知道外国人为什么管它叫中国的"华尔街"吗？

司　机：兴许是这儿的银行多呗！中国人民银行、中国银行、中国工商银行、中国建设银行、中国交通银行、中国人民保险公司、中国证券公司……总之是国家级银行总部和非银行金融机构总部,几乎都在这条街上安家落户。

爱德华：啊,你开快一点儿,我禁不住想立即见到这条中国的"华尔街"！

司　机：那可是块宝地,作为金融街,没准儿比美国华尔街还有历史呢！

爱德华：你是说，这条街已经建成很久了？

司　机：不，你们就要看到的金融街，是从 20 世纪 90 年代初才开始
建设的。

亨　特：你是说，那儿在很久以前就是中国的金融中心？

司　机：是。早在我国的明、清时代，那儿就叫"金城坊"，也就是今
天说的金融街。除了国家的银号外，巨商富豪都是在那儿
发迹致富的。

亨　特：这里面一定有很多有趣的故事。

司　机：那可是三天三夜都说不完！

爱德华：你给我们讲一两个。

司　机：唉，在那个年代，无非是几家欢乐几家愁！噢，到了，下次
再坐我的车，我再给你们讲吧！

亨　特：我就爱跟北京的出租车司机聊天儿，能长很多见识。

司　机：我也爱跟客人聊，特别是外国朋友，都想了解咱北京，我得
当好这主人不是！

爱德华：太谢谢你了，坐你的车，很愉快！

司　机：别客气，要是有缘，我们下次再见！

二、访中国人民银行

爱德华：朱先生，我们刚游览了金融街，确实十分宏伟壮观。

朱宝山：这是一个以金融机构办公、营业为主的街区，同时有股票、证
券、资金、黄金、外汇调节、金融抵押、租赁、期货等各类金融
市场，以及具有金融特色的律师事务所和会计师事务所。

爱德华：这可是一个名副其实的金融中心！

朱宝山：是的。这里将成为功能完善，设施先进，配套齐全的全国
性金融管理、融资、结算和信息中心，并逐步发展成为国际
金融中心。

亨　特：那么，金融家们可以在这里把握高速发展的中国经济脉

搏,观察瞬息万变的世界金融动态。

爱德华:目前,有外国金融机构进驻金融街吗?

朱宝山:这儿有得天独厚的优势,众多外资营业性金融机构和中介机构,都相中了这块宝地。

亨　特:中国政府不断加大开放金融市场的步伐,为他们开了方便之门。

朱宝山:是的。我们正在积极、稳妥地推进金融业的对外开放,我们已经取消了外资银行在中国设立营业性分支机构的地域限制。

爱德华:难道以前有地域限制吗?

亨　特:开始只有北京、上海和深圳允许设立外资金融机构。

朱宝山:现在外资银行在华设立经营性分支机构的地域,从北京等二十几个城市扩大到了全国所有中心城市。

爱德华:那么,是不是也取消了对外资银行业务范围的限制呢?

朱宝山:当然也只能是陆续开放。不过,一些外资银行驻华代表处、办事处,现在已经获准升格为分行。

爱德华:也有我们美国的银行吗?

亨　特:有大通银行驻北京代表处,花旗银行也早就可以从事同业拆借业务。

朱宝山:从2006年12月起,外国银行在中国的分行,可以申请将分行转为在中国注册的法人银行,发展中国境内公民的人民币业务。人民币业务已经对外资银行全面开放。

亨　特:从2007年4月起,一些外资银行已经完成了这种转型,获准正式营业。

朱宝山:是的。这些银行的业务范围也在迅速扩大,从人民币储蓄、贷款、资金拆借、楼房按揭,已发展到担保、承兑、贴现、重大项目融资和国债交易。

爱德华:啊,这种开放态势太诱人了! 这些运作,激活了资本流动,必然给中外企业注入大量资金,带来新的发展机遇。

亨　特:中国一直实行稳健的货币政策,保持人民币不贬值和低通货膨胀,对稳定世界金融形势作出了很大贡献,赢得了全世界的广泛赞誉。我们对中国经济的发展前景充满了信心。

朱宝山：我国宏观经济运行良好，国际收支盈余，外汇储备充裕，经
　　　　济多年保持持续、高速发展。我们将以更加开放的姿态，
　　　　吸引更多的外国企业家来华投资。

爱德华：不用说，也包括金融业的进一步开放？

朱宝山：是的。当然，为了防范和化解金融风险，这种开放只能是
　　　　稳妥的、循序渐进的。

亨　特：可以理解。用中国话说，性急喝不得热粥，一口吃不成胖
　　　　子嘛！

生　词

1. 巡礼	xúnlǐ	sight-seeing; tour; visit a sacred land
2. 自豪	zìháo	be proud of
3. 亮丽	liànglì	bright and beautiful
4. 风景线	fēngjǐngxiàn	scenic line
5. 兴许	xīngxǔ	perhaps, maybe
6. 证券	zhèngquàn	securities
7. 安家落户	ān jiā luò hù	make one's home in a new place, settle
8. 禁不住	jīnbuzhù	can't help
9. 坊	fāng	lane
10. 银号	yínhào	banking house
11. 富豪	fùháo	rich and powerful people
12. 发迹	fājì	gain fame and fortune
13. 致富	zhìfù	become rich, make a fortune
14. 欢乐	huānlè	happy, joyous
15. 有缘	yǒuyuán	be predetermined by fate; have an affinity
16. 宏伟	hóngwěi	magnificent

17. 壮观	zhuàngguān	grand
18. 股票	gǔpiào	share，stock
19. 黄金	huángjīn	gold
20. 调节	tiáojié	adjust，regulate
21. 期货	qīhuò	futures
22. 设施	shèshī	installation，facilities
23. 齐全	qíquán	complete；all in readiness
24. 融资	róngzī	financing
25. 把握	bǎwò	hold，grasp；certainty
26. 脉搏	màibó	pulse
27. 观察	guānchá	observe
28. 动态	dòngtài	trends，dynamic state
29. 得天独厚	dé tiān dú hòu	be richly endowed by nature
30. 中介	zhōngjiè	intermediary
31. 相中	xiāngzhòng	settle on；take a fancy to
32. 稳妥	wěntuǒ	safe，reliable
33. 推进	tuījìn	push forward
34. 分支	fēnzhī	branch
35. 所有	suǒyǒu	all
36. 陆续	lùxù	one after another；in succession
37. 升格	shēnggé	upgrade
38. 态势	tàishì	situation，posture
39. 激活	jīhuó	activation
40. 注入	zhùrù	inject
41. 稳健	wěnjiàn	firm，steady
42. 贬值	biǎnzhí	devaluate，depreciate
43. 通货	tōnghuò	currency
44. 膨胀	péngzhàng	inflate，expand
45. 赞誉	zànyù	praise，acclaim
46. 宏观	hóngguān	macro
47. 盈余	yíngyú	surplus
48. 储备	chǔbèi	reserve
49. 充裕	chōngyù	abundant，plentiful
50. 防范	fángfàn	be on guard；take precautions

| 51. 化解 | huàjiě | dispel, dissolve |
| 52. 性急 | xìngjí | impatient, short-tempered |

专　名　Proper Nouns

1. 华尔街	Huá'ěr Jiē	Wall Street
2. 明代	Míngdài	the Ming Dynasty
3. 清代	Qīngdài	the Qing Dynasty
4. 大通银行	Dàtōng Yínháng	Chase Manhattan Bank
5. 花旗银行	Huāqí Yínháng	the Citibank

 练　习

A

禁不住

动补结构词组。①"承受不住",用于人或事物。与"禁不住"相对应是"禁得住"。②"抑制不住、忍不住",后面必带动词、小句做宾语,主语限于人。"禁得住"没有这个义项的对应用法。

Be unable to bear or endure; cannot help doing something. It is a phrase formed by verb + complement and has two meanings. One is "be unable to bear", which is used to refer to a person or a thing. The opposite of 禁不住 is 禁得住. The second meaning is "cannot control" or "cannot help doing something". It takes a verb or a clause as its object and the subject is restricted to people. 禁得住 does not have the corresponding use here.

一、熟读下列各句,体会并说出"禁不住"、"禁得住"的意义和用法。

　　1. 你这样的身体禁不住这么折腾。

　　2. 他禁不住一阵伤心,哭了起来。

　　3. 公司资金雄厚,禁得住这次打击。

　　4. 银行提供楼房按揭,我禁不住也想贷款买房了。

　　5. 经济实力不强大的国家,禁不住如此严峻的金融危机的冲击。

6. 不管国际资本市场汇率怎么波动,我们禁得住风险。

二、请用"禁不住"或"禁得住"完成下列句子。

1. 这是一家有近百年历史的证券交易所,没想到在 20 世纪最后一次全球金融危机中＿＿＿＿＿＿＿＿＿＿。

2. 每一位参加国际比赛的运动员,赛前、赛后都要接受尿样检查,＿＿＿＿＿＿＿＿＿＿＿＿＿＿＿。

3. 中国老一代夫妻,彼此很少说"我爱你",但他们风雨同舟几十年,＿＿＿＿＿＿＿＿＿＿＿＿＿＿。

4. 很多吸毒者戒毒后＿＿＿＿＿＿＿＿＿＿＿＿＿＿。

5. 这家百年老店,经营传统的手工艺品,享有极高的信誉,卖出的商品＿＿＿＿＿＿＿＿＿＿＿＿。

6. 在 20 世纪最后一次全球性金融危机中,他苦心经营的＿＿＿＿＿＿＿＿＿＿＿＿＿＿。

没准儿

口语,意思是"不一定",表示不能肯定。但"不一定",偏重于否定,而"没准儿"偏重于肯定。

It is a colloquial expression, meaning 不一定 (uncertain), indicating that one is not sure about something. But 不一定 leans towards negation, while 没准儿 leans towards affirmation.

一、熟读下列各句,体会"没准儿"、"不一定"的意义和用法。

1. 他不一定能来。
   他没准儿能来。

2. 这种产品不一定能打开销路。
   这种产品没准儿能打开销路。

3. 贷款消费,现在还不一定是中国人过日子的好办法。
   贷款消费,现在没准儿是中国人过日子的好办法。

4. 你们的申请,不一定能获得批准。
   你们的申请,没准儿能获得批准。

二、请用"没准儿"或"不一定"完成下列句子。

1. 20 世纪最后一次全球金融危机,对不少国家而言是一场灾难,但好好儿总结经验_____能促进人们进一步完善金融管理体系。

2. 中国改革开放后,宏观经济运行良好,国际收支盈余,外汇储备充裕,经济多年保持持续、高速发展,以后_____还会保持在8%左右的发展速度。

3. 他善于把握金融市场的脉搏,_____有一天会成为金融市场的鳄鱼。

4. 天气预报_____准确,你还是带上伞吧。

5. 签了合同也_____没问题,你可别高兴得太早。

6. 他什么时候回家,_____,你就不要等他了。

几

数词。在询问数目时,"几"所指的数限于1~9,如:"这个小孩几岁了?""你买了几斤苹果?"但"几"可以用在"十"之后,说"十几、二十几"等;也可以放在"十、百、千、万、亿"之前,说"几十、几百、几千、几万、几亿"。"几"还可以表示不定数目,后面要跟量词。课文中"几家欢乐几家愁"句中的"几",就是这种用法,不是说的"几家、几十家",而是一个不确定数。

Several. It is a numeral. When used to inquire about numbers, 几 is restricted to 1~9. For instance, 这个小孩几岁了? 你买了几斤苹果? However, 几 can be used after 十(ten), as in 十几(more than ten), 二十几(more than twenty), etc. It can also be placed in front of 十(ten), 百(hundred), 千(thousand), 万(ten thousand), 亿(hundred million) to form 几十(a few dozen), 几百(several hundred), 几千(several thousand), 几万(tens of thousands), and 几亿(several hundred million). 几 is also used to indicate an indefinite number, to be followed by a measure word. In the text, when expressing the meaning of "some families being happy and others sad", the word 几 is used this way, expressing an indefinite number, rather than several or several dozen.

一、熟读下列各句,体会"几"的意义和用法。

1. 据有关资料,现在居民个人储蓄存款已高达几千个亿。

2. 据说,今天有好几百万人参加了街头咨询。

3. 我看你有几招,都使出来吧!

4. 他总是喜怒无常,就像春天的天气,几天晴朗几天阴。

5. 谁能说得清楚,在这场金融危机中,有几人暴富,几人跳楼。

二、请用"几"和括号里的词语完成下列句子。

1. 金融市场瞬息万变,_____。(把握)

2. 这儿有得天独厚的优势，＿＿＿＿＿＿＿＿＿＿＿＿＿＿。（相中）

3. 为了防范和化解金融风险，中国政府准备分＿＿＿＿＿＿＿＿＿＿＿。（推进）

4. 美国微软大王比尔·盖茨＿＿＿＿＿＿＿＿＿＿＿＿。（发迹致富）

5. 改革开放以来，中国经济＿＿＿＿＿＿＿＿＿＿＿＿。（宏观调控）

6. 20 世纪最后一次全球金融危机，中国政府＿＿＿＿＿＿＿＿
＿＿＿＿＿＿＿＿＿＿＿＿＿＿＿＿＿＿＿＿。（贬值）

7. 麦当劳、肯德基已经在北京＿＿＿＿＿＿＿＿＿＿＿＿。（陆续）

8. 中国政府不断加大开放金融市场的步伐，据我所知，现在已有一些外资银行驻华代表处、办事处获准升格为分行，而且已有＿＿＿＿＿＿＿＿
＿＿＿＿＿＿＿＿＿＿＿＿＿＿＿＿。中国的金融市场为外商、外企普遍看好，＿＿＿＿＿＿＿＿＿＿＿＿。（广泛赞誉）

不用

　　副词，口语中说的"甭"，就是"不用"的合音。①表示不需要。②表示劝阻、禁止。

　　Need not. It is an adverb. 甭, a colloquial word is actually the combination of 不 and 用. It expresses 1) need not, or 2) dissuasion or prohibition.

一、熟读下列各句，体会"不用"的意义和用法，试用"甭"替换"不用"，再读一读。

　　1. 你告诉她，从明天起，她不用来上班了！

　　2. 你不用理他，他过一会儿就会高兴起来。

　　3. 你不用多说了，我都明白。

　　4. 不用派人去催债了，欠款已经汇过来了。

二、请用"不用"与括号里的词语完成下列句子。

　　1. 这是一家资信很好的跨国银行，业务范围很广，＿＿＿＿＿＿＿
＿＿＿＿＿＿＿＿＿＿＿＿＿＿＿。（储备）

　　2. 通过宏观调控，中国政府保持了人民币不贬值，＿＿＿＿＿＿＿
＿＿＿＿＿＿＿＿＿＿＿＿＿＿。（通货膨胀）

　　3. 改革开放后，中国人民生活水平普遍提高，他们开始关注出国旅游＿＿＿＿
＿＿＿＿＿＿＿＿＿＿＿＿＿＿＿＿。（设施齐全）

　　4. 自从计算机进入家庭，＿＿＿＿＿＿＿＿＿＿＿＿＿＿＿。（观察动态）

　　5. 个人买得起豪华车和住宅＿＿＿＿＿＿＿＿＿＿＿＿＿。（资金充裕）

B

一、请用下列词语组成短语。

注入　　陆续　　流动　　升格　　充裕　　获准
贷款　　拆借　　防范　　资金　　盈余　　储备

二、熟读下列短语,并选择适当的短语填空。

宏伟壮观　　得天独厚　　　　一道亮丽的风景线
安家落户　　几家欢乐几家愁　　性急喝不得热粥,
　　　　　　　　　　　　　　　一口吃不成胖子

1. 上海浦东开辟成开发区后,世界各大企业、公司相中了那块宝地,纷纷
   在那儿_____。

2. 天安门城楼_____,是首都北京的中心。现在获准允
   许参观登临,千万别错过机会。

3. 期货交易风险极大,一天之内,有人巨富,也有人成了穷光蛋,真是
   _____。

4. 你看,北京八达岭、慕田峪长城脚下,个体摊位一个挨一个,卖的都是手
   工纺织品、艺术品,成了吸引外国游人的_____。

5. 学好汉语必须在听、说、读、写上下工夫,希望尽快学好,可以理解,但
   _____。

6. 生活在改革开放的时代,生活在北京,可谓_____,我
   们应该、也可以做前人没有做过的事情。

三、完成下列句子。

1. 在北京金融街,金融家们可以在这里_____。

2. 中国政府正在积极、稳妥地推进金融业的开放,我们已经取消了
   _____。

3. 为了防范和化解金融风险,中国金融业开放只能是_____。

4. 中国金融业开放的态势太诱人了。人民币业务对外资银行全面开放,
   外资银行的业务范围也在迅速扩大,这些运作,激活了资本流动,必然
   _____。

5. 中国宏观经济_____。外商、外企对中国经济的发展
   前景充满了信心。

四、想一想,谈一谈。

1. 为什么外国人管北京的金融街叫中国的"华尔街"?

2. 司机为什么兴致勃勃地向两位外国朋友讲北京的金融街没准儿比美国华尔街还有历史?他言之有据吗?

3. 北京的金融街有什么特色,它为什么吸引各国金融家?

4. 中国政府在推进金融业开放中有哪些举措?

5. 中国政府在 20 世纪最后一次全球金融危机中作出了什么贡献?

五、阅读下面的短文,然后回答问题。

信 用 卡

由于计算机和网络技术的发展,持"卡"消费,早已成为发达国家最普通的消费方式,如今在中国也流行起来。不过,持"卡"消费,是建立在信用基础上的,一旦信用受到怀疑,也会有麻烦。

英国的达西先生来中国洽谈生意,当天上午住进中英合资五星级饭店 A,每晚 108 美元,他用信用卡预付了 10 天的房费,共折合 520 英镑。办好住房手续,达西先生就逛商场去了。他在商场挑选了一大堆商品,准备带回国去。当他付款时,被收银员告知,信用卡已经全额透支了。"不可能!我的信用卡上有 2 000 英镑的额度,今天预付饭店房费后,还应该有一千多英镑。""对不起,先生的信用卡确实全额透支了。"达西先生只好把商品一一放回货架,他感到众多顾客从四面八方射过来的目光像火一样烤着他,他的自尊心受到了极大伤害。回到饭店,达西先生立即挂通了英国 TSB 银行的电话,查询是怎么回事儿。银行回答说,他卡上的资金在同一天、被同一单位先后两次转走,第一笔 520 英镑,第二笔 1 480 英镑,两笔支取时间相隔不到三分钟。

达西先生立即找饭店英方经理布斯先生诉说此事,并请饭店作出解释。"这不能由我们来作解释,我们饭店根本不可能出现这种事情。"布斯说。"你至少应该查一查。""不,没有这个必要!"布斯断然拒绝。在达西先生的坚持下,布斯同意与 TSB 银行联系。TSB 银行证实确有此事,但布斯仍然以饭店从未发生过此类事件为由,不作进一步调查。

达西先生身无分文,只有一张无法消费的信用卡,他寸步难行。一天过去了,两天过去了,他不能请朋友吃饭,不能谈生意,不能打电话,甚至连房门也不能出……

1. 达西先生的信用卡究竟出了什么问题？是谁的错？什么性质的错？
2. 在达西向布斯诉说了情况后，布斯作出了什么反应？你怎么评价布斯的反应？
3. 你设想一下，这个"信用卡"事件会有什么结果？
4. 谈谈你使用信用卡的情况，有类似经历吗？

资本市场 29

Capital Market

一、经济增长的动力

爱德华：朱先生，我们前面进行了非常有益的谈话，我还有一个问题，也请你不吝（吝惜）赐教。

朱宝山：爱德华先生太客气了，我们一起探讨吧。

爱德华：中国有充分自由化的资本市场吗？

朱宝山：噢，我想，所谓资本自由化也是一个相对概念，就是美国资本市场的自由化程度，也是处在不断发展的进程中，你说是吧？

爱德华：朱先生说得有道理。那么，就请朱先生谈谈贵国的资本市场吧。

朱宝山：我国的资本市场还在培育和发展的过程中。

亨　特：中国对发展资本市场好像持非常谨慎的态度。

朱宝山：我们是谨慎的，但又是积极的。我们要建立一个规范的、有监控能力和自律能力的资本自由化市场。

爱德华：这需要有非常完善的法制和市场游戏规则。

亨　特：这恐怕是让全世界都头痛的事情。

朱宝山：是的。人类进入20世纪90年代以来，国际资本急剧膨胀，资本流量和流速都达到前所未有的规模，市场交易空前活跃。

亨　特：据资料统计，企业在全球资本市场融资，每天超过了50亿美元，外汇市场的日交易额和短期资金的流动量都在10万亿美元以上。如此庞大的资金和流量，任何国家和国际力量都难以驾驭。

朱宝山：这就是地区性和全球性金融危机频频发生的原因。但是世界各国也不是无所作为。

爱德华：事实上，每一次金融危机都给大家一次教训，资本市场的立法也就更健全。

朱宝山：这就说明，我们可以有所作为，可以防范和化解金融风险。

亨　特：看来，朱先生对中国的资本市场自由化十分乐观。

朱宝山：我们有许多出色的老师啊！

爱德华：谁？

朱宝山：你们哪！

爱德华：我们？

朱宝山：是你们！中国有句古话，叫"前事不忘，后事之师"嘛。你们的资本市场已经有两百多年历史，你们说，这中间有多少经验和教训？

亨　特：我明白了，中国最善于借鉴别人的经验和教训。

爱德华：我们这些老师的形象好像并不好，有时可能还是一个很坏的典型，就是你们所说的"反面教员"，是不是？

朱宝山：啊，坏事可以变成好事嘛，经验和教训，同样是宝贵的。

二、叫人又爱又恨的资本市场

爱德华：朱先生，你刚才的一席话，让我产生了无限感慨。

朱宝山：哦？

爱德华：细想一下国际资本市场的历史和现状，真是叫人又爱又恨。

朱宝山：我的话，怎么会让你产生这样的感慨呢？

爱德华：你想想，多少国家、多少人不是靠资本市场发财致富的？这不叫人爱吗？

亨　特：但一次次金融危机，也叫无数人破产、跳楼，许多国家的经济陷入绝境。

爱德华：所以又叫人恨。

朱宝山：爱德华先生这种感慨是有道理的。不过，世间的爱与恨很复杂，很难说得清。

爱德华：哦？你好像也有很多话要说？

朱宝山：是啊。我想，你们也注意到了国际资本市场的现状和发展趋势。

亨　特：在国际资本市场，美元、欧元、日元等少数几种货币，仍然占据着绝对的主导地位。

朱宝山：美元地位尤其坚挺，投资者始终乐于购买以美元计值的资产。国际资本市场上，对美元金融资产的需求最为强劲。

爱德华：贵国的人民币早晚也会成为国际市场上的硬通货的。

朱宝山：我们也深信不疑，不过还需要时间。就目前来说，发展中国家在国外交易和举债时，就不仅要承受利率和汇率风险，而且还要承受少数国家的政治、经济政策的影响。

爱德华：这是没有办法的事。

朱宝山：这就在国际资本市场造成了事实上的不平等。

亨　特：啊，我明白了。在国际资本市场，几家欢乐几家愁，爱与恨，确实不是三言两语说得清的。

朱宝山：当然，我们并不因此而感伤，更没有理由悲观。

亨　特：在 20 世纪末的金融危机中，中国表现出的自信心、能力以及发挥的作用，一扫全球悲观气氛，至今让人记忆犹新。

朱宝山：能量巨大的国际资本市场，确实有它脆弱的一面，那场波及全球的金融危机，教我们学会了许多东西。

爱德华：很多人经历了那场灾难，都变得聪明起来了。

朱宝山：少数人的过度投机，特别是操纵市场行为，常使国际资本市场发生剧烈震荡。

亨　特：为了实现资本利润最大化，市场中存在适度投机行为是不可避免的。

朱宝山：但是，遏制过度投机，也是绝对必要的。

爱德华：是的。巨额短期资金无监控地自由流动，虽然使国际资本市场交易异常活跃，但少数人疯狂投机，恶意炒作，正是导致金融危机的一个重要原因。

朱宝山：受害最深的是发展中国家。这些国家,建设资金严重短缺,需要吸纳大量外资。资本市场一旦发生剧烈震荡,投资信心下降,外资突然抽逃、撤回,后果就不堪设想。

爱德华：你说得很对,发展中国家应该加强对短期资金自由流动的管理和监控。

朱宝山：经验告诉我们,适度限制短期投资,鼓励长期投资,特别是对基础设施建设的长期投资,可以有效防范和化解金融风险。

爱德华：全世界都注意到,中国具有吸引外资的巨大潜力。

朱宝山：我国正在积极培育和发展资本市场,不断扩大市场规模,开发各种金融工具及金融衍生产品,完善立法,加强监管,保证资本市场良好运转。

爱德华：如果是那样,全世界的资金就会源源不断流入中国了。

生 词

1.	吝惜	lìnxī	grudge, stint
2.	赐教	cìjiào	condescend to teach, grant instruction
3.	培育	péiyù	cultivate
4.	谨慎	jǐnshèn	prudent, cautious
5.	规范	guīfàn	standard, norm
6.	自律	zìlǜ	self-discipline
7.	法制	fǎzhì	legal system
8.	游戏	yóuxì	game
9.	人类	rénlèi	mankind
10.	急剧	jíjù	rapid, sharp, sudden
11.	流量	liúliàng	volume of flow
12.	流速	liúsù	velocity of flow
13.	前所未有	qián suǒ wèi yǒu	unprecedented
14.	庞大	pángdà	huge, colossal

15. 驾驭	jiàyù	control, drive
16. 频频	pínpín	again and again, repeatedly
17. 无所作为	wú suǒ zuòwéi	be in a state of inertia; attempt nothing and accomplish nothing
18. 立法	lìfǎ	make laws, legislate
19. 借鉴	jièjiàn	use for reference, draw lessons from
20. 反面	fǎnmiàn	reverse side, negative side
21. 宝贵	bǎoguì	precious
22. 无限	wúxiàn	infinite, boundless
23. 感慨	gǎnkǎi	sigh with emotion
24. 陷入	xiànrù	sink into; be lost in
25. 绝境	juéjìng	hopeless situation, blind alley
26. 主导	zhǔdǎo	leading, dominant
27. 坚挺	jiāntǐng	strong
28. 强劲	qiángjìng	powerful, forceful
29. 硬通货	yìngtōnghuò	hard currency
30. 深信不疑	shēn xìn bù yí	firmly believe and have no doubt
31. 举债	jǔzhài	borrow money, raise a loan
32. 感伤	gǎnshāng	sad, sorrowful
33. 悲观	bēiguān	pessimistic
34. 自信心	zìxìnxīn	self-confidence
35. 记忆犹新	jìyì yóu xīn	remain fresh in one's memory
36. 能量	néngliàng	energy, capabilities
37. 脆弱	cuìruò	weak, fragile
38. 波及	bōjí	spread to, affect
39. 灾难	zāinàn	disaster, catastrophe
40. 过度	guòdù	excessive
41. 投机	tóujī	speculation
42. 操纵	cāozòng	manipulate, control
43. 剧烈	jùliè	violent, fierce
44. 震荡	zhèndàng	shake, quake
45. 适度	shìdù	appropriate; moderate degree
46. 遏制	èzhì	contain, keep within limits
47. 异常	yìcháng	abnormal; exceedingly

48. 疯狂	fēngkuáng	insane, frenzied
49. 炒作	chǎozuò	speculate
50. 吸纳	xīnà	absorb
51. 抽逃	chōutáo	take out and flee
52. 撤回	chèhuí	recall, withdraw
53. 衍生	yǎnshēng	derive
54. 运转	yùnzhuǎn	revolve, operate
55. 源源不断	yuányuán bú duàn	in an endless stream; continuously

专 名 Proper Noun

| 欧元 | ōuyuán | euro |

A

早晚/迟早

　　副词。预知某事必然发生,但还不能说出发生的确切时间,有"或者早或者晚,但总有那么一个时候"的意思。

Sooner or later. 早晚 or 迟早 are adverbs, indicating a prediction that something will surely happen, but the exact time of occurrence cannot be told yet. It has the meaning of "either sooner or later, but there will definitely be such a time".

一、熟读下列各句,体会"早晚"、"迟早"的意义和用法。

　　1. 你早晚会知道我是什么人的。

　　2. 你早晚会理解我的。

　　3. 他迟早是要走的,你留不住他。

　　4. 请不要伤感,我们早晚还会再见的。

二、请用"早晚"或"迟早"和下列短语造句。

　　1. 疯狂炒作

2. 如此庞大的资金和流量

3. 一个规范的、有监控能力和自律能力的资本自由化市场

4. 资金严重短缺

5. 金融危机

一

数词,如"一、一十、一百一十"。但"一"字常常用得很活,在句子中,它还常常表达"全、满、每一"等意思。"一"有时也是副词,如"一见就爱"。

It is a numeral, as in 一(one),一十(ten), and 一百一十(one hundred and ten). But 一 can often be used very flexibly. In a sentence, it often expresses the meanings of 全(whole),满 (full),每一(every). Sometimes 一 is an adverb, as in 一见就爱.

一、熟读下列各句,体会并分别指出句中"一"的意义和用法。

1. 我一有空就去看你。

2. 他的话刚说完,一屋子的人都气炸了。

3. 这样的机会一生中也许只有一次。

4. 你看他一头白发,岁月不饶人啊!

5. 一到冬天,他总要生病。

6. 悲观气氛一扫而光。

二、请用"一"和下列短语造句。

1. 投机心理

2. 转变观念

3. 悲观失望

4. 难以驾驭

三、请指出下列短语中"一"的大概意思。

一手泥　　　一席话　　　一人一份

一口否定　　一手操纵　　一脸不高兴

一贯认真　　一见就爱　　讲一口标准的美音

异常

副词,修饰形容词和少数表示心理活动的动词,说明性状和程度不同一

般,不平常。"异常"同副词"非常"近似,但"异常"一般不修饰单音节词,而"非常"没有这个限制。"非常"后面还可以加"之",如说"非常之好",而"异常"不这么用。"异常"也可以做形容词用。

Unusual;abnormal. It is an adverb used to modify adjectives and a few verbs indicating psychological activities. It indicates that the properties and extent are unusual or extraordinary. It is very similar to the adverb 非常,but 异常 does not normally modify monosyllabic words, while 非常 is not thus restricted. What's more, 非常 can be followed by 之,as in 非常之好,but 异常 cannot be used this way. 异常 can also be used as an adjective.

一、熟读下列各句,体会并分别指出句中"异常"的意义和用法。
1. 他的情况异常特殊。
2. 现在,资本市场的发展势头异常强劲。
3. 我注意到,他今天的表现有些异常。
4. 外国公司对在中国投资的前景异常乐观。
5. 最近出现的许多异常现象,使我们不得不持谨慎态度。
6. 本来十分坚固的经济基础,受这场金融危机的冲击,变得异常脆弱了。

二、请用"异常"和括号里的词语完成下列句子。
1. 现在年轻人的思想_____。(自信心)
2. 中国对投资国际资本市场所持态度_____
_____。(难以监管)
3. 外国企业家、金融家对中国的资本市场自由化前景_____
_____,_____。(稳健的货币政策)
4. 细想一下国际资本市场的历史和现状,_____
_____。(陷入绝境)
5. 当今世界,生态环境破坏严重,_____
_____。(没有理由悲观)

B

一、请用下列词语组成短语。
抽逃　适度　资金　吸纳　运转
震荡　限制　操纵　投机　遏制
疯狂　炒作　过度　剧烈　谨慎

二、熟读下列词语,并从中选择适当的词语填空:

> 前所未有　　源源不断　　一席话
> 无所作为　　记忆犹新　　坏事可以变成好事
> 三言两语　　深信不疑　　前事不忘,后事之师

1. 改革开放以来,中国经济建设取得了＿＿＿＿＿＿＿＿＿＿成就。

2. 20世纪末的金融危机,给东南亚各国的经济打击,人们＿＿＿＿＿＿＿＿
＿＿＿＿＿＿＿＿。

3. 从计划经济到市场经济,人们思想观念方面的变化,不是＿＿＿＿＿＿
＿＿＿＿＿＿说清的。

4. 中国的经济建设成就和发展蓝图,向世界展示出无限的经济贸易合作
机会,对此我＿＿＿＿＿＿＿＿＿＿。

5. 江总经理的＿＿＿＿＿＿＿＿＿＿彻底打消了我对贵国投资的疑虑。

6. ＿＿＿＿＿＿＿＿＿＿,只要我们不断总结,善于吸取经验教训,我们
就能不断前进。

7. 中国的技术贸易起点低,与发达国家的差距大,所以发展的潜力也大。
在技术贸易领域,外商不会＿＿＿＿＿＿＿＿＿＿,而是大有作为的。

8. 1998年7~8月,长江中下游发生了百年不遇的特大洪水,全国各地的
救灾物资＿＿＿＿＿＿＿＿＿＿送往灾区。

9. 认识到抽烟对身体的危害,自己戒了烟,还用自己的行为规劝别人戒
烟,这应该说是＿＿＿＿＿＿＿＿＿＿。

三、完成下列句子。

1. 中国的资本市场还在＿＿＿＿＿＿＿＿＿＿。

2. 人类进入20世纪90年代以来,国际资本＿＿＿＿＿＿,资本流量和流速
都达到＿＿＿＿＿＿,市场交易＿＿＿＿＿＿。

3. 发展中国家应该加强对短期资金＿＿＿＿＿＿＿＿＿＿。

4. 就目前来说,发展中国家在交易和举债时,不仅要＿＿＿＿＿＿
而且还要＿＿＿＿＿＿＿＿＿＿。

5. 少数人的疯狂投机和恶意炒作,是导致＿＿＿＿＿＿＿＿＿＿。

四、想一想,谈一谈。

1. 中国对资本自由化的态度是什么?

2. 进入20世纪以来,地区性和全球性的金融危机频频发生,为什么?金

融危机给人们带来什么危害?

3. 你认为金融危机是怎么造成的?

4. 发展中国家与发达国家在国际资本市场是不平等的,为什么?发展中国家如何保护自己利益?

5. 中国如何培育和发展资本市场?

五、阅读下面的短文,然后回答问题。

守株待兔

古代有一个寓言,说的是一个农民,下地干活儿的时候,看见一只兔子突然蹿了出来,一头撞到树上,死了。这个农民捡到兔子,心中大喜,于是再也不想耕地种庄稼,每天都到这棵树下来守候,希望再捡到兔子,等啊等,也不知等了多少天,可是他再也没有捡到兔子。这个农民成了天下人嘲笑的对象。

现代商场中,到处都能看到商品促销的广告大战,争夺中央电视台黄金时段的广告播放权,尤其激烈。1995 年,在公开竞标中,山东秦池酒厂以 6666 万元成为标王。全国各地媒体,竞相报道,狂热爆炒,一时间,秦池名声大振。一个月后,秦池就收到销售代理保证金一千多万,头两个月的销售收入突破两个亿,超过了 1994 年全年的销售额。到年终,销售额比上年增长了五倍,利税增长了六倍,成为全国少见的超常发展企业。尝到争夺中央电视台标王甜头的秦池酒厂,以更大决心和投入,参加 1996 年的竞标。最终,以 3.2 亿的天价再夺标王。这一次,媒介不仅失去了炒作新闻的狂热,而且还不断提出质疑,如秦池以 3.2 亿天价夺标是否值得?中国已有四万多家白酒厂,中国人一年能喝几斤秦池酒?在新的一年里秦池能否创造 3.2 亿元利润?果然,1996 年秦池没有完成预订销售额,3.2 亿元广告费又一分不能少,秦池陷入了困境。

秦池是怎么陷入困境的?是市场疲软,还是投资决策的失误?是媒体"质疑"产生了消极导向,还是市场"无形的手"翻云覆雨?

1. 秦池两次中标,结果完全不同,为什么?
2. 1996 年,秦池该不该以 3.2 亿元的巨大投入去争夺标王?
3. 秦池争夺标王的故事与寓言"守株待兔"有何相似之处?
4. 你读了这个故事有什么感想?

证券和股票市场 30

Markets of Securities and Stocks

一、股 民 说 股

亨　　特：嗨,你们都是来买卖股票的吗?

股民甲：来玩儿玩儿。

爱德华：玩儿玩儿?

亨　　特：中国老百姓把冒险叫玩儿命,把买卖股票叫玩儿股。

爱德华：噢,有意思。可股市并不好玩儿。

股民乙：好玩儿! 股价看涨时,那是挡不住的诱惑,让你激动发狂;
　　　　股价看跌时,仿佛大难临头,让你心惊胆战。

股民甲：这多刺激! 许多人成天泡在股市,玩儿的就是这种心跳。

股民丙：他们这种人是钱烧的,也有炒股经验,所以敢这么玩儿,我
　　　　可没有这个经济实力和心理承受力。

爱德华：你刚进股市?

股民丙：是。我连什么是牛市,什么是熊市都还说不清。

股民乙：嗨,牛市也叫多头市场,就是股价上扬,人气旺盛;熊市也
　　　　叫空头市场,就是股价趋跌,股市趋淡。

股民甲：你以后就跟我玩儿股吧。看见我一脸牛气,你就满仓杀进。

股民乙：你要看见他一脸熊样儿,就赶紧抛售清仓,溜之大吉。

股民甲：你别损我! 不过,割肉,跳楼,那滋味儿确实不好受。我有
　　　　过这种惨痛教训,所以我才有今天的心理承受力。

股民丙：你是大庄家,不管是赚是赔,总是一脸不在乎,面不改色心
　　　　不跳,我怎么跟你?

股民乙：投资股市，有股息，有红利，盈利率大，你见人家大把大把赚钱，还是禁不住眼馋，硬要往股市里钻。

股民丙：是。谁不眼红？谁会嫌钱多？但股市风险大，我也害怕。

股民甲：依我看，风险风险，跟风才有险，跟风必有险。

亨　特：你这样解释"风险"？

股民甲：刚进股市的人，没有股市知识和经验，最容易盲从，一味追涨杀跌，结果不是被深度套牢，就是被摔得粉身碎骨，这不是盲目跟风的"风险"吗？

股民丙：所以，我最好还是不要看别人的喜怒哀乐行事。可是怎样才能不盲目跟风呢？

爱德华：纽约股票交易所俱乐部有一座雕像，是一头牛和一头熊的拼搏。从正面看，像是公牛战胜了北极熊，可稍一变换角度，你看见的就是北极熊正在给公牛致命一击。

亨　特：股票市场就是这样，没有永远的熊市，也没有永远的牛市，而且牛市熊市，瞬息即变。这就是这座雕像给玩儿股者的忠告。

股民甲：所以，玩儿股是门学问，不能光靠运气，而要靠知识，要善于分析大盘基本状况和未来走势，要随时掌握各种指数，如道·琼斯工业指数、恒生指数、沪指、深指、中经指数等。这样，成功的概率就会大大提高。

爱德华：华尔街一位股市预言家还说过，股票市场服从地球引力定律，一级一级爬楼梯登帝国大厦，到顶层要两个半小时，但从顶层往下跳，八秒半钟就能到达地面。

股民甲：是这样，是这样！我现在知道，股市上疯狂投机，暴涨暴跌，一夜之间就可以使百万富翁变成穷光蛋。

爱德华：这也是经济学家们所说的"郁金香现象"。在荷兰，作为国花的郁金香，由于市场上的投机狂热，曾经在一两年里总上涨幅度高达 5 900%。但一夜发生雪崩，就使价值连城的郁金香价格几乎等同于一只普通的洋葱头。

股民甲：所以我的成功秘诀，就是选择好进入和退出的时机。当股价持续飙升时，就是该出手之时；当股价下探、景气处于循环低潮、舆论普遍悲观时,十之八九反弹有望,这时倒是买进的最佳时机。

爱德华:看来,你是一位很成熟、很老练的股民。

股民甲:过奖了。噢,开市了!

股民乙:现在的股市邪了,大盘缩了又缩,垃圾股炒了又炒,今天开盘垃圾股就比上一个交易日收盘上涨了53点。我去交割完,也来炒炒垃圾股。

股民甲:对不起,二位先生,我也该进大户室了,再见!

二、经济学家说股

亨　特:于先生,你是中国著名的经济学家,有些问题,我们想向你请教。

爱德华:请问,中国证券市场上,都有哪些金融工具?

于任之:主要是三大类,包括债券(国家债券、金融债券、企业债券)、股票(A股、B股、H股)和基金。

亨　特:B股是中国企业在境内上市、由外国人认购的股票吗?

于任之:是的。H股是中国企业在香港挂牌上市的股票。B股和H股的发行,为国家重点建设筹集了大量外资,为我国证券市场与国际资本市场接轨发挥了很大作用。

爱德华:除了你提到的三大类以外,也有期货、期权、可转换公司债券和其他一些衍生金融工具吗?

于任之:我们的证券品种正在不断增加。

爱德华:那么,进出中国证券市场的都是什么人呢?

于任之:与国际证券市场的结构基本一样,有法人、机构、证券承销商和代理商以及自然人。

亨　特:中国是一个人口大国,如果像我们美国那样,家家都有人炒股,那有多少股民?

于任之:从理论上可以计算出来,但事实上是无法计算的。

爱德华:不管怎么说,中国永远是国际资本垂青的大市场。

于任之:中国是一个发展中国家,需要大量建设资金,一个发展健康、秩序良好、运行安全的证券市场,对我国优化资源配置、调整经济结构、筹集更多的社会资金、促进国民经济发展具有重要作用。

亨　特:著名经济学家凯恩斯说过,在人类几千年的商业文明中,最伟大而又精巧的发明,就是股票。

于任之:是的。它在近当代世界经济中的巨大作用完全证明了这一点。

亨　特:近当代资本市场的资本疯狂膨胀和高速流动,给世界经济发展注入了无限活力,但也使世界经济日益变得难以驾驭。

爱德华:因此,如何防范和最大限度地降低资本市场的潜在风险,是世界各国都面临的重大问题。

于任之:是的。中国已经出台了《证券法》等一系列法律法规。中国证券监督管理委员会正在有效行使它的职能,加强对证券期货业的监管,提高市场透明度和信息披露质量,防范和化解风险,维护市场的稳定和健康发展。

生　词

1. 冒险	màoxiǎn	take a risk
2. 玩儿命	wánrmìng	gamble with one's life, risk one's life needlessly
3. 激动	jīdòng	excite, agitate
4. 发狂	fākuáng	go mad, go crazy
5. 大难临头	dà nàn líntóu	with great disaster hanging over one; be faced with imminent disaster
6. 心惊胆战	xīn jīng dǎn zhàn	tremble with terror, shake with fright
7. 实力	shílì	actual strength
8. 牛市	niúshì	bull market

9. 熊市	xióngshì	bear market
10. 多头	duōtóu	a long market
11. 空头	kōngtóu	short-sellers
12. 牛气	niúqi	bullish
13. 满仓	mǎncāng	full stock
14. 熊样儿	xióng yàngr	bearish
15. 抛售	pāoshòu	sell in big quantities and/or at low prices
16. 溜之大吉	liū zhī dà jí	sneak away, slink off
17. 惨痛	cǎntòng	distressingly grievous, excruciatingly painful
18. 庄家	zhuāngjiā	banker (in a gambling game)
19. 股息	gǔxī	dividend
20. 红利	hónglì	bonus, extra dividend
21. 嫌	xián	dislike, complain of
22. 盲从	mángcóng	follow blindly
23. 一味	yíwèi	invariably
24. 套牢	tàoláo	be tightly bound up
25. 粉身碎骨	fěn shēn suì gǔ	have one's body smashed to pieces and one's bones ground to powder
26. 盲目	mángmù	blindly
27. 喜怒哀乐	xǐ nù āi lè	happiness, anger, grief and joy
28. 俱乐部	jùlèbù	club
29. 雕像	diāoxiàng	sculpture, statue
30. 拼搏	pīnbó	struggle hard
31. 变换	biànhuàn	change
32. 角度	jiǎodù	angle
33. 致命一击	zhìmìng yì jī	a deadly blow
34. 忠告	zhōnggào	sincere advice
35. 大盘	dàpán	the composite index
36. 走势	zǒushì	trend
37. 指数	zhǐshù	index
38. 预言家	yùyánjiā	prophet
39. 服从	fúcóng	obey, abide by

40. 地球	dìqiú	the Earth
41. 引力	yǐnlì	gravitation
42. 定律	dìnglǜ	law
43. 穷光蛋	qióngguāngdàn	pauper
44. 郁金香	yùjīnxiāng	tulip
45. 雪崩	xuěbēng	snow slide, avalanche
46. 价值连城	jiàzhí lián chéng	worth several cities — invaluable
47. 洋葱头	yángcōngtóu	onion
48. 秘诀	mìjué	secret (of success)
49. 飙升	biāoshēng	go up violently
50. 下探	xià tàn	go down
51. 反弹	fǎntán	bounce back
52. 邪	xié	evil, weird
53. 垃圾股	lājī gǔ	junk shares, shares of firms that are losing money
54. 开盘	kāipán	opening quotation
55. 收盘	shōupán	closing quotation
56. 交割	jiāogē	complete a business transaction
57. 债券	zhàiquàn	bond
58. 基金	jījīn	fund
59. 挂牌	guàpái	listing; put up one's brass plate
60. 发行	fāxíng	offering; issue, distribute
61. 筹集	chóují	accumulate, raise
62. 接轨	jiēguǐ	join tracks
63. 期权	qīquán	options
64. 法人	fǎrén	legal person
65. 自然人	zìránrén	natural person
66. 理论	lǐlùn	theory
67. 垂青	chuíqīng	show appreciation for somebody, look upon somebody with favor
68. 优化	yōuhuà	optimize
69. 配置	pèizhì	configuration; deploy, dispose
70. 精巧	jīngqiǎo	exquisite, ingenious
71. 发明	fāmíng	invention

72. 活力	huólì	vigor, vitality
73. 面临	miànlín	be faced with
74. 披露	pīlù	publish, disclose

专 名 Proper Nouns

1. 道·琼斯工业 指数	Dào·Qióngsī Gōngyè Zhǐshù	the Dow Jones industrial average
2. 恒生指数	Héngshēng Zhǐshù	the Hang Seng index
3. 沪指(上海证券 交易所指数)	Hùzhǐ(Shànghǎi Zhèngquàn Jiāoyìsuǒ Zhǐshù)	the index of the Shanghai Stock Exchange
4. 深指(深圳证券 交易所指数)	Shēnzhǐ(Shēnzhèn Zhèngquàn Jiāoyìsuǒ Zhǐshù)	the index of the Shenzhen Stock Exchange
5. 中经指数 (中国《经济 日报》指数)	Zhōngjīng Zhǐshù (Zhōngguó《Jīngjì Rìbào》Zhǐshù)	the index of China's *Economic Daily*
6. 帝国大厦	Dìguó Dàshà	the Imperial Tower
7. 荷兰	Hélán	the Netherlands
8. 凯恩斯	Kǎi'ēnsī	John Maynard Keynes
9. 中国证券监督 管理委员会	Zhōngguó Zhèngquàn Jiāndū Guǎnlǐ Wěiyuánhuì	the China Securities Regulatory Commission

练 习

A

是赚是赔

动词"是",在表示选择时,常有两种格式:"是……还是……","是……

是……"。回答选择问句,都必须作肯定的回答。

To win or lose. The verb 是, when used to indicate a choice, has two patterns: 是……还是……or 是……是……When answering alternative questions of this kind, the answer should always be in the positive.

一、熟读下列各句,体会动词"是"表示选择时的用法。
    1. 你是作现货交易还是作买空卖空交易?
    2. 这家公司年报披露的信息是真是假,天知道!
    3. 公司今年经营业绩是好是坏,现在很难预测。
    4. 看你这样子,是赚了还是赔了?
    5. 他非要去冒这个险,是死是活,也只好由他去了。

二、请用"是……还是……"或"是……是……"和下列短语造句。
    1. 做多头　　做空头
    2. 降低成本　　提高商品价格
    3. 逃避责任溜之大吉　　勇敢站出来承担责任
    4. 买债券　　玩儿股票
    5. 百万富翁　　穷光蛋

硬是

副词,表示不听劝阻、不顾条件非要做某事。常含有"勉强"、"强行"、"坚决"、"固执"等意思。

Actually; simply. It is an adverb indicating insistence on doing something regardless of dissuasion or conditions. It often implies such meanings as 勉强 (manage with an effort), 强行 (force), 坚决 (determined), or 固执 (stubborn).

一、熟读下列各句,体会"硬"、"硬是"的用法,并分别指出各自在句中的意思。
    1. 这家商店连年亏损,现在只是硬撑着。
    2. 股市这么震荡,他硬是没有趴下。
    3. 都说股票市场风险太大,可他硬是不信这个邪。
    4. 他退休了,可硬是闲不住,总想找地方发挥余热。
    5. 他硬是要往股市钻,都快把家里那点儿钱折腾光了。
    6. 我对炒股一点儿兴趣也没有,是朋友硬拉我来的。

二、请用"硬是"和括号里的词语完成下列句子。
    1. 退休后他成天泡在股市,＿＿＿＿＿＿＿＿＿＿＿＿＿＿＿。(成熟、老练)

2. 股价下跌、景气处于循环低潮,舆论普遍悲观时＿＿＿＿＿＿＿＿＿＿
＿＿＿＿＿＿＿＿＿＿＿＿＿＿＿＿＿＿＿＿＿＿＿。(反弹、抛售)

3. 一次次惨痛教训＿＿＿＿＿＿＿＿＿＿＿＿＿＿＿。(一味盲从)

4. 20 世纪波及全球的最后一次金融危机中,资金空前短缺,＿＿＿＿＿
＿＿＿＿＿＿＿＿＿＿＿＿＿＿＿＿＿＿＿＿＿＿＿。(筹集大量外资)

5. 你得承认玩儿股是门学问,不能光靠运气,也不能靠书本上的那点儿知
识,＿＿＿＿＿＿＿＿＿＿＿＿＿＿＿＿＿＿＿＿＿。(分析、掌握)

嫌

动词,意思是"不喜欢"、"不满意",在句中做谓语时可带名词、形容词或动词宾语。"嫌+名",还可带时态助词"过",名词宾语限于指人,指物要用"不喜欢"。

It is a verb that means "dislike" or "dissatisfy". When used as the predicate in the sentence, it takes a noun, an adjective or a verb as its object. "嫌 + noun" can be followed by the tense particle 过. Its nominal object only refers to people. When talking about things, 不喜欢 should be used instead.

一、熟读下列各句,体会"嫌"的意义和用法。
1. 你别嫌我的话多,我是为你好。
2. 你炒一年股票,就赚了十几万,还嫌少?
3. 你那么喜欢跳迪斯科,不嫌吵得慌?
4. 谁也没有嫌过她,全是她多心。
5. 这家商店的售后服务真好,顾客有求必应,他们从来不嫌麻烦。

二、请用"嫌"和下列短语造句。
1. 饭菜不好
2. 风险大
3. 配置不好
4. 没有活力
5. 做得不精巧

一味

副词,表示不顾客观条件和情况,固执地坚持某种行为或动作。用"一味"的句子,常含有贬义。

Invariably. It is an adverb, indicating persistence in acting in a certain way. A sentence with 一味 often carries a derogatory meaning.

一、熟读下列各句,体会"一味"的意义和用法。

1. 不敢冒险就别玩儿股,可一味冒险,总有一天要玩儿完。
2. 如果一味强调客观条件,那就什么事都做不成。
3. 服装设计一味求新求奇,不可能得到多数人认同。
4. 股市行情,瞬息万变,一味疯狂投机,后果不堪设想。

二、请用"一味"和下列短语造句。

1. 服从上级领导
2. 玩儿命
3. 追求利润
4. 忍气吞声
5. 谨慎从事

B

一、请用下列词语组成短语。

发行　抛售　信息　垂青　配置　走势
股票　披露　债券　证券　盲目　股价

二、熟读下列词语,并选择适当的词语填空。

> 大难临头　　价值连城　　面不改色心不跳
> 心惊胆战　　人气旺盛　　滋味确实不好受
> 粉身碎骨　　喜怒哀乐　　提高……透明度
> 致命一击

1. 他多年在股市沉浮,练出了胆气和心理承受力,是赔是赚,股价是上扬还是下跌,他都能做到 _____。

2. 股市风险冉大,我也不害怕,我已下定决心,不达目的誓不罢休,哪怕 _____。

3. 总经理是个性格十分内向的人,_____从不表现出来。

4. 20 世纪末波及全球的金融危机给这家百年证券公司_____,公司不得不宣布破产。

5. 近年来多家博物馆＿＿＿＿＿＿＿＿＿＿＿的名画儿被盗,是什么原因?

6. 有话憋在心里不能对自己最亲爱的人说,这＿＿＿＿＿＿＿＿＿＿＿。

7. 据可靠消息,最近股市稳定,股价看涨,＿＿＿＿＿＿＿＿＿＿＿,我劝你满仓杀进。

8. 市场经济竞争激烈,更要求信息反馈及时、准确,＿＿＿＿＿＿＿＿＿＿＿。

9. 好丈夫应该是每当＿＿＿＿＿＿＿＿＿＿＿之时,他都走在前面,用他自己的身体保护家人,而不是只想自己,溜之大吉。

10. 每当金融市场波动,金融危机来临时,金融家们都禁不住＿＿＿＿＿＿＿＿＿＿＿
＿＿＿＿＿＿＿＿＿＿＿。

三、完成下列句子。

1. 股票市场就是这样,没有永远的熊市,＿＿＿＿＿＿＿＿＿＿＿。

2. 牛市也叫＿＿＿＿＿＿＿＿＿＿＿,熊市也叫＿＿＿＿＿＿＿＿＿＿＿。

3. 股票市场没有永远的赢家,因为＿＿＿＿＿＿＿＿＿＿＿。

4. 玩儿股、炒股不外乎两种心情:股价看涨时,＿＿＿＿＿＿＿＿＿＿＿;股价看跌时,＿＿＿＿＿＿＿＿＿＿＿。

5. 玩儿股是门学问,不能光靠运气,而要靠知识,头脑冷静,要善于分析＿＿＿＿＿＿＿＿＿＿＿,要随时＿＿＿＿＿＿＿＿＿＿＿。

四、想一想,谈一谈。

1. 为什么中国老百姓把买卖股票叫炒股、玩儿股?

2. 你认为炒股者成功的秘诀是什么?

3. 中国证券市场上,都有哪些金融工具?进出中国证券市场的是哪些人?

4. 股票在近当代世界经济中有什么作用?

5. 股票对中国国民经济发展有什么作用?中国政府对股票这类的证券市场持什么态度?

五、阅读下面的短文,然后回答问题:

太太炒股

"又怎么啦?"我睡得正香,半夜被太太摇醒。"唉,我前天刚抛了的股票,明天准要上扬,你说我该死不该死!我怎么就这么蠢,一点儿眼光都没有……""我的好太太,你能不能让我睡个安稳觉?""你说,我真是那种头发长见识短的女人吗?或者简直就是臭苍蝇,见利就贪……""得了吧,好太太,你要是臭苍蝇,我是什么?睡吧!"我被半夜推醒已经不是第一次了。赚了,她会兴奋得让你一夜睡不成;赔了,她也把你摇醒,让你听她把自己骂得狗血淋头。这个世界上,除了她自己,没有人敢这么骂她。

"爸,怎么还没做饭?待会儿我上学又该迟到了!"我正在埋头写作,放学回来的儿子冲我大喊大叫。"你妈不是在厨房做吗?""哪儿啊! 你去看看。"我知道,老婆又是做了一半,扔下去股市了。自她炒股以来,我就成了家庭"主妇",一家的饭菜差不多都得我做。劳累不说,还不落好,她跟儿子还总抱怨我做的饭菜不好吃。当我委屈得不行的时候,老婆又安慰我说:"得,再熬熬吧,等我炒股赚了大钱,我们天天下馆子,要不请个小保姆?""你不怕小保姆插足,甚至取而代之,成为这个家的女主人?""谅你也不敢!"她的指头戳得我脑门生疼。

好不容易熬到了年底,企业要进行年终盘点、结算,我的太太也把自己关在屋里,计算炒股业绩。三天后,房门开了。我问:"怎么样?""不赔不赚,瞎忙活了!"太太哭不像哭笑不像笑地说。

唉,股票啊,你究竟是什么东西?

1. "我"的太太骂她自己"见利就贪"。炒股者能不能"贪"? 为什么?
2. 你认为什么时候是买进或卖出股票的最佳时候?
3. 炒股会使人产生什么样的心理变化? 这种变化对家庭生活会有什么影响?
4. 股票究竟是什么?

商业保险市场 **31**

Market of Commercial Insurance

一、商业保险业艰难起步

爱德华：卢先生，贵公司今年的业务怎么样？

卢　鸣：现在保险业竞争很激烈，生意很不好做。

亨　特：我常看见各家保险公司在街头到处设摊招揽客户，好像生意不错嘛！

卢　鸣：那只是场面好看，其实是剃头挑子一头热。

爱德华：这话怎么讲？

卢　鸣：保险公司急着拉客户，可客户还没有那份热情。

爱德华：那是为什么呢？

卢　鸣：这就一言难尽了。我想起步比较晚，是一个重要原因。

亨　特：起步晚并不是坏事。一切从头做起，竞争对手少，商业机会多，潜在市场大。

卢　鸣：有利也有弊。你只说到有利的一面。

亨　特：那么你说的"弊"是指什么呢？

卢　鸣：我想首先是保险业自身的问题，比如从业人员普遍素质不高。

亨　特：保险业不仅需要经验，更需要专业知识，保险公司急于发展业务，难免饥不择食，把什么人都招来当业务员。

卢　鸣：这就埋伏下很多隐患。

爱德华：没有保险业专业知识，很难把保险条款说清楚，使投保人稀里糊涂投保，如因违反告知义务造成削额理赔时，就难免发生纠纷。

卢　鸣：是的。比如意外伤残保险的赔付，按契约规定，投保方通知保险公司并申请赔付，是有时间期限的。如果业务员未尽告知义务，保险公司同投保人、被保人或受益人之间就不可避免地要发生纠纷了。

亨　特：不足额赔付，保险公司就要落得一个骗钱公司的骂名。

卢　鸣：更有甚者，保险公司的有些业务员，为了拉到客户，竟然不择手段。

亨　特：不管黑猫白猫，逮住老鼠就是好猫嘛！

卢　鸣：顾客可不是老鼠！

亨　特：噢，开个玩笑！顾客是上帝，保险公司应该是保护神。

爱德华：争取客户是保险公司的主要业务，在激烈竞争中，保险公司鼓励业务员八仙过海，各显其能，只要拉到客户就是好样儿的。

卢　鸣：可是不能吹牛皮，夸海口，开空头支票，许诺根本就不可能兑现的条件，误导和诱骗客户投保。

爱德华：这是业务员最起码的职业道德，八仙过海，各显其能，也有个合法和非法的界限。

亨　特：业务员的非法行为世界各国都有。有的业务员甚至为投保企业、投保人套现、洗钱，严重扰乱金融市场和保险市场。

卢　鸣：这个问题就很严重了。

爱德华：我想，业务员素质不高，只是起步阶段的一个问题。

卢　鸣：是的。公众对商业保险不了解，缺乏保险意识；保险费用过高，对中低收入阶层，也是一道难以迈过的高门槛；投保后理赔难，也使公众对保险公司产生了不信任。这些都是制约商业保险发展的不利因素。

爱德华：不过，中国是个人口大国，保险业连着千家万户，外国保险公司还是非常看好中国市场的前景。

二、商业保险业正在升温

卢　鸣：爱德华先生，你刚才提到外国保险公司对中国市场的关注，我有一些新的信息告诉你。

爱德华：那太好了！

卢　鸣：随着改革开放的深入，我国保险市场规模不断扩大，对外开放的步伐加快，保险业正在进入一个高速发展时期。

爱德华：能说得具体一点儿吗？

卢　鸣：你了解我国传统的社会保障体系吗？

亨　特：我知道一点儿。职工的医药费用全部向企业和单位报销，生老病死都由企业和单位负责。

爱德华：是这样。那么公众还需要商业保险吗？

亨　特：职工有国家福利保障，当然没有保险意识，也没有商业保险需求。

卢　鸣：现在的情况不同了。我们正在彻底改革过去的福利制度，比如医疗制度、养老制度、住房分配制度，建立起真正的社会保障体系。

爱德华：这种改革，必然给商业保险的发展带来机遇。

亨　特：名列全世界保险费收入前十名的日本，城镇居民的投保率高达 560%，美国为 148%，而中国目前还只有 5%。中国拥有巨大的物质财富和人口总量，保险市场是日本、美国无法比拟的。

卢　鸣：是的。就拿建立养老基金一项来说，假定我国有四亿人参加养老基金，人均每月交费 80 元，全国每年收养老基金将是 4 000 亿，而给付高峰要在近 20 年后才到来，届时养老基金聚集的资金可能超过八万亿。

爱德华：在美国，养老基金一直是资本市场最大的投资者，中国有如此庞大的养老基金，对建设资金相对匮乏的中国来说，应该是更具有特殊意义。

卢　鸣：除了养老保险,还有财产保险、健康保险、儿童成长保险、失业保险、汽车保险、意外灾害保险等等,各种商业保险产品都有广阔的潜在市场,都有待于大力开发。

爱德华：这个前景太诱人了! 作为国际贸易服务之一的保险业,中国对开放国内保险市场有什么打算呢?

卢　鸣：不是"打算"。事实上,美国、加拿大、英国、日本等国家的保险公司已经获准进入中国市场,有独资公司,有股份制公司,有中外合资公司。

爱德华：这些公司经营什么业务呢?

卢　鸣：主要是财产保险、人寿保险、人身保险、水灾火灾保险、航空旅客人身意外伤害保险等等。

亨　特：据我所知,他们服务的主要对象是外国人和外资企业。

卢　鸣：对外开放国内保险市场,当然只能是逐步的。不过,在上海的街头巷尾,就活跃着几千名美国友邦保险有限公司的业务员,经营人身险和财产险。

爱德华：中国的这种开放态势令人鼓舞!

卢　鸣：现在,一个以我国国有商业保险公司为主、中外保险公司并存、多家保险公司竞争的市场格局已经初步形成。

爱德华：好的开始就是成功的一半儿。中国的保险市场,会跻身世界保险业前列的。

卢　鸣：我们很清醒。我们起步晚,基础薄弱,经验不足,资深人才匮乏,险种单调,公证人、经纪人等中介作用尚未充分发挥。总之,我们还有很多工作要做。

爱德华：航船已经起锚,胜利到达彼岸的时间还远吗?

 生　词

1. 艰难	jiānnán	difficult , hard
2. 招揽	zhāolǎn	solicit , canvass

3. 剃头	tìtóu	have a haircut, have one's head shaved
4. 挑子	tiāozi	loads carried on a shoulder pole
5. 一言难尽	yì yán nán jìn	hard to explain in a few words
6. 利弊	lìbì	advantages and disadvantages
7. 饥不择食	jī bù zé shí	a hungry person is not picky and choosy
8. 埋伏	máifú	ambush, hide
9. 投保人	tóubǎorén	policy-holder
10. 稀里糊涂	xīlihútú	in a daze; not knowing what one is about
11. 违反	wéifǎn	violate
12. 告知	gàozhī	notification
13. 削额	xuē é	reduce the amount
14. 伤残	shāngcán	wounded and disabled
15. 赔付	péi fù	compensation, indemnity
16. 受益人	shòuyìrén	beneficiary
17. 落得	luòde	get, end in
18. 骂名	màmíng	bad name, infamy
19. 更有甚者	gèng yǒu shèn zhě	what is more
20. 逮住	dǎizhù	capture, catch
21. 老鼠	lǎoshǔ	rat, mouse
22. 保护神	bǎohù shén	guardian
23. 八仙过海，各显其能	bāxiān guò hǎi, gè xiǎn qí néng	each shows his or her special prowess like the Eight Immortals crossing the sea
24. 好样儿的	hǎoyàngrde	great fellow, fine example
25. 吹牛皮	chuī niúpí	boast, brag, talk big
26. 夸海口	kuā hǎikǒu	boast about what one can do
27. 许诺	xǔnuò	make a promise
28. 误导	wùdǎo	misguide
29. 诱骗	yòupiàn	trap, trick
30. 界限	jièxiàn	demarcation line
31. 套现	tàoxiàn	obtain cash by illegal means

32. 洗钱	xǐqián	money laundry
33. 扰乱	rǎoluàn	disturb, create confusion
34. 阶层	jiēcéng	stratum
35. 门槛	ménkǎn	threshold
36. 千家万户	qiān jiā wàn hù	innumerable households, every family
37. 升温	shēngwēn	warm up
38. 关注	guānzhù	follow with interest, pay close attention to
39. 随着	suízhe	along with
40. 体系	tǐxì	system
41. 报销	bàoxiāo	apply for reimbursement
42. 福利	fúlì	welfare, material benefits
43. 彻底	chèdǐ	thoroughly
44. 养老	yǎnglǎo	provide for the aged
45. 分配	fēnpèi	distribution
46. 给付	jǐfù	pay out
47. 高峰	gāofēng	peak
48. 聚集	jùjí	gather
49. 匮乏	kuìfá	short of, deficient
50. 成长	chéngzhǎng	grow up
51. 失业	shīyè	unemployment
52. 有待	yǒudài	remain(to be done), await
53. 股份	gǔfèn	share, stock
54. 寿	shòu	long life, old age
55. 水灾	shuǐzāi	flood
56. 火灾	huǒzāi	fire disaster, conflagration
57. 街头巷尾	jiē tóu xiàng wěi	streets and lanes
58. 并存	bìngcún	coexist
59. 初步	chūbù	initial, preliminary
60. 前列	qiánliè	front row, forefront
61. 资深	zīshēn	veteran
62. 单调	dāndiào	monotonous, dull
63. 起锚	qǐmáo	weigh anchor, set sail
64. 彼岸	bǐ'àn	the opposite shore

专 名 Proper Noun

美国友邦保险有限公司	Měiguó Yǒubāng Bǎoxiǎn Yǒuxiàn Gōngsī	American International Group, Inc.（AIG）

 练习

 A

剃头挑子一头热

　　这是一句歇后语。在中国有现代理发馆以前,有的理发师挑着一副担子,一头是一个小火炉,上面有锅,烧着热水,便于为客人剃头时洗头;担子的另一头是剃头用的工具,刀剪、围巾、凳子之类。那时的理发师只给客人剃头,所以叫"剃头匠",他挑的担子就叫"剃头挑子"。因为一头有火、有热水,所以叫"剃头挑子一头热",以后就用这句话来比喻在两人或两方之间,只有一方愿意、有热情,而另一方不愿意、甚至很冷淡。歇后语因为是熟语,在说话时,常常只说出前半句(如说"剃头挑子"),后半句不一定说出来,人们也能懂。

Just like barber's shoulder pole, only one end is warm. This is a two-part allegorical saying. Before China had modern barber shops, some barbers went along the street shouldering a pole with loads on both ends. On one end were a small stove and a cauldron to heat water up so that the barber could wash his customers' hair when shaving it. On the other end were the barber's tools, such as scissors, razors, apron, stool, etc. At that time, the only thing a barber did was to shave his customers' hair, and so they were called "shavers", and the shoulder pole was referred to as that of the shaver(剃头挑子). As there were fire and hot water on one end, hence the saying that only one end was warm. Later on, the saying was used as an allegory that of the two people or two parties, only one is willing and enthusiastic to do something, while the other is unwilling. As this kind of two-part allegorical saying is idiomatic, people often say only the first part(e. g. 剃头挑子)with the second part unstated, and the saying is still understood.

一、熟读下列各句,体会"剃头挑子一头热"的意思和用法。

　　1.你这是剃头挑子一头热,我看那姑娘并不爱你。

　　2.A公司想同B公司联合,那是剃头挑子一头热,B公司还不愿意呢!

　　3.他们两个人的事儿呀,还是剃头挑子——一头热,一头冷。

　　4.现在的关系,就像那剃头挑子,我们心里烧着一把火,可人家怀里揣着一团冰。

二、请用"剃头挑子一头热"或"剃头挑子"和下列短语造句。

　　1.技术转让　　转让方和受让方

　　2.父母在子女身上的智力投资

　　3.不受欢迎的商品广告

　　4.为招徕顾客,高声叫卖的个体摊贩

　　5.滞销商品推销员

竟/竟然

　　副词,表示违反常情、事理,出乎意料,语气较重,有"不应该这样而这样了"的意思。

　　Unexpectedly;go so far as to. 竟 or 竟然 is an adverb,indicating a violation of the general rule or the common sense,or something out of expectation. Its tone is fairly strong,carrying with it the meaning of "it should not turn out like this but it is like this now".

一、熟读下列各句,体会"竟"、"竟然"的意义和用法。

　　1.老板叫他去,他竟敢不去!

　　2.他是一个很有教养的人,竟然说出这种话来。

　　3.他提出的无理要求,老板竟然答应了。

　　4.你竟然忘记了以前的教训,能不犯错误吗?

二、请用"竟然"和括号里的词语完成下列句子。

　　1.保险公司的有些业务员,为了完成定额,＿＿＿＿＿＿＿＿＿＿＿＿＿

　　＿＿＿＿＿＿＿＿＿＿＿＿＿＿＿＿＿＿＿＿＿＿。(误导、诱骗)

　　2.不法金融家、银行家,为了巨额利润＿＿＿＿＿＿＿＿＿＿＿＿＿＿＿

　　＿＿＿＿＿＿＿＿＿＿＿＿＿＿＿＿＿＿＿＿＿＿。(扰乱、洗钱)

　　3.没想到他的那些辉煌成就＿＿＿＿＿＿＿＿＿＿＿＿。(吹牛皮)

4. 中国的保险业起步晚,加上人们的保险意识薄弱,保险费用对中低收入
阶层来说还偏高,所以各保险公司的业务员＿＿＿＿＿＿＿＿＿＿＿＿
＿＿＿＿＿＿＿＿＿＿＿＿＿＿＿＿＿＿＿＿＿。(招揽、谨慎)

5. 不法商人为了私利,知法犯法,卖假烟假酒,更有甚者,＿＿＿＿＿＿＿
＿＿＿＿＿＿＿＿＿＿＿＿＿＿＿＿＿＿＿＿＿。(落得骂名)

随着

　　介词,后带宾语,组成的介词结构表示条件,多置于句首。"条件"在前,
在这个条件的影响下,"结果"跟着产生了。"条件"和"结果"之间,是"水涨
船高"的关系。"随着"组成的介词结构,也可以放在句中。

Along with. It is a preposition and always followed by an object. The prepositional phrase formed with it gives a condition, and is normally placed at the beginning of a sentence. Influenced by this condition, there emerges a result. The relation between the condition and the result is the same as the one that "the boat goes up when the river rises". The prepositional phrase formed with 随着 can also be placed in the middle of a sentence.

一、熟读下列各句,体会"随着"的意义和用法。
　　1. 随着年龄的增长,知识和经验也丰富起来。
　　2. 随着国家经济的发展,人民的生活水平不断提高。
　　3. 中国人的保险意识,随着社会保障体系改革的深化,正在逐步加强。
　　4. 商品是随着交换需求的产生而产生、随着社会的发展而发展的。

二、请用"随着"和下列短语造句。
　　1. 人民生活水平的提高
　　2. 福利制度改革
　　3. 现代化步伐加快
　　4. 经济结构调整
　　5. 对中国加深了解

B

一、请用下列词语组成短语。
　　扰乱　许诺　匮乏　人才　隐患

界限　理赔　聚集　资金　埋伏

二、熟读下列词语,并选择适当的词语填空。

> 饥不择食　　稀里糊涂　　有利也有弊
> 夸下海口　　街头巷尾　　资深人才匮乏
> 千家万户　　无法比拟　　八仙过海,各显其能
> 埋伏隐患

1. 改革开放后的中国,挑战与机遇并存,＿＿＿＿＿＿＿＿＿＿＿,人人都有施展才华的机会,人人都受到竞争的压力。

2. 随着改革开放的深入,各方面都需要高级管理人才,尤其是＿＿＿＿＿＿＿＿＿＿＿＿＿＿＿＿＿＿,必将影响我国国民经济高速发展。

3. 现在,在＿＿＿＿＿＿＿＿＿＿＿,人们议论的话题已由昔日的柴米油盐变成上网、汽车、房子、股票。

4. 人们现在的生活质量是二三十年前＿＿＿＿＿＿＿＿＿＿＿。

5. 以前只有极少数人家才有的电话,现在已走进＿＿＿＿＿＿＿＿＿＿＿,手机也不是什么稀罕物了。

6. 基础建设工程一味图快,不严格把关,必然给工程质量＿＿＿＿＿＿＿＿＿＿＿＿＿＿＿＿＿。

7. 大学生下海开公司,＿＿＿＿＿＿＿＿＿＿＿。

8. 物质匮乏,缺吃少穿,＿＿＿＿＿＿＿＿＿＿＿的时代一去不复返了。

9. 他第一次被朋友拉进赌场,＿＿＿＿＿＿＿＿＿＿＿输了两万多元人民币,他永远不会忘记这次惨痛教训。

10. 他向父母＿＿＿＿＿＿＿＿＿＿＿,别人有的他要有,别人没有的他也要有。为此他成了工作狂。

三、完成下列句子。

1. 我认为中国保险业起步晚并不是坏事,一切从头做起,＿＿＿＿＿＿＿＿＿＿＿＿＿＿＿＿＿。

2. 保险公司的业务员不仅需要经验,更需要＿＿＿＿＿＿和＿＿＿＿。

3. 中国正在彻底改革过去的福利制度,建立起＿＿＿＿＿＿＿。

4. 中国是个人口大国,保险业＿＿＿＿＿＿＿＿＿＿＿。

5. 中国保险市场格局已初步形成。这是一个以＿＿＿＿＿＿＿＿＿＿＿为主,＿＿＿＿＿＿＿＿＿＿＿并存,＿＿＿＿＿＿＿＿＿＿＿竞争的格局。

四、想一想,谈一谈。

1. 为什么中国保险业起步晚? 现状如何?

2. 保险公司对业务员要经过严格的专业培训方可上岗,为什么?

3. 为什么中国的商业保险业起步艰难?

4. 你对中国商业保险业前景怎么看?

五、阅读下面的短文,然后回答问题。

海底沉船

美国电影《泰坦尼克号》,讲了一个美丽动人的爱情故事;我们这儿要说的"海底沉船",则是一个颇有戏剧性的保险诈骗案。

某年某月的一天,一艘驶往香港的远洋货轮,正在印度洋上航行。风和日丽,海天一色,船上八男二女,在甲板上享受着海风的吹拂。突然,一声巨响从船仓深处传来,八男二女还没有作出任何反应,就飞上了天。船爆炸了,船体在几分钟后,完全沉没!

这是一艘载有"核能机器设备"的货船,在奥地利投保,保险金额2 000万美元,如果出事,投保人可获得4 000万美元赔偿。人们有理由怀疑,这是一起保险诈骗案。

奥地利保险公司和国际刑警组织开始了大量调查。原来,船上装载的根本不是什么"核能机器设备",而是700吨废钢铁。上交保险公司的"核能机器设备"图样以及装船清单是欧洲一个码头的黑社会头目提供的。从3 000米海底发现的沉船查明爆炸是在船仓内发生的,而后来在装船地点发现的一张海图,上面清晰、准确标有货船爆炸沉没的地点,这显然是有人预谋。

货船爆炸沉没后,案犯被捕,但不久因查无实据被释放。以后,案犯逃亡,做整容手术,使用假护照。在证据确凿后,国际刑警却找不到他的踪影。一天,他竟然偕女友飞回了维也纳,在机场,他旧时一位熟人,听出了他那熟悉的声音,报告了警方。最后,案犯被判终身监禁。

1. 为什么说货船沉没是一起保险诈骗案?

2. 诈骗者最终是什么下场?

3. 保险业、金融业中的欺诈案件时有发生,你有所见闻吗? 请举例说说。

32 环保产业市场

Market of Environmental Protection Industry

一、环保意识

亨　　特：啊，就是这儿了。

孙玉敏：亨特先生，爱德华先生，你们好!

亨　　特：让你久等了。

孙玉敏：不用客气。爸，妈，客人来了。

孙宝洁：啊，欢迎二位先生来家做客!

宁秀丽：快请进屋里坐。

亨　　特：谢谢。

爱德华：你们这个小院儿很漂亮，满院子的绿色和花香。

亨　　特：还有鸟儿叫! 啊，这树上挂着一只鸟笼!

孙玉敏：那是我爸养的宠物。

孙宝洁：我的宠物不是小狗小猫，是会唱歌儿的云雀。

爱德华：孙老先生这个家不像在大城市里。

孙玉敏：我爸就喜欢个花儿呀、草呀、鸟儿呀什么的，现在天天讲保
　　　　护环境，回归自然，他就更来情绪了。

孙宝洁：人类只有一个地球，地球是我们共同的家园，是我们生存
　　　　的环境，我们不爱护谁爱护?

宁秀丽：可惜不爱护我们家园的人还太多，打野物(野生动物)吃野
　　　　味儿啊，滥砍滥伐森林哪，到处倒污水扔垃圾呀，没有一点
　　　　儿环保意识。锻炼身体，倒也知道去公园，可有人就拿树
　　　　枝练拳脚、荡秋千……

孙玉敏：那算什么！仅我们北京市，每天排放的工业和生活废水就是两百多万吨，而全国 90% 以上的废水、污水都排放进了大大小小的河流和湖海，全国 532 条主要河流中已有 436 条受污染，大连、天津面对的渤海，因为周边工业污染，可能在不远的将来变成臭海、死海。

亨　特：情况有这么严重？

孙玉敏：问题还不只这些，还有水土流失，农田和草原荒漠化，城市大气污染、垃圾污染，塑料包装物和农用塑料造成的"白色污染"等等。据报载，我国 2006 年因污染造成的直接经济损失就高达 20 000 亿元。

爱德华：情况确实很严重，但我并不感到吃惊。全世界进入工业化时代以后，对环境的污染和破坏就日甚一日。

亨　特：对自然资源的肆意掠夺和无节制开采，造成生态环境急剧恶化，人类已经感到日益迫近的生存危机。

孙宝洁：所以，环境与发展是全人类面临的共同问题。

亨　特：可喜的是，全世界的环保意识正在觉醒。

爱德华：在保护环境方面，我们每一个人都有责任，各国政府及其决策人当然具有更重要和决定性的作用。

孙宝洁：是的。我国政府已经制定了一个《全国生态环境建设规划》，把保护和建设好生态环境、实现可持续发展，作为我国现代化建设的一项基本方针，同时还颁布了森林法、水土保持法、野生动物保护法等一系列法律法规。

孙玉敏：大地啊母亲，我要还你蓝天白云、青山绿水、鸟语花香！

爱德华：啊，孙小姐是诗人！

二、正在升起的朝阳

爱德华：史先生，我们注意到国家环保局对环境保护产品实行认定制度，你能给我们介绍一些这方面的情况吗？

史开继:可以。不知你们想了解哪些情况？

爱德华:比如,贵国为什么要实行环保产品认定呢?

史开继:你知道,环保产业发展很快,现在全球环保市场价值已达到 6 000 亿美元,还有差不多同样数额的资金将投入环保业。

爱德华:环保业已经远远超过旅游、软件等新兴产业。

亨　特:像一轮耀眼的、正在升起的朝阳!

史开继:是的,环保业是具有灿烂前景的朝阳产业,它不仅是各国国内经济新的增长点,而且是国际贸易新的增长点。

爱德华:确实如此。比如席卷全球的"绿色消费浪潮",就已经在各国引起深刻的产业革命,开发和培育出许多新兴产业。

亨　特:单拿治理城市机动车尾气污染来说,尾气监控、测试需要专用仪表仪器;太阳能和其他新能源的开发与应用,电动汽车的研制等等。

史开继:还有家用电器,可防放射性、电磁辐射的电脑、电视,保护臭氧层的无氟制冷技术,低噪音、能消毒杀菌的洗衣机。

亨　特:哈,如果再说到"绿色食品",生产、加工、包装、运输、储存,哪一个环节都需要环保产业支持。此外,还有垃圾、废水污水和废旧固体物资的回收与利用。

爱德华:环保产业,已经并将继续衍生出无以计数的新兴产业和服务部门,并推动多学科高科技的发展。

亨　特:无论开发领域、应用前景,还是潜在市场都无限广阔。

史开继:是啊,发展环保产业,已经成为世界各国重新调整经济结构、振兴老产业、培育新兴产业、实现国家经济可持续发展的根本战略和重要手段。

亨　特:尤其引人瞩目的是,环保产业带动了国际环境贸易的迅猛发展。

爱德华:世贸组织从诞生之日起,就成立了贸易和环境委员会。国际标准化组织推出了 ISO14000 环境管理国际标准系列。有无绿色标志、环境标志、生态标志,产品能否通过 ISO14000 认证,已经或正在成为国际贸易的重要条件。

史开继:随着环保标准日益严格,有的国家以环境保护为由,推行"绿色"贸易保护主义,在国际贸易中设置新的非关税壁垒。

爱德华:因环保壁垒导致的贸易纠纷,是近年来国际贸易中的一大特点,这大概就是贵国要对进入中国市场的境外环保产品实行认定的原因吧。

史开继:我们应该与世界接轨,当然也为了保护我国消费者利益,发展我们自己的环保产业,是不是?

亨　特:世界环保业和国际环境贸易的蓬勃发展,形成了新的竞争局面。

史开继:世界环保产业发展极不平衡,在环保产业较发达的国家,某些环保市场正日趋饱和,环保企业纷纷向境外市场进军,对环保产业相对落后的发展中国家,又是一个新的挑战。

爱德华:用你们的话说,同时也是一个新的发展机遇,对不对?

史开继:对,我们也会抓住这个发展机遇。

生 词

1.	鸟笼	niǎolóng	bird cage
2.	宠物	chǒngwù	pet
3.	云雀	yúnquè	skylark
4.	回归	huíguī	return
5.	情绪	qíngxù	feeling, mood, sentiment
6.	家园	jiāyuán	home, homeland
7.	生存	shēngcún	existence
8.	爱护	àihù	treasure, take good care of
9.	野生	yěshēng	wild
10.	野味	yěwèi	wild animal
11.	滥	làn	excessive, indiscriminate
12.	砍伐	kǎnfá	cut down
13.	污水	wūshuǐ	waste water, sewage
14.	荡	dàng	swing, sway, wave

15. 秋千	qiūqiān	swing
16. 排放	páifàng	discharge
17. 废水	fèishuǐ	liquid waste
18. 周边	zhōubiān	periphery
19. 污染	wūrǎn	pollution
20. 流失	liúshī	be washed away; run off
21. 草原	cǎoyuán	grassland
22. 荒漠化	huāngmòhuà	desert encroachment
23. 大气	dàqì	atmosphere
24. 塑料	sùliào	plastic
25. 肆意	sìyì	wantonly, willfully
26. 掠夺	lüèduó	plunder, rob
27. 节制	jiézhì	control, check; be moderate in
28. 开采	kāicǎi	extract, exploit
29. 恶化	èhuà	deteriorate
30. 迫近	pòjìn	approach, draw near
31. 觉醒	juéxǐng	awaken
32. 规划	guīhuà	plan
33. 颁布	bānbù	promulgate
34. 森林	sēnlín	forest
35. 诗人	shīrén	poet
36. 朝阳	zhāoyáng	morning sun
37. 认定	rèndìng	recognition; believe, set one's mind on
38. 耀眼	yàoyǎn	dazzling
39. 灿烂	cànlàn	magnificent, brilliant
40. 席卷	xíjuǎn	sweep across, roll up like a mat
41. 浪潮	làngcháo	wave, tide
42. 治理	zhìlǐ	harness, bring under control
43. 机动车	jīdòngchē	motor vehicle
44. 尾气	wěiqì	tail gas
45. 仪表	yíbiǎo	meter
46. 仪器	yíqì	instrument
47. 应用	yìngyòng	apply
48. 放射性	fàngshèxìng	radioactivity

49. 电磁	diàncí	electromagnetism
50. 辐射	fúshè	radiation
51. 臭氧	chòuyǎng	ozone
52. 氟	fú	fluorine
53. 制冷	zhìlěng	refrigeration
54. 噪音	zàoyīn	noise
55. 消毒	xiāodú	disinfect
56. 杀菌	shājūn	disinfect
57. 固体	gùtǐ	solid
58. 物资	wùzī	goods and materials
59. 推动	tuīdòng	push forward, promote
60. 学科	xuékē	discipline
61. 振兴	zhènxīng	rejuvenate, develop vigorously
62. 引人瞩目	yǐn rén zhǔmù	noticeable, conspicuous, spectacular
63. 迅猛	xùnměng	swift and violent
64. 诞生	dànshēng	birth
65. 标志	biāozhì	sign, mark, symbol
66. 生态	shēngtài	ecology
67. 认证	rènzhèng	legalization, authentication
68. 蓬勃	péngbó	vigorous, full of vitality
69. 日趋	rìqū	gradually; with each passing day
70. 饱和	bǎohé	saturation
71. 进军	jìnjūn	march, advance

专 名 Proper Noun

| 渤海 | Bó Hǎi | the Bohai Sea |

 练习

A

情绪

名词。①指人从事某种活动时心理产生的一种兴奋。课文中出现的"情绪"即用的这个意思。②指人的情感,尤指不愉快情感。在句子中可做主语、宾语和定语。

Morale;mood. It is a noun. 1) It refers to the psychological excitement when one is engaged in a certain kind of activity,as is used in the text(he is in high spirits). 2) It refers to the mood of a person,especially an unhappy mood. It can be used as the subject,object or an attribute in a sentence.

一、熟读下列各句,体会"情绪"的意义和用法。

1. 这几天她的情绪有点儿失控。
2. 他不肯说你,是为了照顾你的情绪。
3. 职工们听了公司的发展规划,情绪特别高涨。
4. 我看得出来,她这几天正在闹情绪。

二、请用"情绪"与下列短语造句。

1. 难控制
2. 不公平待遇
3. 影响工作　　影响健康
4. 在谈判中
5. 在激烈的比赛中

单

副词,跟"仅"、"只"的意义相当,用来限定行为、事物的范围,并说明这个范围是狭窄的。多用于口语。"单"可重叠为"单单",意义和用法与"单"相同,但语气更重,多用于书面。

One;single;only. It is an adverb. Its meaning is similar to that of 仅 or 只(only).

used to delimit the scope of an action or a thing, indicating that it is a narrow one. It is colloquial. It can also be repeated as 单单, whose meaning is the same as 单, with a stronger tone. 单单 is more often used in the written form.

一、熟读下列各句,仔细体会"单"、"单单"的意义和用法。

1. 我知道,单靠有钱并不一定能得到她的爱。

2. 单就提高服务质量来说,我们就还有很多事情可做。

3. 单单有一个好的计划,是远远不够的。要实现计划,还需要很多条件。

4. 为了改善生态环境,单是污水处理一项,就需要投入大量资金。

二、请用括号里的词语完成下列句子。

1. 环境保护单靠国家治理还不行＿＿＿＿＿＿＿＿＿＿＿。(觉醒、爱护)

2. 环保业是有灿烂前景的朝阳工业,它已经并将继续衍生出无数新兴产业和服务部门,并推动多学科和高科技的发展。单拿开发绿色食品来说＿＿＿＿＿＿＿＿＿＿＿＿＿＿＿＿＿＿。(无限广阔)

3. 人类对自然资源的肆意掠夺和无节制开采,造成了生态环境急剧恶化,臭氧层出现空洞,单天气变暖＿＿＿＿＿＿＿＿＿＿＿。(无可挽回)

4. 环境保护不单单是我们这一代的事,它关系到＿＿＿＿＿＿＿＿＿＿＿＿＿＿＿＿＿＿＿＿＿＿＿＿＿＿＿＿＿＿＿＿＿＿＿＿。(生存危机)

5. 一个企业、一个国家单是领导人有责任心还不够,＿＿＿＿＿＿＿＿＿＿＿＿＿＿＿＿＿＿＿＿＿＿＿＿＿。(拼搏、竞争意识)

无论

连词,表示结论或结果在任何条件下都不会改变,后面常有"也"、"都"、"总"等副词跟它相呼应。主要有两种格式。①"无论"后面跟"谁"、"什么"、"怎么"、"多少"等疑问词。但这些疑问词并不表示疑问。②"无论"后面跟一个并列结构,并列结构之间可用连词,有时也不用连词。

No matter. It is a conjunction, indicating that the conclusion or result will not change no matter under what circumstances. It is often echoed by such words as 也 (as well), 都 (all), or 总 (after all) that comes afterwards. It is mainly used in two patterns. 1) It is followed by such interrogative words as 谁 (who), 什么 (what), 怎么 (how) or 多少 (how many/much). But these interrogative words no longer express interrogation. 2) 无论 can also be followed by a coordinated structure, with or without a conjunction between the two parts.

一、熟读下列各句,仔细体会"无论"的意义和用法。

1. 无论什么人,他今天都不接见。
2. 无论是谁都不能无视城市环境污染的严重性。
3. 无论多少次失败也不能改变我们前进的方向。
4. 无论怎么困难我们也要把环保产业搞上去。
5. 你放心,这件事无论成与不成,我都会尽力去办。
6. 回到家,无论大事小事,妻子都要问个没完。
7. 无论当官的还是普通老百姓,都需要增强环保意识。

二、请用"无论"和下列短语造句。

1. 不杀害野生动物
2. 不能滥砍滥伐树林
3. 情绪激动时
4. 面对水土大量流失,农田和草原荒漠化
5. 求情、送礼　　坚持原则

以……为……

"以",介词,有"拿"、"把"、"按照"等意思。"以……为……":①表示"拿(把)……作为(当作)……"的意思,"以"和"为"的宾语,多是名词性成分;②有"要算"、"要数"的意思,表示一种比较,"为"的宾语一般是形容词性成分。

Take...as;regard...as. 以 is a preposition,whose meaning is 拿(take),把(a preposition used to shift the object before the verb),or 按照(according to).1)以……为……means"take...as" or "regard...as",with both 以 and 为 taking a nominal as the object.2) It has the meaning of 要算(consider),要数(be reckoned as),indicating a comparison. Here 为 normally takes an adjectival object.

一、熟读下列各句,体会并说明各句中"以……为……"的意义和用法。

1. 这家公司以生产环保产品为主。
2. 我们这几个人中,以王总的经验最为丰富。
3. 今年,我市以治理大气污染、净化空气为主要目标。
4. 他总是以帮助别人为自己的最大快乐。
5. 为了防止水土流失,这块地还是以植树种草为宜。
6. 在我们这样一个人口大国,如果以每年每人出一元钱支持环保业来计算,那将是多么巨大的投入。

二、请用"以……为……"和下列短语造句。

1. 他是工作狂
2. 论业务水平
3. 这是个非营利性机构
4. 环保意识
5. 购买商品

B

一、请用下列词语组成短语。

排放　肆意　废水　环境　噪音　持续
治理　开采　污染　标志　周边　推动
日趋　蓬勃　发展　饱和　恶化　规划

二、熟读下列词语,并选择适当的词语完成下列句子。

引人瞩目	日甚一日	可持续发展
回归自然	无以计数	新的增长点
前景灿烂	席卷全球	与世界接轨
日趋饱和	关税壁垒	蓝天白云、青山绿水、鸟语花香

1. 为了保护民族工业,许多国家找各种理由设置_____,必须承认,这样做不符合全球经济一体化的时代潮流。
2. 北京一万平米以上超大型豪华商场_____。
3. 早上上班高峰只要一堵车,自行车_____。中国真是自行车王国!
4. 男人留长发、女人剪短发,人们已见怪不怪,再也不会像以前那样_____。
5. 起点低、基础薄弱的中国商业保险市场_____,为外国保险公司普遍看好。
6. 为了经济_____,我们不能不保护我们的生存环境。
7. 环保产业已经远远超过旅游、软件等新兴产业,它不仅是各国国内经济_____,而且是国际贸易_____。
8. 中国的对外贸易日益_____,已经并还在不断制定和完善各种经济法规。

9. 尽管城市现代化程度越来越高,设备越来越完善,工作累了的人们还是喜欢到＿＿＿＿＿＿＿＿＿＿＿＿＿＿＿＿＿的大自然中去放松放松。

10. 一次次＿＿＿＿＿＿＿＿＿＿＿＿的金融危机,提醒人们加强对证券期货业的监管,防范资本市场的风险。

11. 商场如战场,竞争的残酷程度＿＿＿＿＿＿＿＿＿＿＿＿＿＿,如何抓住机遇,稳步发展,每个成功者都有自己的秘诀。

12. 工业化时代,各种商品＿＿＿＿＿＿＿＿＿＿＿＿＿,吃的、穿的都讲质量,讲科学,消费者对商品的要求越来越苛刻,越来越挑剔了。

三、完成下列各句。

1. 不能不引起人们关注的是,全世界进入工业化时代以后,对自然资源的＿＿＿＿＿＿＿＿＿＿＿＿＿＿造成生态环境＿＿＿＿＿＿＿＿＿＿＿＿＿＿,地球母亲已经不堪承受。

2. 环保产业,已经并将继续衍生出无以计数的＿＿＿＿＿＿＿＿＿＿＿。

3. 发展环保产业,已经成为＿＿＿＿＿＿＿＿＿＿＿＿＿。

4. 随着环保标准日益严格,有的国家以环境保护为由,推行＿＿＿＿＿＿＿＿＿＿＿＿＿＿＿＿＿。

5. 日甚一日的"绿色消费浪潮"已经在各国＿＿＿＿＿＿＿＿＿＿＿＿＿＿。

四、想一想,谈一谈。

1. 现在世界上环境污染主要有哪些?

2. 你认为中国的环保形势如何? 中国人的环保意识如何?

3. 谈谈环保产业对国民经济发展的深远意义和在国际贸易中的巨大影响。

4. 你认为我们每个人在环境保护方面有什么责任,可做哪些事儿?

五、阅读下面的短文,然后回答问题。

特殊审判

今天是 5 月 31 日——"世界无烟日",本中级人民法院现在正式开庭,审理成日病先生状告香烟中毒案。法官宣布开庭之后,被告带进了法庭。听众席上顿时哗然,原来,被告是一个巨人的香烟盒儿,上面那金发碧眼的漂亮女郎图像,特别惹眼。

"被告,你为什么到处毒害人?"法官问。

"我没有毒害人,我是大家的朋友。"香烟女郎说。

"你看,原告席上那个人,因为受了你的诱惑,现在得了肺癌,活不了多久了,你还说是他的朋友吗?"法官又问。

"法官大人,我曾经给他很多帮助。他工作时,我帮他提神;他烦恼时,我帮他解闷;他需要交朋友时,我成了他拉关系、联络感情的最好助手……"香烟女郎甜甜地说。

法官打断了香烟女郎的话,一声冷笑:"这么说,你还很有功啰!"

"法官大人,我的功劳可大了,您知道吗,我一年要为国家带来多少税收?"

原告的代理律师沉不住气了,站起来:"法官大人,我可以发言吗?我要请教让人爱不释手的香烟小姐,你含二十多种有毒物质,吸烟者的死亡率,因得肺癌致死的比不吸烟者高出 10 倍,因得喉癌致死的高出 5.4 倍,因得食道癌致死的高出 3.4 倍。尤其不能容忍的是,你毒害了成千上万的青少年。"

香烟女郎说:"先生,我有那么可怕吗?他们的死一定与我有关吗?你有什么证据呢?"

律师立即拿出一沓儿文件,说:"我这里有大量受害者的医院化验报告。"

法官说:"拿上来。被告,你还有什么话说?"

被告沉默了。律师说:"我要求被告赔偿原告经济损失 100 万元人民币。"

听众席上立即响起了热烈的掌声。

1. 你认为香烟污染环境吗?
2. 你认为吸烟对人的健康有多大危害?
3. 你如果不吸烟,怎样同吸烟者相处?
4. 你如果吸烟,你对上面的故事有什么看法?

33 信息产业市场

Market of Information Industry

一、中国的硅谷

爱德华：亨特，你说我们现在去参观中国硅谷？

亨　特：是！孙小姐是一位很好的向导，你会乐而忘返的。

孙玉敏：那是一个很特殊的地区。

亨　特：你在中国听到"硅谷"这个名字，不感到新鲜吗？

爱德华：我正奇怪呢！我们美国旧金山市有一个"硅谷"，没想到中国北京也有一个地方叫"硅谷"。

亨　特：旧金山市的"硅谷"，本来叫圣克拉拉谷，你知道人们为什么叫它"硅谷"吗？

爱德华：你这是故意拿我开心还是怎么的？这是连三岁小孩儿都知道的常识。

亨　特：那你说说。

爱德华：谁不知道，美国主要微电子工业都集中在那里，而微电子工业最关键的材料是硅片，所以圣克拉拉谷别称"硅谷"。

亨　特：答案完全正确，计10分！

爱德华：你这是在搞智力测验嘛！

孙玉敏：其实，"硅谷"之所以在全世界享有盛誉，主要因为它是美国信息产业的发祥地，是美国高科技人才云集的圣地。

爱德华：孙小姐解释得很好。难道我们现在要去参观的也是这样一个地方？

亨　特：说得不错，这儿本来是北京市海淀区的一块地方，以中关村为中心向四周辐射,现在大约覆盖了100平方公里,聚集了几千家高新技术企业。

爱德华:这儿是中国信息产业的发祥地和高科技人才云集的地方?

亨　特:可以当之无愧地称为"中国的硅谷"!

孙玉敏:世界知名的北京大学、清华大学、中国人民大学等十几所高等学府以及中国科学院的高新技术和尖端科学研究所都在这里。

亨　特:这里人才济济,科研实力和成果同美国硅谷相比,毫不逊色!

孙玉敏:这里的激光照排技术、大型集成电路、计算机主机与软件等新兴信息产业,或者处于世界领先地位,或者与世界发展保持同步。同美国硅谷一样,中关村地区信息产业的发展正反映了中国信息产业的发展轨迹。

亨　特:开始,这里叫电脑一条街,街两边一个小门脸儿就是一家电脑销售商店。

孙玉敏:当然也经销与电脑相关的产品,如软件啦、打印机啦、缆线啦等等。总之是门脸儿小,规模小,大多是国外电脑名牌产品的代销部。

爱德华:如果是这样,还不能同我们的硅谷比美。

孙玉敏:凡事都有一个发展过程,现在的情况可就大不相同了!

亨　特:一座座现代化的高楼正拔地而起。

孙玉敏:更重要的是,像联想、方正等大型信息产业集团,已经有了自己的实业和自己的品牌生产基地。

亨　特:他们已经集研制、开发、生产和营销为一体。

爱德华:哦?有这样巨大的变化?

孙玉敏:不仅如此,美国微软中国公司的总部就设在这里,并用最优惠的条件招揽人才,准备在这里与中国同行展开竞争。

爱德华:俗话说,耳听为虚,眼见为实,我倒要认真看看中国硅谷是什么样儿!

亨　特:你的认真劲儿,我可领教过了,怕又要累坏孙小姐了。

二、迎接信息时代

孙玉敏：爱德华先生，这儿就是联想集团微机事业部，请进吧！

何云龙：欢迎，欢迎，请坐吧！

爱德华：何先生，孙小姐今天陪同我们来参观，一路上对贵公司赞不绝口，让我对贵公司产生了无限敬意。

何云龙：孙小姐恐怕有些言过其实了。

亨　特：联想集团确实是中国信息产业的龙头企业。

何云龙：信息产业已经成为当代经济的主导产业，在全世界从工业化时代向信息时代迈进的过程中，美国等发达国家已经占尽了先机，我们必须加速发展电子信息产业，推进国民经济信息化。

孙玉敏：在20世纪末的全球金融危机中，西方的一些经济强国风光不再，一派委靡不振的景象，唯独美国经济长盛不衰，就因为得到蓬勃发展的信息产业的支撑。

爱德华：孙小姐说得很对。美国新的就业机会中，有37%的岗位是信息产业及相关行业提供的。

何云龙：还不只是这些。首先是信息产业本身就是知识技术密集型产品和高附加值产品，无论是信息设备制造，还是以计算机为主要平台的信息服务，如信息资源的发掘、采集、储存和传输，都可以创造巨大的经济效益。

孙玉敏：光缆、计算机、多媒体、移动通讯、程控交换、卫星导航和电视接收等信息产品创造的价值，在国民经济总收入中都占有很大比重。

何云龙：如果扣除信息产品的贡献，美国国民经济将成为负增长。

亨　特：事实确实如此，正因为信息产业能创造如此巨大的经济效益，所以在美国股票市场上，最吃香的股票是高新技术股，股价最高的是信息产业股票。

孙玉敏：庞大的资金来源，使电子信息产业成为产品升级、更新换代最快的产业。

爱德华：比尔·盖茨说，微软距离破产只有18个月，这说明信息产业的竞争异常激烈。

何云龙：谁拥有最先进的技术，谁才有市场。数字化浪潮正在使信息产业发生根本性突破，我们的时代正在加速向数字化、网络化和智能化过渡。

亨　特：眼下，信息家电正在崛起，从智能卡到可视电话，从可随身携带的掌上电脑到家庭网络装置……

何云龙：日常生活的各方面都需要一种简单方便的小玩意儿，一种数字、语音智能产品，像口香糖一样大小的模块儿，像巴掌一样大小的机顶盒儿。

亨　特：你在厨房或卧室可以上网浏览，看看是否有当日棒球比赛门票，在哪家餐馆就餐有免费葡萄酒。当你走进家门时，电视或音响就认出了你，开始播放你最喜欢的节目或音乐。

孙玉敏：听起来，简直像天方夜谭！

亨　特：不，这类产品已经问世，完全不懂电脑的人，只要触摸、点击一下，或只要拿起电话，就能享受到这一切。

何云龙：谁能预料，信息产业在未来还会有多少新奇发明，还会上演多少有声有色的活剧！

爱德华：确实很难预料，但可以肯定，它不仅将空前促进社会经济繁荣，也将极大地改变我们的生活！

生　词

1. 向导	xiàngdǎo	guide
2. 乐而忘返	lè ér wàng fǎn	enjoy something so much that one does not want to come back
3. 微电子	wēidiànzǐ	microelectronic
4. 硅片	guīpiàn	siliconchip
5. 智力	zhìlì	intelligence

6. 测验	cèyàn	test
7. 发祥地	fāxiángdì	birthplace
8. 圣地	shèngdì	sacred place
9. 覆盖	fùgài	cover
10. 当之无愧	dāng zhī wúkuì	deserve the name of
11. 学府	xuéfǔ	seat of learning;institution of higher learning
12. 尖端	jiānduān	acme;most advanced
13. 人才济济	réncái jǐjǐ	an abundance of talented people, a galaxy of talent
14. 成果	chéngguǒ	achievement, fruit
15. 激光	jīguāng	laser
16. 照排	zhàopái	photolithography
17. 集成电路	jíchéng-diànlù	integrated circuit
18. 新兴	xīnxīng	new and developing, rising
19. 领先	lǐngxiān	in the lead
20. 反映	fǎnyìng	reflect
21. 轨迹	guǐjì	orbit
22. 打印机	dǎyìnjī	printer
23. 缆线	lǎnxiàn	cable
24. 拔地而起	bá dì ér qǐ	rise steeply from level ground
25. 实业	shíyè	industry
26. 耳听为虚，眼见为实	ěr tīng wéi xū, yǎn jiàn wéi shí	what you hear may be false, but what you see is true
27. 敬意	jìngyì	respect
28. 言过其实	yán guò qí shí	overstate, exaggerate
29. 龙头	lóngtóu	lead; tap
30. 先机	xiānjī	early opportunities
31. 委靡不振	wěimí bú zhèn	lose their grandeur and momentum
32. 景象	jǐngxiàng	scene, picture
33. 唯独	wéidú	only, alone
34. 长盛不衰	cháng shèng bù shuāi	be always vigorous without a decline
35. 支撑	zhīchēng	support, prop up

36. 岗位	gǎngwèi	post, station
37. 平台	píngtái	platform
38. 发掘	fājué	explore, excavate
39. 采集	cǎijí	gather, collect
40. 储存	chǔcún	storage
41. 传输	chuánshū	transmission
42. 光缆	guānglǎn	optical fiber
43. 移动	yídòng	mobile
44. 程控	chéngkòng	program-controlled
45. 接收	jiēshōu	reception
46. 负	fù	negative, minus
47. 更新换代	gēngxīn huàndài	updating and upgrading
48. 突破	tūpò	break through
49. 崛起	juéqǐ	rise abruptly
50. 携带	xiédài	carry, take along
51. 装置	zhuāngzhì	installation, device
52. 玩意儿	wányìr	toy, thing
53. 口香糖	kǒuxiāngtáng	chewing gum
54. 模块	mókuài	module
55. 巴掌	bāzhang	palm
56. 机顶盒	jīdǐnghé	a box on top of(the TV)
57. 棒球	bàngqiú	baseball
58. 天方夜谭	Tiānfāng yè tán	*the Arabian Nights*
59. 问世	wènshì	come out；be published
60. 触摸	chùmō	touch
61. 点击	diǎnjī	hit, click
62. 预料	yùliào	predict
63. 新奇	xīnqí	novel
64. 肯定	kěndìng	certain

专　名　Proper Nouns

1. 硅谷	Guīgǔ	the Silicon Valley
2. 旧金山	Jiùjīnshān	San Francisco

3. 圣克拉拉谷　　Shèngkèlālā Gǔ　　Santa Clara Valley
4. 海淀　　　　Hǎidiàn　　　　　Haidian
5. 中关村　　　Zhōngguāncūn　　Zhongguancun
6. 中国科学院　Zhōngguó Kēxuéyuàn　Chinese Academy of Sciences
7. 联想集团　　Liánxiǎng Jítuán　　the Lenovo Group
8. 北大方正　　Běidà Fāngzhèng　　Founder Group of Peking University
9. 比尔·盖茨　Bǐ'ěr·Gàicí　　　Bill Gates

 练 习

A

之所以

这是一个固定格式,可当做一个词来看,意思相当于现代汉语的"……的原因"。"之所以……"小句后,常有"为了"、"因为"一类词领起的小句来解释这个原因。

The reason why.... This is a set expression which can be regarded as a single word, with the meaning equivalent to "the reason why...". After the clause introduced by 之所以, there is usually a clause introduced by 为了(for) or 因为(because) to explain the reason.

一、熟读下列各句,体会"之所以"的意义和用法。

1. 他之所以下海经商,是为了赚更多的钱。
2. 我们之所以常常争吵,就因为我们性格不合。
3. L 公司之所以破产,只因为他们不善经营。
4. 公司之所以现在还没有辞退他,是想再给他一次机会。
5. 大家之所以纷纷上网,是希望从网上获得更多信息。

二、请用"之所以"和下列短语造句。

1. 环境污染
2. 无愧地称为"中国的硅谷"
3. 人才流失

　　4. 这里叫食品一条街

　　5. 美国微软中国公司的总部设在这里

唯独

　　副词,表示"只有"、"独一无二"的意思,用来限定事物的范围,一般放在做主语的名词性词语前。

　　Only；alone. It is an adverb，meaning 只有（only）, or 独一无二（unique）. It is used to delimit the scope of something，being placed before the nominal subject.

一、熟读下列各句,体会"唯独"的意义和用法。

　　1. 我们老板什么都好,唯独脾气太大。

　　2. 大家都同意,唯独他有意见。

　　3. 她对什么都有兴趣,唯独不肯学电脑。

　　4. 唯独信息产业,无论它的市场前景还是它的应用范围,都足以成为社会经济发展新的增长点。

二、请用"唯独"和下列短语造句。

　　1. 保持了人民币不贬值和低通货膨胀

　　2. 不污染周边环境

　　3. 炒股票不影响情绪

　　4. 稀里糊涂

　　5. 不怕学写汉字

集……为一体

　　这是一个比较固定的用法。"集"是动词,是"集合"、"集聚"、"汇集"的意思。"为",也是动词,意思是"成为"。与"集……为一体"类似的说法还有"集……于一身"。"于"是介词,意思是"在"。

　　Merge…into an organic whole. This is a relatively set expression. 集 is a verb meaning 集合（gather）,集聚（assemble） or 汇集（come together）. 为 is also a verb meaning 成为（become）. Similar to 集……为一体,there is 集……于一身（all these come together on one person）. Here 于 is a preposition,meaning 在（at,in or on）.

一、熟读下列各句,仔细体会"集……为一体"、"集……于一身"的意义和用法。

1. 所谓"多媒体",就是集多种媒介为一体。

2. 一种口香糖大小的模块儿,竟然也集接收、储存、显示等多功能为一体。

3. 我们这位领导,集多种职务于一身。

4. 现在,各种压力集于一身,他怎么承受得了!

二、请用"集……为一体"或"集……于一身"和下列短语造句。

1. 招商银行发行的"一卡通"

2. 营养保健食品

3. 中国的旗袍

4. 古老的汉字

5. 多功能厅

天方夜谭

　　《天方夜谭》又名《一千零一夜》,是一部著名的阿拉伯民间故事集,讲的是东方某国国王山鲁亚尔,生性残暴,他每夜娶一个妻子,到第二天天亮,就把妻子杀了再娶。宰相(相当于现在的政府最高行政长官)的女儿山鲁佐德,美丽聪明,她为了自己不被杀害,也为了拯救其他女子,自愿嫁给国王。成婚后,她就给国王讲故事。她讲的有民间故事、爱情故事、冒险故事、名人轶事、宫廷奇闻,一个接一个,个个故事充满了神奇想象,引人入胜。她一共讲了一千零一夜故事,在这个过程中,国王被深深地感动了,终于悔悟,决心同新婚妻子白头到老。现在,人们常用"天方夜谭"来形容不可思议的新奇事儿或根本不存在的事儿。

　　The Arabian Nights is also named *One Thousand and One Nights*. This is a collection of famous Arabian stories. It is about a cruel oriental King named Schahriar who would marry a girl one night and then kill her the next morning in order to marry a new one. Scheherazade, daughter of the Prime Minister, was both beautiful and intelligent. In order to save her own life as well as the lives of other women, she got married to the King voluntarily. In the evening, she started to tell stories to the King, which included folklore, love stories, adventures, anecdotes of famous people, and fantastic stories of the court. She told one story after another, each being miraculous and fascinating. She told stories for one thousand and one nights, and the King was deeply moved. He repented his error and decided to remain a devoted couple with his wife to the end of their lives. Now people often use 天方夜谭 to describe things that are unimaginable and novel, or things that are nonexistent.

一、熟读下列各句,体会"天方夜谭"的意义和用法。

1. 你以为这是天方夜谭吗? 不,这是现实。

2. 人们有天方夜谭似的想法,才有了许多科学发明。

3. 那都是天方夜谭,你还相信?

4. 我听他讲那些故事,就像听天方夜谭!

二、请用"天方夜谭"和下列短语造句。

1. 短期内想把脏、乱、差的环境治理好

2. 高新科技迅猛发展

3. 传统中草药的独特疗效

4. 他的成功之路充满了艰辛

5. 贫困山区用上了自来水和家用电器

B

一、请用下列词语组成短语。

发掘　储存　资源　突破　尖端
采集　信息　新闻　肯定　领先
发展　轨迹　交换　程控　预料

二、熟读下列词语,并选择适当的词语完成下列句子。

长盛不衰	不可思议	耳听为虚,眼见为实
保持同步	人才济济	更新换代　拔地而起
言过其实	有声有色	委靡不振　最吃香
风光不再	人才云集	乐而忘返　当之无愧

1. 北京是中国的政治文化中心,是知识密集、＿＿＿＿＿＿＿＿的地方。

2. 高等院校、高级科研机构＿＿＿＿＿＿＿＿＿,有时反不如去一般单位更能发挥自己的才能,更容易出成果。

3. 现在学计算机专业的人＿＿＿＿＿＿＿＿＿。

4. 这里几年前还是一片破旧的平房,现在一座座现代化公寓＿＿＿＿＿＿＿＿＿＿＿＿＿,商业网点、娱乐设施应有尽有。

5. 一个＿＿＿＿＿＿＿＿＿＿的人,无论他说得多么天花乱坠,最终也是不能取信于人的。

6. 改革开放后中国经济建设取得了辉煌成果,这一切虽然新闻媒体早有报道,但我仍劝你来中国作一次商业旅行,要知道＿＿＿＿＿＿＿＿＿。

7. 你去了拉萨,看到了那儿的山,那儿的雪,方知道它是＿＿＿＿＿＿＿＿的世界屋脊。

8. 亨特是＿＿＿＿＿＿＿＿＿的中国通,他讲起在中国的亲身经历,真是＿＿＿＿＿＿＿＿＿,令人羡慕。

9. 20 世纪末的最后一次金融危机,波及全球,致使许多国家的经济陷入长期＿＿＿＿＿＿＿＿＿的局面。

10. 北京有些老字号商店在改革开放的大潮中跟不上时代,当年的繁荣景象早已是＿＿＿＿＿＿＿＿＿。

11. 当今＿＿＿＿＿＿＿＿＿最快的商品,要算以计算机为代表的各类电器了。

12. 你想不被淘汰,你想立于不败之地,你就要不断开发新产品,与世界发展＿＿＿＿＿＿＿＿＿。

13. 他是＿＿＿＿＿＿＿＿＿的成功企业家,他让企业＿＿＿＿＿＿＿＿＿＿＿＿＿＿＿的秘诀是不要停步不前,永不满足。

14. 桂林太美了,那儿的青山绿水,风土人情,让人＿＿＿＿＿＿＿＿＿。

15. 金字塔是怎么建成的,至今令人＿＿＿＿＿＿＿＿＿。

三、完成下列句子。

1. 北京中关村地区信息产业的发展＿＿＿＿＿＿＿＿＿。

2. 美国"硅谷"之所以在全世界享有盛誉,主要因为它是＿＿＿＿＿＿,是＿＿＿＿＿＿＿＿＿。

3. 20 世纪末美国经济持续发展,靠的是＿＿＿＿＿＿＿＿＿。

4. 美国微软中国公司的总部设在中关村,为的是＿＿＿＿＿＿＿＿＿。

5. 中国的联想、方正等大型信息产业集团,已经有了＿＿＿＿＿＿＿＿,已经＿＿＿＿＿＿＿＿＿。

四、想一想,谈一谈。

1. 人们为什么把北京中关村称为"中国的硅谷"?

2. 请谈一谈中关村地区信息产业的发展轨迹。

3. 你逛过"中国的硅谷"吗?你对它的现状和发展前景怎么看?

4. 信息产业在当代经济中占什么地位?对国民经济起什么作用?

5. 信息产业和它的产品对我们的生活有什么影响,请举两三个实例说明。

五、阅读下面的短文,然后回答问题。

一 字 千 金

　　古时候,有一本《吕氏春秋》,作者写好后,就在城门上贴出布告,说:"谁看了这本书,能增减、改动一个字,就可以获得千金重奖。"以后,就用"一字千金"来形容诗、文写得完美无缺,不能写得再好了。

　　可是,邓老太太遇到一件事儿,她也说是"一字千金"。

　　这几年股市特热,邓老太太也迷上了炒股。炒股就得时时刻刻注意股市行情,信息不灵怎么成!所以,邓老太太进入股市之前,就先买了一部手机,一可接收信息台发布的股市行情,二可同股友交换情报。你别说,小小手机还真管用,就靠它给的情报,邓老太太炒股三年,还真是赔的少,赚的多。

　　天有不测风云。两个月前,邓老太太的老伴突然一病不起,她天天跑医院,哪里还有心思炒股!两个月来,手机上的股市行情,她连看都没看一眼。一天上午,她的手机响个不停,她打开一看,短信显示的是"关注个股山川,小米"。小米,是邓老太太的股市朋友,人特机灵,有专业知识,平时特别关照邓老太太,大约有两个月没见她了,所以给她发短信。这时,邓老头儿又在哼哼啊啊叫她,她只好关机。下午手机又响起来,"山川危险,小米"。邓老太太突然猛醒,"不好,我还有2 000股山川呢!"她风风火火跑到股市,立即清仓抛出,净赚了4 000块,这以后,山川一路下跌。今天,邓老头儿的病大好了,同老伴聊起股市来,邓老太太说:"多亏了小米,要是到今天我还捏着山川,赔8 000也不止了。"邓老头儿说:"你还得感谢那小东西!"说着,指指手机。"啊,对,它给的信息真是一字千金啊!"

1. "一字千金"的本来意思是什么?
2. 信息就是机会,就是财富,这话对不对?为什么?
3. 邓老太太说的"一字千金"是什么意思?与"一字千金"的原意一样吗?
4. 请你举例说说信息的重要性。

34 知识产权与许可贸易

Intellectual Property Rights and Franchise Trade

一、知识产权保护

爱德华：何先生，信息时代是以知识和高科技为基础的，知识产权是企业最重要的产权，你同意吗？

何云龙：完全同意！知识产权是企业的无形资产，甚至可能是一笔巨大的无形资产。

孙玉敏：据经济学界计算，可口可乐和万宝路的品牌价值高达四五百亿美元。

亨　特：前提是要受到保护，如果仿冒侵权商品充斥市场，对正牌商品销售形成广泛冲击，造成的实际经济损失也将是很可观的。

何云龙：所以，在国际贸易中，知识产权保护越来越受到重视，并且常常成为爆发贸易战的导火线。

爱德华：我们两国曾为计算机软件、激光唱盘、激光视盘发生过不小摩擦。

亨　特：我记得，20 世纪福克斯等八家电影公司的 19 部电影侵权案，就曾经闹得沸沸扬扬。

爱德华：是怎么回事儿？

亨　特：两家商场未经著作权人许可，擅自复制、销售了那 19 部电影的激光视盘。

孙玉敏：我国政府依法保护了著作权人的合法权益。法院经过认真调查和审理，宣判原告胜诉，被告立即停止侵权行为，并赔偿原告经济损失。

何云龙：在知识产权领域，侵权与保护，都不是单方面的。我国也有知名品牌与专利在贵国被侵权。国际间需要在平等互利基础上的相互合作与谅解。

孙玉敏：如果一方借口另一方对知识产权保护不力实施贸易报复，而另一方被迫采取反报复措施，受损害的就不只是某一方了。

爱德华：我想，我们作了努力。

何云龙：在知识产权领域，我们之间的分歧虽然还没有完全消除，但是我们通过耐心磋商，签署了《谅解备忘录》，最终不止一次地避免了贸易战。

孙玉敏：我们不要贸易战，我们要和平！

爱德华：噢，我想，我们今天就是一次很好的沟通。

亨　特：我们在知识产权保护领域，可以达成共识。

何云龙：我们不只有共识，我们国家在保护知识产权方面的立法、司法和实际业绩，也是举世公认的。

亨　特：我们也注意到了这个事实。

二、知识产权协议与公约

爱德华：刚才孙小姐说"我们要和平"，听起来好像在喊口号。

孙玉敏：那不是口号，是我们的真诚愿望。我们不要贸易摩擦，我们要平等互利、公平正当的竞争。

爱德华：但是，良好的愿望不能代替现实，知识产权毕竟具有鲜明的归属性和地域性特征，侵权与反侵权是不可避免的，不以人的意志为转移。

亨　特：一些深受顾客青睐的新技术、新产品，总有人垂涎三尺，未经许可，制假贩假，既损害了消费者利益，又损害了所有权人的利益。

何云龙：但这不是必定发生贸易摩擦或贸易战的理由，相反，倒应该成为知识产权领域国际合作的推动力。

孙玉敏：事实也正是如此。知识产权领域国际性多边公约，不就是这样产生了吗？

爱德华：我承认二位说得对。但是，各国对知识产权的保护水平，总是与一个国家经济、科技发展水平相一致的。

亨　特：发达国家的某些知识产权，在一些国家就很难得到有效保护。

孙玉敏：国情不同，知识产权保护的立场也就不同，意见有分歧，标准自然也有差异，不能把一国的意志和标准强加给另一个国家。

何云龙：所以在知识产权保护领域，不只需要多边国际公约，也需要国家间的双边协议。

爱德华：那么，贵国都签署了哪些多边国际公约呢？

何云龙：就我所知，重要的我们都参加了。我们是世界知识产权组织（WIPO）成员国，我们先后签署了《保护工业产权巴黎公约》、《商标国际注册马德里协定》、《保护文学艺术作品伯尔尼公约》和《世界版权日内瓦公约》以及世贸组织《与贸易有关的知识产权协定》（TRIPS）等等。

亨　特：中国确实取得了显著进展。

何云龙：这是有目共睹的，我们在知识产权保护方面承担的国际义务，几乎涉及了专利、商标、计算机软件、专有技术、高新技术、著作权、商业秘密等等各个领域。

孙玉敏：我国政府还同美国、欧盟、瑞士、日本等签署了保护知识产权的备忘录，相互承诺按照各自的法律，并参考国际公约，保护对方自然人、法人的合法权益。

爱德华：我还想知道贵国的执法情况。如果有法不依、执法不严，仍然会给不法分子以可趁之机。

何云龙：我们保护知识产权的态度是坚决的，执法力度也在不断加强。我国有知识产权协调领导机构，有工商局等行政执法部门，人民法院有知识产权审判庭。

孙玉敏：一旦发现盗窃、仿冒等侵权行为，就坚决收缴、销毁、制止，并给予必要的民事处罚或法律制裁。

何云龙：万宝路香烟和福克斯等公司影视制品的产权，在我国就得到了强有力保护。

爱德华：看来，在知识产权领域，我们有了开展许可贸易的坚实基础。

孙玉敏：雄辩的事实证明，我国已经进入全世界知识产权保护的先进行列。

何云龙：在知识经济时代，许可贸易已经成为国际贸易中最重要和最基本的形式，在知识产权保护方面的谅解与合作，必将大大促进世界各国的经济发展！

生 词

1.	产权	chǎnquán	property rights
2.	无形	wúxíng	intangible
3.	仿冒	fǎngmào	imitations
4.	充斥	chōngchì	flood；be full of
5.	爆发	bàofā	break out
6.	导火线	dǎohuǒxiàn	fuse
7.	摩擦	mócā	friction
8.	沸沸扬扬	fèifèiyángyáng	a lot of bubbling and gurgling
9.	著作	zhùzuò	works
10.	复制	fùzhì	copy
11.	审理	shěnlǐ	try，hear
12.	宣判	xuānpàn	pronounce judgment
13.	原告	yuángào	plaintiff
14.	胜诉	shèngsù	win a lawsuit
15.	被告	bèigào	defendant
16.	停止	tíngzhǐ	stop
17.	报复	bàofù	retaliate
18.	被迫	bèipò	be compelled，be forced
19.	和平	hépíng	peace
20.	司法	sīfǎ	administration of justice

21. 业绩	yèjì	outstanding achievement
22. 举世公认	jǔshì gōngrèn	universally acknowledged
23. 口号	kǒuhào	slogan
24. 代替	dàitì	replace, substitute for
25. 现实	xiànshí	reality
26. 鲜明	xiānmíng	bright, clear-cut, distinctive
27. 归属	guīshǔ	belong to, come under the jurisdiction of
28. 特征	tèzhēng	characteristic
29. 意志	yìzhì	will, determination
30. 青睐	qīnglài	favor
31. 垂涎三尺	chuíxián sān chǐ	spittle three feet long; drool with envy
32. 立场	lìchǎng	stand, position
33. 强加	qiángjiā	impose, force
34. 有目共睹	yǒu mù gòng dǔ	be obvious to anyone who has eyes, be perfectly obvious
35. 秘密	mìmì	secret
36. 参考	cānkǎo	reference
37. 协调	xiétiáo	coordinate
38. 行政	xíngzhèng	administration
39. 审判庭	shěnpàn tíng	judicial court
40. 盗窃	dàoqiè	steal; theft
41. 收缴	shōujiǎo	take over, capture
42. 销毁	xiāohuǐ	destroy by melting, burning, etc.
43. 制止	zhìzhǐ	check, curb, prevent
44. 民事	mínshì	civil
45. 制裁	zhìcái	sanction, punish
46. 坚实	jiānshí	solid, strong, substantial
47. 雄辩	xióngbiàn	convincing argument, eloquent speech

专 名 Proper Nouns

1. 20 世纪福克斯	Èrshí Shìjì Fúkèsī	the 20th Century Fox
2. 万宝路	Wànbǎolù	Marlboro

3.《保护工业产	Bǎohù Gōngyè Chǎn-	Paris Convention on the
权巴黎公约》	quán Bālí Gōngyuē	Protection of Industrial Property
4.《商标国际注册	Shāngbiāo Guójì Zhùcè	Madrid Agreement for International
马德里协定》	Mǎdélǐ Xiédìng	Registration of Trade Marks
5.《保护文学	Bǎohù Wénxué	Bern Convention for the
艺术作品	Yìshù Zuòpǐn	Protection of Literary and
伯尔尼公约》	Bó'ěrní Gōngyuē	Artistic Works
6.《世界版权	Shìjiè Bǎnquán	Geneva Convention on
日内瓦公约》	Rìnèiwǎ Gōngyuē	Universal Copyright
7.《与贸易有关的	Yǔ Màoyì Yǒuguān de	Agreement on Trade-Related
知识产权协定》	Zhīshi Chǎnquán	Aspects of Intellectual
	Xiédìng	Property Rights（TRIPS）
8.瑞士	Ruìshì	Switzerland

A

将

副词。①单纯表示时间,相当于"快要"、"就要",说明某种情况或动作就要发生或完成。②用来对事情发展的未来情况进行判断,含有"一定"、"一定会"的意思。

Be going to;will. It is an adverb. 1）It can be used to indicate time only,equivalent to 快要（soon;before long）, or 就要（be about to;be going to）,indicating that a certain situation or action will soon occur or finish. 2）It is used to give a judgment about the future situation of an affair,implying the meaning of 一定 or 一定会（certainly;surely）.

一、熟读下列各句,体会并说明句中"将"的意义和用法。

    1. 会议将在下午3时结束。

    2. 如果不刻苦努力,将一事无成。

    3. 这个计划将分几个步骤实施。

    4. 如果我们的知识产权得不到保护,我们将不得不中止这项贸易。

    5. 知识产权许可贸易,必将大大推动接受方的经济技术现代化进程。

二、请用"将"和下列短语造句。

    1. 环境保护

    2. 信息产业

    3. 商业保险

    4. 金融市场委靡不振

    5. 股价上扬

    6. 对手顶不住

举世公认

    "举"：①动词，往上托起，如"举手、举重"；提出，如"举例、列举"；还有其他一些动词意义，如"举行、举办、一举一动、一举两得"等等。②形容词，意思是"全"，如"举家"就是全家，"举国"就是全国，"举世"就是全世界，等等。

    1）举 can be used as a verb, meaning "lift or hold up"，as in 举手(put up one's hand)and 举重(weight lifting). It can also mean 提出(raise；put forward)，as in 举例(give an example)，and 列举(enumerate). It may have other verbal meanings as in 举行(hold)，举办(run)，一举一动(every action)，一举两得 (gain two ends at once)，etc. 2）It can be used as an adjective, meaning 全(whole；entire)， as in 举家(the whole family)，举国(the whole country)，举世(the entire world)，etc.

一、熟读下列各句，体会并说明"举"的扩展词的意义和用法。

    1. 大家纷纷举手向会议主持人提问。

    2. 去年，我们举家南迁，把家搬到了上海。

    3. 名人的一举一动都受到新闻媒体的关注。

    4. 我们这次磋商，既消除了分歧，又达成了新的合作意向，真是一举两得。

    5. 这项尖端技术，目前还是举世无双。

    6. 这只是举手之劳，算不得什么，不用谢。

    7. 我们自己研制的探月卫星顺利升空，举国上下一片欢腾。

二、想一想下列短语中"举"是什么意思，然后用所列短语造句。

    1. 举目远望

    2. 举措

    3. 举棋不定

    4. 举止不礼貌

    5. 举座皆惊

加强/强加

"加强",动词,是使受者更坚强或更有效,如"加强领导、加强信心、加强责任感、加强执法力度"等;"强加",动词,是强迫对方接受某种意见或做法,后面跟介词"于"或"给"带出的宾语,如"强加于人"、"强加于对方"、"强加给别人"等。

加强(strengthen) is a verb, meaning to make it stronger or more effective, as in strengthening the leadership, enhancing the sense of responsibility, reinforcing the dynamics in law enforcement, etc.

强加(impose) is a verb, meaning to force the other party to accept a certain opinion or way of doing things. It is followed by objects introduced by such prepositions as 于 or 给, as in 强加于人 (imposing on others), 强加于对方, (imposing on the other party), 强加给别人 (imposing on other people), etc.

一、熟读下列各句,体会"加强"、"强加"的意义和用法。

1. 企业应该加强管理。
2. 我们商定,以后要通过各种渠道加强联系。
3. 这是我个人的看法,不想强加于大家。
4. 任何问题都应该协商解决,把少数人的意见强加于绝大多数人的做法,已经行不通了。

二、请用"加强"或"强加于/给"和下列短语造句。

1. 环境污染的治理
2. 谈判失败的责任
3. 金融市场监管
4. 不履行合同
5. 日程安排
6. 运输途中的损耗

B

一、请用下列词语组成短语。

无形　宣判　产权　报复　制裁

充斥　摩擦　胜诉　制止　盗窃
秘密　仿冒　行为　被迫　许可

二、熟读下列词语,并选择适当的词语完成下列句子。

沸沸扬扬　　　有目共睹　　　垂涎三尺
达成共识　　　举世公认　　　受顾客青睐
可趁之机　　　不以人的意志为转移

1. 全球气候变暖被新闻媒体炒得_____。
2. 为了经济可持续发展,加强对环境的保护,人们越来越_____。
3. 我们要坚持保护知识产权,加强执法力度,不给不法分子_____。
4. 股票市场股价的上扬与下跌是_____的。
5. 不受污染的新开发出来的绿色食品,越来越_____。
6. 为了扩大保险市场,商业保险公司必须下大力气培训业务员,同时加强对商业保险的宣传,打消公众对保险公司的不信任,只有公众与保险公司_____,中国的保险业才能进入一个高速度发展时期。
7. 中国在保护知识产权方面所作的努力是_____的。
8. 中国一直实行稳健的货币政策,保持人民币不贬值和低通货膨胀,在20世纪末的金融危机中作出了很大贡献,赢得了全世界的广泛赞誉,这是_____的。
9. 有些人对美色与金钱总是_____,被押上审判庭是迟早的事儿。
10. 中国悠久文化的魅力,中国市场的潜力,中国改革开放后的吸引力是_____的。

三、完成下列句子。

1. 知识产权是企业的_____。
2. 如果仿冒侵权商品充斥市场,对正牌商品销售_____。
3. 各国对知识产权的保护水平,总是与_____。
4. 在知识经济时代,许可贸易已经成为_____。
5. 知识产权保护越来越受到重视,并且_____。

四、想一想,谈一谈。

1. 在知识产权领域,为什么侵权与保护不是单方面的?
2. 为什么知识产权领域侵权与反侵权是不可避免的?

3. 为什么知识产权保护领域不只需要多边国际公约,还需要国家间的双边协议?

4. 中国在保护知识产权方面做了哪些工作? 对此你怎么看?

五、阅读下面的短文,然后回答问题。

谁 不 会 做

　　哥伦布发现新大陆后,回到西班牙,受到了热烈欢迎,可也有人不以为然,一天,他们在小酒馆里见到哥伦布,就对哥伦布说:"你有什么了不起,不就是驾着船沿着海岸走吗? 谁不会做?"哥伦布没有反驳,只是拿过一个鸡蛋对大家说:"谁能把这个鸡蛋立在桌子上?"那些看不起哥伦布的人,传了一圈,也没有人能把鸡蛋立在桌子上。哥伦布拿过鸡蛋,在桌子上轻轻一磕,就把鸡蛋稳稳地立在桌子上了。"啊? 就这么简单!""是啊,我做给你们看了,你们就觉得简单了。"

　　无独有偶。20 世纪初,美国福特公司的一台电机出了故障,可怎么也找不到毛病出在哪里,公司只好请著名物理学家斯坦门茨帮忙。斯坦门茨检查后,用粉笔在电机外壳上画了一条线,说:"打开电机,在画线处把里面的线圈减少 16 圈。"工程人员照办后,故障果然排除了。经理问:"多少酬金?"斯坦门茨说:"一万美元。画一条线 1 美元,知道在哪儿画线 9999 美元。"福特公司二话没说,立即开出一张一万美元的支票,并许以重金聘请斯坦门茨。有人在一边议论起来:"画一条线就值一万美元?""这太容易了,谁不会?"

1. 为什么"画一条线"只值"1 美元","知道在哪儿画线"值"9999 美元"? 价值差别为什么这么大?

2. 有的人为什么说哥伦布和斯坦门茨能做的事,谁都会做? 他们的错误在哪里?

3. 你读了这个故事后有什么感想?

35 倾销与反倾销

Dumping and Antidumping

一、规范不正当贸易

爱德华：史先生，非常感谢你邀请我参加这次商事法律研讨会。

史开来：不必客气！通过讨论，可以消除分歧，增加彼此的理解嘛。

亨　特：倾销与反倾销，确实是一个非常复杂的法律问题，可又是一个不能回避的问题。

史开来：无庸讳言，这里有许多人为因素。

爱德华：那当然，事儿都是人做的嘛！

史开来：我不是这个意思。比如补贴和倾销，是两种扭曲竞争条件的不公平贸易行为，国际贸易中的反补贴与反倾销法，就是为了规范这两种行为的。

爱德华：这个宗旨是不容置疑的。

史开来：但事实上，滥用反倾销法的就大有人在。

亨　特：这就是你说的人为因素了。

史开来：是的。你们二位知道，国际贸易中的倾销行为，是指一国（地区）的生产商或出口商以低于其国内市场的价格或低于成本的价格，挤进另一国（地区）市场的行为。

爱德华：这种低价倾销，给进口国相关产业造成了重大损害。

史开来：而且是实质性损害。

爱德华：是的。或是构成了重大损害威胁，或是对这种产业的建立构成了严重障碍。

史开来：还必须证明，倾销行为与这种实质性损害存在直接的因果关系。

爱德华：是的，必须有这几种条件，才能被视为倾销。

史开来：倾销的完整过程是，降价出口——挤占市场——挤垮对方产业——垄断市场——获取垄断利润。

亨　特：因此，倾销违背了公平竞争和公平贸易的原则，严重扰乱正常的贸易秩序，理所当然要受到进口国的抵制。

史开来：但抵制倾销必须是合理的，如果超过了合理范围和合理程度，反倾销也就会成为一种贸易歧视和新的保护主义。

爱德华：史先生认为，什么是合理范围和合理程度呢？

史开来：例如把本不存在倾销的商品武断地定为倾销商品，或任意夸大倾销幅度，从而无理地实施反倾销措施，或不适当地提高反倾销税率，这就超过了合理范围和合理程度。

亨　特：哈，这恐怕就难免"公说公有理，婆说婆有理"了。

史开来：但是事实终究是事实。

爱德华：好在现在有了反倾销法，可以依法办事，弄清事实真相。

亨　特：受损害企业可以提出反倾销申诉，政府当局可以据此立案调查，并作出裁决。

史开来：是的，根据反倾销法，被指控方也有应诉和辩护的机会。但是，这仍然不能排除许多人为的因素。

爱德华：史先生，我注意到，你对你所说的"人为因素"十分在意，能说说这是为什么吗？

史开来：噢，现在休息，我们是不是去喝点儿什么？

爱德华：这是个好主意！

二、正常价值与"替代国"

史开来：二位先生可能知道，不合理反倾销，已经对我国的出口商品构成严重威胁，我们不得不给予极大关注。

爱德华：我们美国的某些商品也曾被列入反倾销调查对象。

亨　特：贵国的第一起反倾销案，就是对来自美国、加拿大、韩国的新闻纸反倾销案嘛。

史开来：没错儿。但是截至目前为止，在世贸组织成员国之间发生的数千起反倾销案，绝大多数是西方发达国家发起的，其中相当一些案件，存在着价格歧视。

亨　特：确定倾销成立的基础是出口商品的正常价值和出口价格，如果出口价格低于该产品的正常价值时，就应当视为倾销。

爱德华：这可以用出口国正常贸易中旨在用于消费的相同产品的可比价格来衡量，也可以通过生产成本加上合理数额的管理、销售和一般费用以及利润来计算。

亨　特：实在找不到正常价值，还可以用替代国相同产品来计算。

史开来：问题恰恰就出在这里。

爱德华：问题出在这里？

史开来：就以我们国家一些出口商品遭"反倾销"为例。一些国家非要人为地用替代国的相同产品价格，来衡量中国产品是否构成倾销，计算倾销幅度，从而征收高额倾销税。

爱德华：这是世贸组织反倾销法认可的。

史开来：但是，他们选择"替代国"，就像手中拿着一把有弹性的尺子，可以随心所欲地伸缩。

爱德华：我不明白你的意思。

史开来：各国国情不同，许多"替代"是极不合理的。比如曾有一件反倾销案，为我们定的替代国是日本和瑞士，岂不荒谬！

亨　特：这或许是一个很特殊的案例。

史开来：不，还有更荒唐的事儿。同一个"反倾销"案，竟以马来西亚的劳动力、印度的煤、恒河的运费来计算中国产品的正常价值。

爱德华：各国的资源不同，劳动力成本不同，有时确实很难比较。

史开来：一些人就是不肯承认这样一个事实，低廉的劳动力和原材料，使中国产品具有无可比拟的比较成本优势。

亨　特：寻找"替代国"时，不能不考虑这个重要因素。

史开来：更重要的是，一些国家根本无视我国经济改革对市场政策和价格体制的影响。

亨　　特：中国过去实行计划经济,现在确实在努力建设市场经济新体制。

史开来：但是,一些国家不愿正视这个事实。他们不肯承认,我国的商品价格就是市场价格,反映了商品的正常价值。从所谓"替代国"寻找"公平价格",或完全脱离中国实际情况推算出所谓"公平价格",都是不可取的。

亨　　特：现在的情况有了变化。许多国家已经注意到中国经济体制发生的巨大变革。有的国家已经承认中国为转型经济国家,欧盟等也已把中国从非市场经济国家的名单中划掉。

爱德华：关贸总协定乌拉圭回合谈判后,各国进口关税不断下调,非关税壁垒措施逐步减少,反倾销、反补贴已经成为世贸组织多数成员国对外贸易政策与法律的重要组成部分。

史开来：我们赞成按照国际贸易规范促进出口,反对以倾销方式扩大出口;但同时也反对以反倾销为借口,推行新的贸易保护主义。

爱德华：我很欣赏你们的立场。

 生　词

1.	倾销	qīngxiāo	dumping
2.	回避	huíbì	evade, avoid
3.	无庸讳言	wúyōng huìyán	no need for reticence
4.	人为	rénwéi	artificial, man-made
5.	补贴	bǔtiē	subsidy
6.	扭曲	niǔqū	twist, distort
7.	不容置疑	bù róng zhìyí	allow of no doubt; be beyond doubt
8.	大有人在	dà yǒu rén zài	such people are by no means rare
9.	相关	xiāngguān	be interrelated
10.	障碍	zhàng'ài	obstacle, barrier
11.	因果	yīnguǒ	cause and effect

12. 完整	wánzhěng	complete
13. 垮	kuǎ	break down
14. 理所当然	lǐ suǒ dāng rán	as a matter of course
15. 抵制	dǐzhì	resist, boycott
16. 歧视	qíshì	discrimination
17. 武断	wǔduàn	arbitrary; subjective assertion
18. 任意	rènyì	willful
19. 夸大	kuādà	exaggerate
20. 从而	cóngér	thus, thereby
21. 公说公有理， 婆说婆有理	gōng shuō gōng yǒulǐ pó shuō pó yǒulǐ	both parties claim to be in the right
22. 终究	zhōngjiū	eventually; after all
23. 真相	zhēnxiàng	the real situation, truth
24. 申诉	shēnsù	appeal
25. 立案	lì'àn	place a case on file for investigation and prosecution
26. 指控	zhǐkòng	accuse, charge
27. 应诉	yìngsù	respond to the lawsuit
28. 辩护	biànhù	defense
29. 排除	páichú	remove, eliminate
30. 在意	zàiyì	take notice of, take to heart
31. 截至	jiézhì	up to
32. 发起	fāqǐ	initiate, sponsor
33. 确定	quèdìng	determine, define
34. 衡量	héngliáng	weigh, measure
35. 恰恰	qiàqià	exactly, precisely
36. 遭	zāo	meet with
37. 弹性	tánxìng	elasticity
38. 随心所欲	suí xīn suǒ yù	follow one's inclinations, do as one pleases
39. 伸缩	shēnsuō	expand and contract, lengthen and shorten
40. 荒谬	huāngmiù	absurd
41. 荒唐	huāngtáng	ridiculous, preposterous

42. 无视	wúshì	ignore, defy
43. 体制	tǐzhì	system
44. 正视	zhèngshì	face squarely
45. 脱离	tuōlí	break away from
46. 推算	tuīsuàn	calculate, reckon
47. 变革	biàngé	transform, change
48. 转型	zhuǎnxíng	transform
49. 划掉	huàdiào	delete, remove

专 名 Proper Nouns

1. 马来西亚	Mǎláixīyà	Malaysia
2. 恒河	Héng Hé	the Ganges
3. 乌拉圭回合	Wūlāguī Huíhé	the Uruguay Round

A

无庸讳言

"无庸",文言副词,相当于现代汉语口语里的"用不着、没有必要"。"无庸讳言"意思是"用不着忌讳说出"。此外还常用"无庸置疑",意思是"不必怀疑";"无庸赘(zhuì 多余地)述",意思是"用不着多说"等。

No need for reticence. 无庸 is an adverb in classical Chinese, equivalent to 用不着(no need) or 没有必要(not necessary) in modern Chinese. 无庸讳言 means "there is no need to avoid saying it". Other often used phrases include 无庸置疑(no need for doubt), 无庸赘述(no need to go into details), etc.

一、熟读下列各句,体会并说明句中"无庸……"的意义和用法。

1. 无庸讳言,我们双方在一些问题上还存在着分歧。

2. 合同已经写清楚了,我就无庸赘述了。

3. 我们今年的经营业绩是无庸置疑的。

4. 我无庸说出他的尊姓大名,也不想对他加以评论,我只是想告诉大家,他做的这件事,对我们造成了很大伤害。

二、用"无庸讳言"、"无庸置疑"或"无庸……"和下列短语造句。
1. 股市风险大
2. 保护消费者合法权益
3. 环境污染对国民经济发展
4. 在技术贸易谈判中,合同价格
5. 工程承包中,承包人的不正当行为

从而

连词,表示结果或进一步行动。用"从而"引出这种结果或进一步行动,表示这是在前面已经提到的基础上产生的,所以"从而"置于后一小句的开头。

Thus；thereby. It is a conjunction，indicating a result or further action. The result or further action introduced by 从而 is produced on the above-mentioned basis. Therefore、从而 is placed at the beginning of the second clause.

一、熟读下列各句,体会"从而"的意义和用法。
1. 公司的经营理念变成了每一个职员的思想,从而大大提高了公司的经营效益。
2. 我们要善于通过调查研究发现问题,从而找到解决问题的方法。
3. 由于我们建立了预警机制,并聘请了高水平律师,从而在反倾销案中争取到了主动。
4. 中国经济体制的深刻变革,极大地解放了生产力,从而加速了中国经济的现代化进程。

二、请用"从而"完成下列句子。
1. 世界上许多大型企业,都在境外建立加工基地,＿＿＿＿＿＿＿＿＿＿＿＿。
2. 世界超大型跨国连锁公司以雄厚的资金做后盾,以低价位的进入策略挤占中国零售市场,＿＿＿＿＿＿＿＿＿＿＿＿。
3. 中国正在彻底改革过去的福利制度,建立起真正的社会保障体系,
＿＿＿＿＿＿＿＿＿＿＿＿。
4. 全世界进入工业化时代以后,对环境的污染和破坏日甚一日,＿＿＿＿＿＿＿
＿＿＿＿＿＿＿＿。

5.国情不同,知识产权保护的立场也就不同,＿＿＿＿＿＿＿＿＿＿＿＿＿。

终究

副词,强调事物的性质、状况,不因出现某种新情况而改变,不管怎样都是如此,或基本事实不可否认。

Eventually; after all. It is an adverb, emphasizing that the nature or state of affairs of a certain thing will not change as a result of some new circumstance, that it will remain the same no matter what, or that the basic fact cannot be denied.

一、熟读下列各句,体会"终究"的意义和用法。
1.孩子终究是自己的,再不好,也得爱他、疼他。
2.技术落后的产品终究是要被淘汰的。
3.一切荒谬的言论,终究是站不住脚的。
4.《反倾销法》虽然被一些人滥用,但终究是一部不可随意歪曲的国际贸易法。

二、请用"终究"完成下列句子。
1.人类肆意破坏生态环境＿＿＿＿＿＿＿＿＿＿＿＿＿＿＿＿＿＿。
2.陈旧落后的观念＿＿＿＿＿＿＿＿＿＿＿＿＿＿＿＿＿＿＿。
3.假冒伪劣产品＿＿＿＿＿＿＿＿＿＿＿＿＿＿＿＿＿＿＿＿。
4.全球一体化是时代潮流,关税壁垒＿＿＿＿＿＿＿＿＿＿＿＿。
5.随着科学进步,癌症、艾滋病＿＿＿＿＿＿＿＿＿＿＿＿＿＿。

恰恰

副词,表示事件、情况发生的巧合,有"正好"、"合适"的意思。

Just; exactly. It is an adverb, indicating the coincidence of events or situations, with the meaning of 正好(just right; happen to) or 合适(right; appropriate).

一、熟读下列各句,体会"恰恰"的意义和用法。
1.现在同我们竞争的对手,恰恰是我们过去的合伙人。
2.他们的反倾销公告,恰恰说明我们的商品不存在倾销。
3.不是我们没有诚意,恰恰相反,正是我们的诚意才促成了这次合作。
4.市场占有率雄辩地证明,在科技含量方面最具有优势的恰恰是我们,而不是别的什么人。

二、请用"恰恰"完成下列句子。

1. 老父亲怎么也没想到,女儿的男朋友_____。

2. 人们有没有想到,保护地球、保护环境、保护野生动物_____。

3. 大自然带给人类的灾难,如洪水、酸雨等,_____。

4. 你别小看,就是这些普普通通的超市,它的服务对象是普普通通的群众,_____。

5. 这些衣着朴素、态度谦虚的人,_____。

B

一、请用下列词语组成短语。

抵制　倾销　歧视　排除　价格
回避　指控　荒唐　障碍　补贴
衡量　变革　体制　确定　转型

二、熟读下列词语,并选择适当的词语完成下列句子。

不可取　　不容置疑　　弄清(事实)真相
随心所欲　理所当然　　截至目前为止
人为因素　岂不荒谬　　给予极大的关注
大有人在　弹性的尺子　公说公有理,婆说婆有理

1. 在激烈的市场竞争中,保险公司鼓励业务员八仙过海,各显其能。但业务员为了拉到客户,竟然不择手段,这就是_____的了。

2. 我们每个人对环境保护应该也必须_____。

3. 有些人打着反倾销的旗帜,却把本不存在的倾销商品武断地定为倾销产品,又任意夸大倾销税率,从而无理地实施反倾销措施,_____。

4. 中国在努力保护知识产权,并取得了很大成绩,这是_____的事实。

5. 既然制定了环境保护法,_____,要对一切违法行为进行严肃处理。

6. 供货商与推销商发生争执时,常常_____,最后只能提交仲裁委员会依据法律仲裁。

7. _____,是作出一切决定的前提。

8. 我们主张公平竞争和公平贸易的原则,滥用反倾销法,并把它变成一把
_____,是对出口国的价格歧视。

9. 制定和执行法律,是为了保护绝大多数人的利益,绝不能_____
_____。

10. 尽管我们已经接受了服务贸易这个崭新的概念,但不重视商业服务还
是_____。

11. 不履行合同,_____应该赔偿损失。

12. 国际资本市场发生剧烈震荡,不能排除_____。

三、完成下列句子。

1. 倾销和反倾销,确实是一个非常复杂的法律问题,可又是_____。

2. 倾销,理所当然要受到进口国的抵制,因为它违背了_____。

3. 确定倾销成立的基础是_____。

4. 低价倾销对进口国_____但抵制倾销必须是合理的,如果超过了
_____。

四、想一想,谈一谈。

1. 具备哪些条件才能被视为倾销?

2. 抵制倾销的合理范围和合理程度是什么?

3. 倾销与反倾销不仅是一个非常复杂的法律问题,而且不能排除人为因
素,为什么?

4. 中国在倾销与反倾销中持什么立场?

5. 有些国家立案调查中国商品有倾销行为,我们认为是不合理的,为什
么? 对此你怎么看?

五、阅读下面的短文,然后回答问题。

正理与歪理

"公说公有理,婆说婆有理",有时可能都说得有道理,有时则有人讲的是
正理、真理,有人讲的是歪理、谬论。

一个教师有两个学生。他特别喜欢其中一个学生,而特别讨厌另一个。
一天,在上课的时候,两个学生都手拿着书睡着了。教师走到他讨厌的学生跟
前,啪地就是一巴掌,把学生打醒,教训说:"看看你,一拿起书本就睡着;你看
看人家,睡着了还拿着书!"

中国古时候有一个两小儿辩日的故事。一个孩子说:"太阳刚出来时离

人近,到中午时离人远。"另一个孩子说:"不对,太阳刚出来时离人远,到中午离人近。""太阳刚出来时大,中午小,难道不是近的大远的小吗?""不对。太阳刚出来时冷飕飕的,到中午就热得烤人,难道不是近的感觉热远的感觉凉吗?"最近,又听说一个类似两小儿辩日的故事。一个孩子问:"你说美国远还是山东远?"一个孩子理直气壮地说:"当然是美国远山东近。""不对,是美国近山东远。""你瞎说。""我问你,你在北京能买到山东煎饼和高粱饴糖吗?可你在北京能买到美国的爆米花儿和杏仁儿糖,你说山东远还是美国远?"

在一家旅馆,客人与经理在结账的时候发生了纠纷。客人问:"我们一点儿水果都没吃,账单上的水果费是怎么回事儿?"经理说:"先生,我们每天都送水果到你们房间去了,吃没吃是你们的事儿,但水果钱不能不付。"客人立即说:"噢,是这样!"他拿过账单,划去 150 美元,说:"你吻我的妻子,每天收费 50 美元,我们在贵店住了三天,一共是 150 美元。"经理连忙辩解说:"我没有吻你的妻子。我是有良好教养的人,怎么可能做那种事儿?"客人说:"你每天都进我们的房间,至于吻没吻我的妻子,那是你的事儿。"

1. 第二个故事里,两个人讲的都是什么理?
2. 第三个故事里,两个人讲的都是什么理?
3. 第四个故事里,两个人讲的都是什么理?
4. 你遇到过"公说公有理,婆说婆有理"的事儿吗?请说说。

第三十六课

农业产业化与贸易机会 36

Industrialization of Agriculture and Trade Opportunities

一、中国农业的历史与现状

肖玉兰：爱德华先生，我们一边参观一边谈吧！

爱德华：谢谢肖女士今天陪同我们来参观。

肖玉兰：我们农业部的人工作对象在农村，同外国朋友下乡，一来可以了解下边的情况，二来可以听听你们的建议，这是一举两得的事儿。

亨　特：中国是一个农业大国，有7.4亿人，也就是大约57%的人口在农村，农村经济的好坏，对整个国民经济有举足轻重的影响。

肖玉兰：是的。我们一直把农业当做国民经济的基础，优先考虑，优先发展。

爱德华：看得出来。我们眼前这一望无际的农田，显然实现了高度机械化作业。你们已经有很先进的农业经济。

肖玉兰：不，我国绝大多数地方，还基本上是传统农业经济。一家一户，一把锄头一张犁，用简单原始劳动从事动植物生产，经营目的也还没有彻底摆脱自给自足的局限。

爱德华：这不奇怪，即使是农业产业化程度最高的国家，也走过这条道路。

亨　特：这是老祖宗留下来的嘛！

肖玉兰：但是，这种传统的粗放型经营，早就该进历史博物馆了！

亨　特：迟早是要送进博物馆的，只是有的地方早一点儿，有的地方晚一点儿罢了。

爱德华：20 世纪 90 年代后,高科技潮流不仅促使全球工业经济向知识经济转变,而且有力地推动传统农业进入产业化时代。

亨　特：全球性创汇农业迅速崛起,传统农业生产正在走向工厂化、产业化。

肖玉兰：我国的农业经济必须顺应这个历史趋势。

亨　特：我想,你们已经和正在这样做。

肖玉兰：是的,近些年,我国农业已经发生了根本性变化。过去,农业经营,产前、产中、产后,生产、加工、销售,完全是分割的,农民收入只是原料生产和初级产品创造的价值。

亨　特：而加工、运输、销售的利润,可能是农民所得的几倍、几十倍。

爱德华：你知道我们的杏仁儿吗?

肖玉兰：知道,美国杏仁儿在中国市场很贵、很畅销。

爱德华：我们的杏仁儿从种植、收获、工厂加工到销售,完全实现了一条龙,出口到九十多个国家和地区,全球 80% 的杏仁儿供应量来自加州,每年出口创汇占美国农产品出口总额六百多亿美元的 1% ~ 1.5%。

亨　特：种植商从销售中也能分享可观的利润。

肖玉兰：这就是农业产业化效益! 我国经济较发达的地区,现在也正在走农、工、贸相结合的道路,并且已经涌现出一大批农工贸一体化企业。

爱德华：看来,中国传统农业正在走向产业化。你能带我们去看看这样的企业吗?

肖玉兰：当然可以。不过,我们还是先去访问一个种田能手吧!

二、产业化拉动巨大的潜在市场

方兴农：啊,肖主任来啦!

肖玉兰：我来介绍一下,这是爱德华先生,这是亨特先生,这是方兴农先生!

方兴农：欢迎，欢迎，快请进！

爱德华：谢谢！这是你的家？

方兴农：是，请不要客气！

爱德华：嗬，这么大一栋楼！这么大一座花园儿！比我们美国那些种植业主的还气派嘛！

方兴农：这不是托改革开放的福嘛！

亨　特：你是怎么致富的呢？

方兴农：农村开始实行家庭承包责任制，我承包了五十亩农田，一百余亩荒山，又种农作物，又种果树。几年下来，就从温饱走上了小康。

肖玉兰：他是我们国家最早觉悟的新一代农民。

方兴农：过去我们只知道精耕细作，多打粮食夺高产。

肖玉兰：为了追求农产品产量最大化，不惜围湖造田、毁林开荒、过度放牧，造成水土严重流失，自然灾害频繁。

方兴农：一味追求产量最大化，破坏了生态环境，能不受老天惩罚吗？

肖玉兰：他有文化，信息灵，懂科学技术，没有再走我国农民走了几千年的老路。

爱德华：哦？真了不起！

方兴农：我只是以市场为导向，把生产计划和实施建立在市场需求的基础上，注重农副产品的深加工，产品流通尽力突破地区界限，从一镇、一乡，走向全国，走向世界。

肖玉兰：他生产的绿色食品和水果，已经远销欧美。

爱德华：你不是一个普普通通的农民，你是一个聪明的企业家！

亨　特：你已经从个体的、庄园式经营走向了工厂化、企业化。

方兴农：不，还有很大距离。我还没有实现经营规模化、集约化，机械化程度和科技含量都还不高。

爱德华：你要进一步解决农业产业链条的完善与延长问题？

方兴农：正是。

肖玉兰：爱德华先生，他为你提供了一条十分重要的信息。

爱德华：你是说，他告诉我，中国农业在实现产业化的进程中，存在着巨大的商机？

肖玉兰：难道不是吗？我国农业，从种植、收获、干燥、储藏、保鲜、分级，到加工、包装、运输、销售，所有这些环节，都十分薄弱。要实现高度产业化，资金、设备、科技，需要多少投入啊！

方兴农：我们需要各种各样的农业生产和加工机械，需要动植物遗传基因工程技术，需要现代信息技术，通过信息高速公路建立从生产、经营到用户之间的崭新的流通渠道。

肖玉兰：我国幅员辽阔，经济发展极不平衡，我们还要下大力气加强农业基础设施和社会化服务体系建设，加快开发经济相对落后的中西部地区。

爱德华：是啊，中国农业产业化进程，确实存在巨大的潜在市场！

亨　特：好像外国企业家们在这方面还缺少敏锐的眼光和足够的兴趣。

方兴农：我们前进的步伐可不等后来者哟！

生　词

1. 一举两得	yì jǔ liǎng dé	kill two birds with one stone
2. 举足轻重	jǔ zú qīng zhòng	hold the balance, prove decisive
3. 一望无际	yí wàng wú jì	stretch as far as the eye can see
4. 农田	nóngtián	farmland
5. 机械化	jīxièhuà	mechanization
6. 锄头	chútou	hoe
7. 犁	lí	plough
8. 原始	yuánshǐ	primitive
9. 摆脱	bǎituō	shake off, break away from
10. 自给自足	zìjǐ zìzú	self-sufficient
11. 局限	júxiàn	limit, confine
12. 祖宗	zǔzong	ancestor
13. 粗放型	cūfàngxíng	extensive
14. 博物馆	bówùguǎn	museum

15. 罢了	bàle	that's all; nothing else
16. 促使	cùshǐ	urge, spur
17. 创汇	chuànghuì	earn foreign exchange
18. 顺应	shùnyìng	comply with, conform to
19. 分割	fēngē	cut apart, separate
20. 杏仁	xìngrén	almond
21. 种植	zhòngzhí	plant
22. 一条龙	yìtiáolóng	one continuous line, a coordinated process
23. 涌现	yǒngxiàn	emerge in large numbers, spring up
24. 能手	néngshǒu	expert, good hand
25. 托福	tuōfú	thanks to; rely upon
26. 荒山	huāngshān	barren hills
27. 温饱	wēnbǎo	have adequate food and clothing
28. 小康	xiǎokāng	a well-off life
29. 觉悟	juéwù	awakening
30. 精耕细作	jīng gēng xì zuò	intensive and meticulous farming
31. 夺	duó	capture, seize
32. 追求	zhuīqiú	seek, pursue
33. 围湖造田	wéi hú zào tián	reclaim land from a lake
34. 毁	huǐ	destroy, damage
35. 开荒	kāihuāng	open up wasteland
36. 放牧	fàngmù	put out to pasture, graze
37. 频繁	pínfán	frequent
38. 惩罚	chéngfá	punishment
39. 导向	dǎoxiàng	guide
40. 流通	liútōng	circulation
41. 镇	zhèn	town, township
42. 乡	xiāng	village
43. 庄园	zhuāngyuán	manor
44. 距离	jùlí	distance
45. 集约化	jíyuēhuà	intensify
46. 链条	liàntiáo	chain
47. 遗传	yíchuán	heredity, inheritance

48. 基因	jīyīn	gene
49. 高速公路	gāosù gōnglù	highway，expressway
50. 幅员	fúyuán	the area of a country's territory
51. 敏锐	mǐnruì	sharp，acute

专 名 Proper Noun		
加州（加利福 利亚州）	Jiā Zhōu（Jiālìfúlìyà Zhōu）	California

 练 习

A

一来……二来……

连词，连接分句，用来列举原因、目的或条件。"一来……二来……"之后，还可以说"三来……四来……"。书面上常用"一则……二则（再则）……"。

On the one hand...on the other hand. This is a conjunction linking clauses to enumerate reasons，purposes or conditions. After 一来……二来……we can go on to say 三来（thirdly）……四来（fourthly）……. In written Chinese，the form 一则……二则（再则）……is used.

一、熟读下列各句，体会"一来……二来……"的意义和用法。

1. 我一来没资本，二来没那本事去做生意。

2. 我今天来，一来是很久没见面了，想看看你；二来是想向你请教，帮我出出主意。

3. 改变传统的粗放型经营模式，一来可以节省资源，二来可以提高经济效益。

4. 实现农业产业化，一来可以增加大量新的就业机会，二来可以大幅度提高农副产品的附加值，三来可以为人民提供丰富、有营养、卫生的食品。

二、请用"一来……二来……"和下列短语造句。

1. 游览名胜古迹　　农村市场调研
2. 打开商品市场　　获取信息
3. 股市的知识和经验　　良好的心理承受力
4. 锻炼身体　　美化环境
5. 在中国做生意　　同中国人交朋友　　了解中国文化

显然

副词,表示说话人觉得某种情况或道理是很明白或很容易理解的,同时含有强调和加重的语气。"显然"后面如果有停顿,或前面加程度副词"很",这种强调语气更重。

Evidently. It is an adverb, indicating that the speaker thinks that a certain situation or the reason is obvious or easy to understand. It carries with it a tone of emphasis and stress. If 显然 is followed by a pause, or preceded by a degree adverb 很(very), the emphasizing tone is even stronger.

一、熟读下列各句,体会"显然"的意义和用法。

1. 显然,不搞农业产业化,农业发展就没有活力。
2. 我的话他显然一句也没有听进去。
3. 很显然,一个人、一个企业的财力总是有限的,而从股票市场却可以募集来大量资金。
4. 农工贸一体化,生产、加工、销售一条龙,显然,将给农民带来比初级产品价值要高得多的附加值。

二、请用"显然"和括号里的词语完成下列句子。

1. 中国还是一个相对落后的农业国,＿＿＿＿＿＿＿＿＿＿。(农业产业化)
2. 近些年,中国农业已经发生了根本性变化。农业＿＿＿＿＿＿＿＿＿
＿＿＿＿＿＿＿＿＿＿＿＿＿＿＿＿＿＿＿＿。(历史趋势)
3. 中国幅员辽阔,经济发展极不平衡,为了加快中国农业产业化进程,＿＿＿
＿＿＿＿＿＿＿＿＿＿＿＿＿＿＿＿＿。(下大力气)
4. 中国的农业,从种植到收获,从储藏到保鲜,从加工到运输等各个环节,
＿＿＿＿＿＿＿＿＿＿＿＿＿＿＿＿＿＿。(各种各样)
5. 中国的农业在实现产业化的进程中,＿＿＿＿＿＿＿＿＿＿＿＿＿＿＿
＿＿＿＿＿＿＿＿＿＿＿＿＿＿＿＿＿＿。(巨大商机)

罢了

助词,用在陈述句的末尾,有把事情往小里说的意思,对整个句子表示的意思起减轻、冲淡的作用。有时还有轻视甚至鄙视的意味。"罢了"前面常有"不过、只是、无非"等词相呼应。

但注意,"罢了"(bàliǎo)是动词,意思是"作罢、算了"。

It is a particle to be used at the end of a declarative sentence, with a tone of alleviating the thing mentioned, having a function of lightening or weakening the meaning of the whole sentence. Sometimes it carries a sense of belittlement or contempt. 罢了 is often paired with such words as 不过(but),只是(only)or 无非(nothing but)in front. Please note that 罢了(bàliǎo)is also a verb, meaning "give up" or "let it pass".

一、熟读下列句子,体会并说明句中"罢了"的意义和用法。

1. 他不过是说说罢了,你何必当真!

2. 人家是老板,你不服又能怎样,也只好罢了!

3. 她不过跟我一样,也是一个小小的职员罢了,神气什么!

4. 我国农民的生活水平都提高了,我只不过比一些人过得更好一点儿罢了。

5. 我们禁止围湖造田、毁林开荒、过度放牧,无非是要保护好我们赖以生存的环境罢了,决不是要限制农民的生产积极性。

二、请用"罢了"和下列短语造句。

1. 老板说优先考虑聘用技术好的工人

2. 政府要下决心整治城市环境

3. 我只不过是总经理的秘书

4. 他只是觉悟得较早的有文化的新一代农民

5. 无非是坚持锻炼,生活规律

B

一、请用下列词语组成短语。

突破　摆脱　潮流　促使　觉悟
平衡　顺应　局限　崛起　转变
趋势　追求　创汇　频繁　迅速

二、熟读下列词语，并选择适当的词语填空。

> 一举两得　　举足轻重　　顺应历史趋势
> 一望无际　　自给自足　　该进历史博物馆

1. 你这次来中国参加广交会，既推销了贵公司的新产品，又了解了市场信息，真可谓_____。
2. 改革开放结束了中国几千年来_____的小农经济，使广大农村走上了农、工、贸相结合的道路。
3. _____的大沙漠，让你真切地认识到地球正在惩罚人类对它的肆意掠夺。
4. 美国微软公司总裁比尔·盖茨是当今世界计算机领域_____的人物。
5. 一家一户、一把锄头一张犁的农业劳动方式，按说早_____了，可有些地方至今仍然保留着。
6. _____，是一个企业家必须作出的选择。

三、请用括号里的词语完成下列句子。

1. 20世纪90年代后，高科技潮流有力地推动传统农业进入产业化时代，全球创汇农业迅速崛起，_____。（正在走向）
2. 我国农业已经发生了根本性变化。过去，产、供、销完全是分割的，现在正在走农、工、贸相结合的道路，_____。（一条龙）
3. 中国的经济改革首先是从农村开始的，1978年安徽农村开始实行家庭承包责任制，得到了中央的支持。几年下来，_____
_____。（从温饱走上了小康）
4. 计划经济时代_____
_____致使产品大量积压，资金周转困难。（一味追求）
5. 中国农业在实现产业化的过程中，还有很多事情要做，确实存在着巨大商机_____。（敏锐眼光）
6. 中国几千年来是个农业国，大约57%的人口在农村，中国一直把农业
_____。（优先发展）

四、想一想，谈一谈。

1. 你怎么看待中国的农业经济？
2. 改革开放后，尤其是近几年来，中国的农业发生了哪些根本变化？

3. 方兴农是怎么致富的？为什么说他是最早觉悟的新一代农民？

4. 中国农业在实现产业化的进程中，为什么说存在着巨大的商机？对此你怎么看？

五、阅读下面的短文，然后回答问题。

瞄 准 对 象

现在，城市市场似乎日趋饱和，商家们把眼光逐渐转向了广大农村。世人尽知，我国农村市场无比广阔，存在巨大的购买潜力。但是，商家们常常叫苦，说大量商品，如吸尘器呀、消毒柜呀、电烤箱呀等，送下乡后，竟没人问津。最后得出结论说，农民还是没钱，潜在购买力还不能转化成现实购买力。

事情果然是这样的吗？

从前有个读书人进城办事，要买一匹马。来到马市，一个卖主迎上来说："买我的吧，我这是千里马，一口气就能跑一千里！"读书人听了，生气地反问道："你安的是什么心？这儿离城里才几十里，它一口气就要跑一千里，那九百多里，你让我走回来啊？不买，不买！"

有一个足球运动员，球技超人，本是队里的头号射手，但不知为什么，也不知从什么时候起，他射门就没有了准头。一次大赛，他竟三次把球踢进了自家的大门。那天正好是他的生日，他的队友去了礼品商店，根据店主的建议，给他买了一件特殊的生日礼物。他打开一看，竟是一个袖珍指南针！

1. 卖马的主人，为什么没有做成生意？

2. 卖礼品的店主给足球队员们出了个什么主意？

3. 根据上面两个故事的启示，你认为怎样才能打开农村市场？

乡镇企业 37

Village and Township Enterprises

一、异军突起

爱德华：肖女士，我们刚才谈到，中国已经涌现出一大批农工贸一体化企业。

亨　特：中国管这种企业叫乡镇企业。

爱德华：乡镇企业？请问这些企业的特点是什么？

肖玉兰：这个问题，请方先生回答你吧。他现在是全国知名的乡镇企业家。

方兴农：乡镇企业是我国经济改革后出现的新事物，农村实行家庭承包责任制以后，闲散的剩余劳动力要寻找出路，我们这些农民企业家就应运而生了。

肖玉兰：在20世纪80年代，乡镇企业犹如异军突起，经过短短几年，年产值竟高达几千亿元，差不多占国民经济总产值的1/4。

爱德华：噢，这可是一个很大的比例。请问，乡镇企业都经营什么项目呢？

肖玉兰：他们从黄土地上解放出来，就地取材，利用当地的资源和剩余劳动力，办起了各种各样的小工厂。

方兴农：有的从事手工编织，有的从事农副产品加工，有的生产城市大工厂不愿生产的零部件，有的干脆成立包工队进城揽活儿。

肖玉兰：那时是卖方市场，商品严重短缺，市场空白多，市场空间相对大，生产什么都有市场。

亨　特：这是天赐良机，给了乡镇企业的发展机遇，对吧？

方兴农：正是，我们抓住机遇，拾遗补缺，市场需要什么，我们生产什么；市场缺什么，我们卖什么。城里人不愿做的事儿我们都做。

肖玉兰：他们充分发挥了乡镇企业的优势，机动灵活，左右逢源。

方兴农：用我们的话说，这叫船小好掉头。我们的眼睛盯着市场，产品今天适销，我们就生产，明天不对路了，我们就转产，就生产新的适销对路的产品。

爱德华：看来，中国的乡镇企业的确有它独特的经营方式。可是船小也可能经不起大风大浪。

方兴农：爱德华先生说得很对。当市场饱和，空间日趋狭小，出现供求平衡，甚至供大于求的时候，就像风浪骤起，乡镇企业普遍都感到了生存危机。

肖玉兰：这时候，我国乡镇企业经过了几年徘徊、整顿与提高，大批企业关停并转(转产)。

方兴农：但也有不少乡镇企业经受住了大风大浪的考验，彻底抛弃了手工作坊式、家族式的小打小闹，大力引进外资、技术、先进设备和先进管理模式，办起了大规模的现代化企业，走上了外向型经济的道路。

亨　特：中国的科龙、春兰、小天鹅等一批集团，就是乡镇企业。这些集团不仅是中国的大型企业，而且也是世界数一数二的大企业，他们的产品在国际市场上有很强的竞争力。

肖玉兰：20世纪90年代，乡镇企业进入了它的超常发展时期。在1995年，总产值达到了63 500亿，占了全国工业的半壁江山，逼近全社会总产值的1/3。

方兴农：现在，全国性乡镇企业集团数千家，大中型乡镇企业上万家，是国家和地方的利税大户，已经成为农村经济的主体力量和国民经济的重要组成部分。

爱德华：从世界经济发展的历史看，企业曾经何等辉煌，可最终成为昙花一现，这种事例很不少。

亨　特：有统计显示，在日本，企业从创业之初算起，能安安稳稳过

10 年的只有 18.3%，高高兴兴过 20 岁生日的只有 8.5%，风风光光做 30 大寿的则不足 5%。

爱德华：中国的乡镇企业怎样保持自己青春不老呢？

二、乡镇企业发展的新篇章

方兴农：爱德华先生刚才提出的问题，很尖锐，一个企业要保持长盛不衰，确实很难。

肖玉兰：乡镇企业进入超常发展期后，我国市场发生了重大变化，卖方市场变成了买方市场。

爱德华：这个变化，意味着曾经可以任意主宰市场的商家、企业，以后将不得不听从市场规律的无情摆布。

方兴农：是的。一时间，国有企业、乡镇企业以及其他一切企业，都面临着严峻挑战。

亨　特：从市场状况看，首先是内需不旺，消费乏力，产品积压，库存增加。外资企业都受到不同程度的影响，乡镇企业恐怕就更觉艰难了。

方兴农：相当一些企业，效益滑坡，亏损增大，或勉强维持生产，或处于停产、半停产状态；那些效益较好的企业，也是发展速度日趋缓慢，后劲不足。

肖玉兰：这个时候，实现产业结构优化和升级，适应变化了的市场环境，就成为关系到乡镇企业兴衰存亡的关键所在了。

爱德华：那么，你们是怎样做的呢？

肖玉兰：在改善经营的同时，下大力气调整产业结构。

方兴农：产业结构趋同化，是乡镇企业发展的最大障碍。绝大多数乡镇企业都是以第二产业为主，即以机械、纺织、化工、食品等加工工业为主要产业。

亨　特：这么说，乡镇企业不就是乡镇工业的同义语嘛！

爱德华：低水平的重复建设，必然导致产品市场的饱和；产业结构

雷同,又必然引发抢原料、拼价格、争市场,最终造成一荣
俱荣、一损俱损的局面。

肖玉兰:是这样。所以,我们要加大结构调整的力度,发挥各地的
资源优势,大力发展农副产品加工业、农工贸一体化企业,
把发展乡镇企业和推进农业产业化经营结合起来。

方兴农:我们要特别加大投入,发展农业高新技术,比如重要农作
物功能基因组学、抗病虫害、重大生物资源开发利用等等。

肖玉兰:总之,以乡镇企业为龙头,推进整个农业向集约化、规模
化、市场化转变,最终实现农业的高度产业化和现代化。

爱德华:噢,这可是一条崭新的发展道路!

肖玉兰:乡镇企业与农业有割不断的血缘关系,乡镇企业以实现农业
产业化为立足点,有得天独厚的优势。我们坚定不移地沿着
这条道路走下去,必定能开创乡镇企业发展的新局面。

方兴农:谱写出更加辉煌灿烂的新篇章!

爱德华:好啊,我衷心地祝贺你们成功!

 生 词

1. 异军突起	yì jūn tū qǐ	a new force suddenly coming to the fore
2. 事物	shìwù	thing, object
3. 闲散	xiánsǎn	unused, idle
4. 剩余	shèngyú	surplus
5. 应运而生	yìng yùn ér shēng	emerge as the times demand
6. 解放	jiěfàng	liberate
7. 就地取材	jiùdì qǔcái	draw on local resources
8. 编织	biānzhī	weave, knit, plait, braid
9. 包工队	bāogōng duì	contracting team
10. 空间	kōngjiān	space
11. 天赐良机	tiān cì liángjī	heaven-bestowed opportunity

12. 拾遗补缺	shí yí bǔ quē	make good omissions and deficiencies
13. 左右逢源	zuǒ yòu féng yuán	gain advantage from both sides
14. 盯	dīng	fix one's eyes on
15. 狭小	xiáxiǎo	narrow and small
16. 骤	zhòu	suddenly, abruptly
17. 徘徊	páihuái	pace up and down, hesitate
18. 并	bìng	merge
19. 转产	zhuǎnchǎn	change the line of production
20. 经受	jīngshòu	undergo, experience
21. 考验	kǎoyàn	test, trial
22. 作坊	zuōfang	workshop
23. 家族	jiāzú	clan, family
24. 小打小闹	xiǎo dǎ xiǎo nào	small-scale operation
25. 外向型	wàixiàngxíng	export-oriented
26. 超常	chāocháng	extraordinary
27. 逼近	bījìn	approach, draw near
28. 昙花一现	tánhuā yí xiàn	last as briefly as the broad-leaved epiphyllum
29. 安稳	ānwěn	smooth and steady
30. 风光	fēngguāng	grand; scene
31. 青春	qīngchūn	youth
32. 篇章	piānzhāng	chapter
33. 尖锐	jiānruì	sharp, keen
34. 主宰	zhǔzǎi	dominate, decide
35. 无情	wúqíng	merciless
36. 摆布	bǎibù	order about, manipulate
37. 积压	jīyā	overstock
38. 滑坡	huápō	landslide; decline
39. 亏损	kuīsǔn	loss; deficit
40. 勉强	miǎnqiǎng	manage with an effort; reluctant
41. 缓慢	huǎnmàn	slow
42. 后劲	hòujìn	stamina; aftereffect
43. 兴衰	xīngshuāi	flourish and decline

44. 存亡	cúnwáng	live or die, survive or perish
45. 趋同	qūtóng	tend to be the same
46. 同义语	tóngyìyǔ	synonym
47. 重复	chóngfù	repeat
48. 雷同	léitóng	duplicate; identical
49. 一荣俱荣， 一损俱损	yì róng jù róng, yì sǔn jù sǔn	simultaneous prosperity and decline
50. 农作物	nóngzuòwù	crops
51. 抗	kàng	resist, combat
52. 生物	shēngwù	living organism
53. 割	gē	cut
54. 血缘	xuèyuán	ties of blood
55. 立足点	lìzúdiǎn	foothold
56. 坚定不移	jiāndìng bù yí	firm and unshakable
57. 开创	kāichuàng	start, initiate

专 名 Proper Noun

| 科龙 | Kēlóng | Kelong |

A

犹如

介词，跟"好像、就像"意思差不多，用"犹如"组成的介词词组引出比喻，后面还常常用"一样"相配搭。但"犹如"只用于比拟，不表示不确定的感觉或判断，也不与"似的"配搭使用，而"好像"则可以。

Just as; like; as if. It is a preposition with a meaning similar to that of 好像(like) or 就像(just as). The prepositional phrase introduced by 犹如 leads to a simile, and is often paired with 一样(same) coming after. However, 犹如 is only used for analogy, and doesn't express any indefinite feeling or judgment, and is not paired with 似的, while 好像 can be used this way.

一、熟读下列各句,体会"犹如"、"好像"的意义和用法。

   1. 希望犹如肥皂泡破灭了。

   2. 乡镇企业犹如一道亮丽的风景线,举世瞩目。

   3. 在风浪骤起时,他们好像感到了生存危机似的,立即紧张起来。

   4. 企业犹如家庭一样,也需要友情、亲情。

   5. 商场犹如战场,充满了矛盾、对立、争斗、你死我活的拼杀。

二、请用"犹如"和下列短语造句。

   1. 在中国,每年的高考   千军万马挤独木桥

   2. 改革开放后的中国   一头睡狮醒了

   3. 一个个汉字对于欧美学生

   4. 走进交易所

   5. 在严重污染的环境中生活

数一数二

   "数",动词,查点数目或顺序。在"数一数二"这个格式里,"数"是指出名次最前的或程度最大的,意思是不是第一名,也是第二名,虽然不是一个肯定的确数,但名次在最前边。

   Count as one of the very best. 数 is a verb meaning counting or enumerating. In the set phrase 数一数二, 数 is to list the highest in rank or the largest in extent, meaning if it is not the first, then it is the second. Though it is not an exact figure, it is on top of the list.

一、熟读下列各句,体会"数"的意义和用法。

   1. 安娜的学习成绩,在我们班是数一数二的。

   2. 在同类产品中,数他们的质量最好。

   3. 这些年,在众多的乡镇企业中,要数科龙集团最风光。

   4. 他的社交能力,在我们公司不数第一,也要数第二。

二、请用"数一数二"或"数"和下列短语造句。

   1. 在20世纪最后一次全球金融危机中

   2. 像老板这样的中国通

   3. 她左右逢源的能力

   4. 论投资环境和市场潜力

   5. 世界上善于做买卖的

何等

①什么样的。②意思跟"多么"差不多,强调并赞叹程度深。它一般只修饰形容词成分或表心理活动的动词。有时,表面上是赞叹,实际含有讽刺意味。

What kind; how. 1) It means "what kind". 2) The meaning is similar to 多么 (to what an extent), emphasizing and acclaiming the degree. Normally it only modifies an adjectival element or a verb denoting a psychological activity. Sometimes, it expresses admiration on the surface, but carries a sense of satire.

一、熟读下列各句,体会并分别说明"何等"的意义和用法。
   1. 你有这样一个家庭,是何等幸福啊!
   2. 几年前,这家公司是何等风光,现在怎么就破产了呢?
   3. 她是何等人物,我敢同她较量?
   4. 实现乡镇企业与农业产业化相结合,具有何等重要的意义,是显而易见的。

二、请用"何等"和下列短语造句。
   1. 治理环境污染
   2. 提高企业职工素质
   3. 加大结构调整力度
   4. 不作市场调研,盲目投资
   5. 实现农业的高度产业化和现代化

勉强

①动词,使人做不愿意做的事,可带"过",多用于否定句。②形容词,不情愿或能力不够还努力去做,可重叠;凑合,将就达到某种标准。

Manage with an effort; force; inadequate. 1) It can be used as a verb meaning forcing someone to do something he is unwilling to do. It can be paired with 过, and is used more often in a negative sentence. 2) It can be used as an adjective, meaning trying hard to do something one is unwilling or unable to do. It can be reduplicated. It can also mean "passable but inadequate" or "make do with something".

一、熟读下列各句,体会并分别说明"勉强"的意义和用法。

1. 我没有勉强过你,你这样决定,完全是你自愿的。

2. 这个季度,我们勉强完成了生产任务。

3. 他很尊重我,从来不勉强我去做我不愿做的事儿。

4. 企业虽然遇到了一些困难,还是勉强坚持下来了。

二、请用"勉强"和下列短语造句。

1. 这次汉语水平测试

2. 我家人口多,我爸妈工资低

3. 他的汉语听、说能力还不够好

4. 在激烈的市场竞争中

5. 男士皮鞋款式陈旧、品种少

B

一、请用下列词语组成短语。

缓慢	亏损	剩余	主宰	市场	开创
衰落	资金	闲散	兴盛	摆布	局面
无情	滑坡	关键	存亡	效益	积压

二、熟读下列词语,并选择适当的词语填空。

异军突起	就地取材	长盛不衰
应运而生	左右逢源	昙花一现
拾遗补缺	天赐良机	适销对路
半壁江山	小打小闹	一荣俱荣,一损俱损

1. 我刚进股市,没有炒股的知识和经验,也没有足够的经济实力和心理承受力,所以只能_____。

2. 改革开放后,经济高速发展,市场繁荣,充满活力,各行各业的能人_____。

3. 乡镇企业是我国经济改革后出现的新事物,他们_____办起了各种各样的小工厂。

4. 改革开放后,头脑灵活的人,顺应时代潮流,抓住了_____,不仅个人致富了,还带动了本地区经济发展。

5. 不少乡镇企业,经过了徘徊、整顿与提高,办得越来越有生气,不断开发出＿＿＿＿＿＿＿＿＿的新产品。

6. 在激烈的市场竞争中,企业在发展中要想＿＿＿＿＿＿＿＿＿就必须眼睛盯着市场,不断创新。

7. 乡镇企业以它独特的经营方式,充分发挥船小好掉头的优势,市场需要什么就生产什么,在商品市场中起到了＿＿＿＿＿＿＿的作用。

8. 有些乡镇企业家成功后不思进取,最终成为＿＿＿＿＿＿＿＿＿的人物,令人叹息,深思。

9. 企业家要眼光远大,头脑灵活,善于抓住机遇,这样才能保持青春不老,＿＿＿＿＿＿＿＿＿。

10. ＿＿＿＿＿＿＿＿＿的乡镇企业,有的已经从家族式的小作坊变成了现代化企业集团,它们的产品在国际市场上已有相当的知名度。

11. 改革开放后,乡镇企业得到了飞快发展,不论从利税还是产值,它们在国民经济中都举足轻重,可以说占有了＿＿＿＿＿＿＿＿＿。

12. 中国几千年的封建社会,家族之间关系复杂,常是＿＿＿＿＿＿＿＿＿。

三、请用括号里的词语完成下列句子。

1. 乡镇企业抓住了改革开放的天赐良机,在商品严重短缺的卖方市场＿＿＿＿＿＿＿＿＿＿＿＿＿＿＿。(机动灵活)

2. 进入 21 世纪,市场相对饱和,空间日趋狭小,出现了＿＿＿＿＿＿＿＿＿＿＿＿＿＿＿＿＿＿＿的买方市场。(供大于求/供过于求)

3. 20 世纪 90 年代末,在中国市场,外资企业和乡镇企业同中国国有企业一样,感受到了发展的压力,企业兴衰存亡的关键是＿＿＿＿＿＿＿＿＿＿＿＿＿＿＿＿＿＿＿＿。(产业结构优化和升级)

4. 乡镇企业与农业有割不断的血缘关系,所以乡镇企业＿＿＿＿＿＿＿＿＿＿＿＿＿＿＿＿＿＿。(得天独厚)

5. 中国农业＿＿＿＿＿＿＿＿＿＿＿＿＿＿＿＿＿＿＿。(坚定不移)

四、想一想,谈一谈。

1. 中国乡镇企业是怎么发展起来的?

2. 乡镇企业走了一条怎样艰难发展的路?

3. 进入 20 世纪 90 年代后,乡镇企业面临着怎样的生存考验?出路在哪儿?

4. 你用过中国乡镇企业的产品吗?你参观过乡镇企业吗?请谈谈你的看法。

五、阅读下面的短文,然后回答问题。

客串做回生意人

我是个知识分子,做起本行来,还自觉游刃有余,干别的事儿,就难免冒傻气。改革开放后,生意人都交了好运,大把大把赚钱,在社会上吃香得很。我老伴心也活了,时时怂恿我下海。我有自知之明,还是乖乖地干我的老本行。

一天,我在单位上班,老家的一个农民从乡下来找我,说村里办乡镇企业急需机器,新的买不起,城里大工厂淘汰下来的旧机器最好,买到了机器,乡里答应给我20%的中介费。我回家对老伴一说这事儿,老伴就来了劲儿,说:"我们楼下的老马师傅,下岗后专门捣腾机器,我去找他。"不一会儿,老伴回来说:"有戏!老马师傅说了,不管对方给多少好处费,他都按成交额15%提成给我们。他知道我们不懂机器,他说他就直接同对方面谈。"

经过我和老伴牵线,买卖双方在我家见了面。老马师傅同我那老乡在客厅里谈生意,我同老伴忙着给他们准备酒菜。我们酒菜刚准备好,他们也谈完了。大家高高兴兴吃饱喝足,二位客人就告别走了。

一个星期过去了,没有消息;一个月又过去了,还是没有消息。老伴急了,我说:"他们的生意大概没做成吧。""唉,白忙了一阵,空欢喜一场!"老伴叹息说。

一天,邻居王师傅见到我们说:"上回你们给老马介绍的那笔生意,挣了不少钱吧?"我老伴抱怨说:"别提了,没做成!"王师傅吃惊地反问:"什么?没做成?我亲眼见他们把机器拉走了!"我一听,不禁哈哈长笑。"仰天大笑出门去,我辈岂是生意人!哈,哈……"

1. 故事中的"我"为什么没有得到中介费?
2. 应该怎么做中介工作,才能确保得到中介费?
3. 老马师傅是个什么样的人?
4. 请解释一下题目是什么意思。

38 外商投资企业

Foreign-Invested Enterprises

一、投 资 方 式

爱德华：部长助理先生，我这次来贵国考察近一个月，回国之前，我想亲自了解一下政府对外商投资企业的有关政策。

亨　特：爱德华先生这次考察收获很大，对中国市场充满了信心，决心要在中国大干一场。

马君仪：热烈欢迎啊！您已经在中国考察了一个月，我想您对外国商人在华投资情况已不再陌生了吧？

爱德华：那也是走马观花，一知半解而已，问号仍然不少。比如，外商在华投资，目前都有哪些形式？

马君仪：主要形式有外商独资企业、中外合资企业、中外合作经营企业。

亨　特：就是人们常说的"三资企业"。

马君仪：随着我国不断扩大开放，实行"大经贸"战略，外商投资领域已经逐步扩大，合资、合作形式也多种多样。

爱德华：我知道，贵国正在逐步开放零售业、金融业、保险业及其他服务行业；中外合资有股份制；可以同国营企业合资合作，也可以同个体、私营、民营企业合资合作。

马君仪：是的，方正集团与美国数字设备公司、海尔集团与日本三洋电器建立的合资公司，就是令人瞩目的例子。

爱德华：请问，中国目前最欢迎什么样的投资呢？

马君仪：为加速我国国民经济的发展，我们欢迎外国客商以各种形式在华投资。就目前我国经济发展需要来看,我们更欢迎外商在矿山、交通、通讯、能源及高科技领域的长期投资。

爱德华:我很理解。

马君仪:我国地域辽阔,经济发展不平衡,东部及沿海地区经济发达,中西部及偏远地区相对落后,所以我们鼓励外商向中西部地区投资。

爱德华:那里需要资金,投资前景也更广阔,向中西部投资不失为一种好的选择。

马君仪:我们欢迎爱德华先生去那里大干一场!

爱德华:我会认真考虑马先生的建议,我们很愿意为中国的经济发展尽绵薄之力!

二、投资者的责、权、利

爱德华:马先生,不庸讳言,商业活动的终极目的是为了赚钱,我也不能超凡脱俗。请问,外商在华投资利益能得到保障吗?

马君仪:请一百二十个放心!为了确保外商在华投资利益,我国已经制定和出台了一系列涉外经济法规。这些法规,详细、明确地规定了外商享有的权利。

亨　特:据我所知,有《外资企业法》及实施细则、《中外合资经营企业法》及实施条例、《外商投资企业和外国企业所得税法》等等。

马君仪:我们不仅认真执行已出台的各项利用外资政策,而且在保持政策稳定性的同时,不断充实和完善外商投资的法规体系。我国政府一贯依法保护一切在华外商投资企业的合法权益,包括知识产权。

爱德华:具体地说呢?

马君仪:噢,这很复杂。概括地说,外商的财产享有被保护权和自由处置权,外商投资者有生产计划权、经营管理自主权、聘用与解雇职工权等等。

爱德华：那么责任呢？

马君仪：简单地说，就是合法经营。同时，也要注重提高企业中方员工的素质，并保护他们的合法权益。

爱德华：听起来，贵国这些涉外法规，符合国际通行做法，但能够保证不是一纸空文吗？

马君仪：看来，爱德华先生还心存疑虑，您在中国一个月的考察时间太短了。告诉您一个简单的事实吧。

爱德华：什么事实？

马君仪：我国现在的三资企业已经突破55万家，实际利用外资已经超过6 500亿美元，而且绝大多数经营良好，已经获得丰厚利润。有不少外商投资企业，还不急于把利润汇回国去，而用于在华扩大再生产和开拓新业务。更有一些大型跨国公司，把他们的地区总部、研究所和开发中心从境外移到了中国。

亨　特：这表明他们的合法权益得到了切实保障，也表明他们对在华投资充满了信心。

爱德华：我也吃了一颗定心丸儿。

三、投 资 环 境

爱德华：马先生，我还想了解一下投资环境。

马君仪：是硬环境还是软环境？

亨　特：中国改革开放三十年，交通、通讯等基础设施有了长足进步，为吸引外资提供了坚实的物质基础。

爱德华：我想硬环境不成问题，就请谈谈软环境吧。

马君仪：好的。我国政治稳定，社会安定，经济高速发展，潜在市场巨大，政府出台了一系列有利于外商的投资政策。我想，这是最重要的软环境。

爱德华:马先生说得很对。

马君仪:当然,我们还要下硬功夫改善软环境的方方面面。

亨　特:一些职能部门办事效率低下,单位之间互相扯皮的现象严重,公文旅行无休无止,还有官僚主义、形式主义,都是令许多外国人头痛的事儿。

马君仪:我们一直在不断完善外商投资服务体系,提高服务质量和服务效率,比如为外资提供"一条龙"服务、"一站式"办公、计算机联网管理、海关对企业实施分类管理等等。你提到的这些现象,现在已经有了很大改观。

亨　特:这确实是有目共睹的。不过,一些地方"四乱"现象仍然屡禁不止。

爱德华:什么"四乱"现象?

马君仪:噢,就是"乱检查、乱收费、乱摊派、乱罚款"。我们的态度是,坚决杜绝、认真治理和严肃查处,提高政策的可操作性,增加工作透明度,保护守法企业的正常经营活动。

爱德华:谢谢马先生的真诚与坦率,其实,不尽如人意的事儿世界各国都有,我们对贵国也不会苛求。

马君仪:但我们并不因此宽恕自己。我们深知,改善投资环境,特别是投资软环境,是一项长期而艰巨的任务。我们将一如既往,努力为外商在华投资营造一个更加稳定、有利的政策环境和一个更加平等、透明的竞争环境。外国客商会发现,中国是他们最理想的经商、投资场所。

爱德华:我完全相信这一点。

马君仪:我们利用外资的目的,是为了促进我国经济的发展,但同时也要维护外商在华的合法权益,让他们确实有利可图。

爱德华:啊,我希望有利可图,但绝不唯利是图。

马君仪:你是一个好商人。

 **生 词**

1. 部长	bùzhǎng	minister
2. 助理	zhùlǐ	assistant
3. 考察	kǎochá	inspect, make an on-the-spot investigation, observe and study
4. 陌生	mòshēng	strange, unfamiliar
5. 走马观花	zǒu mǎ guān huā	look at flowers while riding a horse — gain a superficial understanding from cursory observation
6. 一知半解	yì zhī bàn jiě	have scanty knowledge
7. 而已	éryǐ	that is all; nothing more
8. 私营	sīyíng	privately-owned
9. 民营	mínyíng	non-governmental
10. 矿山	kuàngshān	mine
11. 偏远	piānyuǎn	remote
12. 不失为	bùshīwéi	can yet be regarded as
13. 终极	zhōngjí	ultimate
14. 超凡脱俗	chāofán tuōsú	avoid earthly concerns and hold oneself aloof from the vulgar
15. 出台	chūtái	appear on the stage, make a public appearance
16. 涉外	shèwài	concerning foreign affairs
17. 条例	tiáolì	regulations, rules
18. 所得税	suǒdéshuì	income tax
19. 充实	chōngshí	substantial, rich
20. 概括	gàikuò	summarize
21. 解雇	jiěgù	discharge, fire
22. 再生产	zàishēngchǎn	reproduction
23. 总部	zǒngbù	headquarters
24. 境外	jìngwài	beyond the border
25. 切实	qièshí	practical, realistic

26.	定心丸	dìngxīnwán	something capable of setting somebody's mind at ease
27.	物质	wùzhì	material, matter, substance
28.	安定	āndìng	stable
29.	硬功夫	yìng gōngfu	masterly skill; great proficiency
30.	扯皮	chěpí	dispute over trifles, argue back and forth
31.	公文	gōngwén	official document
32.	无休无止	wú xiū wú zhǐ	ceaseless, endless
33.	官僚主义	guānliáo zhǔyì	bureaucracy
34.	形式主义	xíngshì zhǔyì	formalism
35.	改观	gǎiguān	change the appearance of
36.	屡禁不止	lǚ jìn bù zhǐ	do not stop despite repeated prohibitions
37.	摊派	tānpài	apportion
38.	杜绝	dùjué	stop, put an end to
39.	查处	cháchǔ	investigate and prosecute
40.	尽如人意	jìn rú rényì	just as one wishes; entirely satisfactorily
41.	苛求	kēqiú	make excessive demands; be over-critical
42.	宽恕	kuānshù	forgive
43.	一如既往	yì rú jì wǎng	as always
44.	有利可图	yǒu lì kě tú	be profitable
45.	唯利是图	wéi lì shì tú	be bent solely on profit

专 名 Proper Nouns

1.	美国数字设备公司	Měiguó Shùzì Shèbèi Gōngsī	American Digital Equipment Corporation
2.	日本三洋电器	Rìběn Sānyáng Diànqì	Sanyo Electric Corporation of Japan

 练 习

A

而已

助词,用在陈述句末尾,有把事情往小里说的意思,有时含有鄙视的意味。常与"只、不过、仅仅、无非"等词相呼应。多用于书面,口语里用"罢了",很多场合,"而已"可换成"罢了"。习用语"如此而已",意思是"只能像这样"、"仅限于此",这是个固定格式,其中的"而已"不能换成"罢了"。

That is all;nothing more. It is a particle used at the end of a declarative sentence, carrying with it a tone of alleviating the thing mentioned. Sometimes it implies a sense of contempt. Often it is paired with such words as 只(only), 不过(no more than), 仅仅(merely), and 无非(nothing but). It is more often used in written Chinese. The colloquial form is 罢了. On many occasions, 而已 can be changed into 罢了. In the idiomatic expression 如此而已, which means "only like this", "only limited to this", 而已 cannot be changed into 罢了 as this is a set expression.

一、熟读下列各句,体会"而已"的意义和用法。
1. 他不过是说说而已,你何必认真。
2. 我刚才只是举例而已,并不是想要批评什么人。
3. 有些人以为可以一夜暴富,那不过是白日做梦而已。
4. 他那点儿本事不过如此而已,有什么了不起!

二、用"而已"和下列短语造句。
1. 只是罚款
2. 仅仅一纸空文
3. 参观一下
4. 为了赚钱
5. 讨个公道

不失为

意思是"还可以算得上"、"还可以被认为是"。"为"在这里做动词"是"用,后面必带有宾语。

Can yet be regarded as. Its meaning is "can yet be counted as" or "can still be regarded as". 为 here is used as a verb, equivalent to the verb "to be", and must take an object after it.

一、熟读下列各句,体会"不失为"的意义和用法。

　　1. 你刚才的话,也不失为一种解释。

　　2. 你的建议,不失为一个好主意。

　　3. 他提出的这些办法,不失为一种可行的应急措施。

　　4. 企业赞助体育比赛,不失为一种善举。

二、请用"不失为"和下列短语造句。

　　1. 同中国人交朋友

　　2. 来中国考察

　　3. 提高员工素质

　　4. 乡镇企业从手工作坊式经营中解放出来

　　5. 中国农业摆脱传统的粗放型经营

因此

　　在很多情况下,我们见到的"因此"是连词,用于表示结果或结论的小句或段落的开头;前一小句有时用"由于"相呼应,组成表因果关系的复句。但本课文中出现的"因此",不是一个词,它实际上是"因 + 此","因"是介词,用来引出行为凭借的对象,意思相当于介词"根据、依、随着、沿"等,后面往往有"而"呼应;"此",代词,"这、这样",指代上文已出现的事情。

Therefore. On many occasions, 因此 is a conjunction, used at the beginning of a clause or a paragraph that states the result or conclusion. It sometimes corresponds with 由于 (because), which introduces the previous clause. Together they form a compound sentence denoting a cause-effect relationship. But 因此 in this text is not one word. It is actually 因 + 此 (because of this). 因 is a preposition, used to introduce the object which the act relies on. Its meaning is equivalent to that of such prepositions as 根据 (on the basis of), 依 (depending on), 随着 (along with), or 沿 (along). It often pairs with 而 (and; but; so that) that comes afterwards. 此 is a pronoun meaning 这 (this) or 这样 (this way), standing for the thing mentioned above.

一、熟读下列各句,体会并分别说明"因"、"因此"的意义和用法。

　　1. 你不能受了一次骗,就因此而怀疑一切人都是骗子。

　　2. 由于他们熟悉市场,因此很快打开了产品的销路。

　　3. 我同他是多年的老朋友了,因此我了解他。

　　4. 这一次你受了表扬,但是千万不要因此就骄傲起来。

　　5. 他只是这一次不小心出了点儿差错,你不能因此就解雇他。

二、请用"因此"和下列短语造句。

　　1. 你不能第一次炒股赚了钱

　　2. 不能有了一次失败的婚姻

　　3. 他们工厂一向奉行"质量第一,顾客至上"

　　4. 乡镇企业真正懂得什么叫市场竞争

　　5. 这是一次非常特殊的考验

一如既往

　　成语。"一",做副词用,是"全、满"的意思,类似的用法还有"一心一意"(全心全意)、"一路平安"(整个行程平安)、"一无是处"(完全没有对的地方)等。"既","已经"。"一如既往",意思是"完全跟过去一样"。

As always. It is an idiom. 一(one;same;all)is used as an adverb, meaning 全(wholly;entirely)or 满(fully;filled). Similar expressions include 一心一意(wholehearted), 一路平安(have a good trip), 一无是处(without a single redeeming virtue), etc. 既 means 已经(already). 一如既往 means "exactly the same as in the past".

一、熟读下列各句,体会"一如既往"的意义和用法。

　　1. 我们将一如既往,保护外商的知识产权。

　　2. 一如既往,我们将努力发展双方的交流与合作。

　　3. 一如既往,本公司现在又争取到了银行的支持和帮助。

　　4. 不论世界格局发生什么变化,中国人民都将一如既往,坚定不移地走自己的路。

二、请用"一如既往"和下列短语造句。

　　1. 热情好客

　　2. 关心环境保护

　　3. 保护外商的合法权益

4. 不断完善外商投资服务体系

5. 产品质量管理

唯利是图

成语。"唯","只、只是",副词;"图","贪图",动词;"是",语中助词,用在倒置的宾语和动词的中间,如成语"唯利是图",意思是只贪图财利,别的什么都不顾。为了强调"利",所以用"是"把宾语"利"提到动词"图"的前边去了。类似的常用成语还有"唯命是从"、"唯命是听"。

Be bent solely on profit. It is an idiom. 唯 is an adverb meaning "only", "solely". 图 is a verb meaning "seek". 是 here is a particle, used between the inverted object and verb. The idiom 唯利是图 means "be bent solely on profit regardless of anything else". In order to emphasize 利(profit), the particle 是 is used to transfer 利 before the verb 图. Similar idioms include 唯命是从(be at somebody's bidding) and 唯命是听(be obedient to somebody).

一、熟读下列各句,体会"唯……是……"格式构成的几个成语的意义和用法。

1. 他是一个唯利是图的商人。

2. 我是一个小小的职员,在老板面前,只能唯命是从。

3. 唯利是图,不讲道德,不讲情义,这种人也算朋友吗?

4. 在家里,太太指东,他不敢往西;让站着,他不敢坐着,真是个唯命是听的丈夫。

二、请用"唯利是图"或"唯命是听"和下列短语造句。

1. 积极主动地工作

2. 孩子在大人面前

3. 假冒伪劣商品多

4. 陈旧的传统观念

5. 充满自信心的人

B

一、请用下列词语组成短语。

涉外　出台　杜绝　扯皮　苛求

条例　法规　摊派　突破　定额

严肃　坚决　宽恕　政策　检查

二、熟读下列词语,并选择适当的词语填空。

> 无休无止　　屡禁不止　　一知半解
> 超凡脱俗　　有利可图　　一百二十个放心
> 不尽如人意　走马观花　　问题仍然不少
> 一颗定心丸儿

1. 我们相信,随着一系列涉外经济法规的制定和出台,经济生活中_____
   _____的事儿,会逐步得到解决。
2. 一些不法商人唯利是图,所以制假贩假的违法行为_____。
3. 中国政府制定和出台了一系列涉外经济法规,并不断充实和完善,使在
   华投资的外商_____。
4. 尽管中国政府在改善软环境方面下了硬功夫、大力气,但一些地方官僚
   主义、形式主义仍然严重,_____。
5. 这次访问,虽然是_____,但我在中国耳闻目睹的许多事情
   是终身难忘的。
6. 中国政府制定和出台了一系列有利于外商的投资政策,使他们对在华
   投资充满信心,像吃了_____。
7. 一些捷足先登的外国公司在中国的成功,充分说明了中国不仅有巨大
   的市场潜力,而且有良好的投资环境,外商确实_____。
8. 在金钱作为标准来衡量一切的当今社会,要想_____,谈何
   容易。
9. 尽管我们已经为外商来华投资极大地简化了手续,但个别地方的职能
   部门办事效率低下;互相扯皮,公文旅行_____。
10. 现在一些年轻人读书满足于_____,这对今后进一步提高
    不利。

三、请用括号里的词语完成下列句子。

1. 通过亲自考察中国市场,公司老板决心长期投资中国高科技领域_____
   _____。(大干一场)
2. 现在普通的中国老百姓已经对上网、炒股、电子邮件_____
   _____。(不再陌生)
3. 中国地域辽阔,经济发展不平衡,中西部及偏远地区相对落后,需要资
   金和技术,_____。(投资前景)

4. 我们深知,改善投资环境,特别是＿＿＿＿＿＿＿＿＿＿。(长期而艰巨)

5. 尽管中国目前仍然存在着令许多外国人头痛的事儿,但我们一直在不断完善外商投资服务体系,提高服务质量和工作效率,＿＿＿＿＿＿＿
＿＿＿＿＿＿＿＿＿＿＿＿＿＿。(大有改观)

6. 我们相信,通过我们的努力,经济生活中一些不尽如人意的事儿会逐步得到解决,对此＿＿＿＿＿＿＿＿＿＿＿。(不会苛求)

7. 中国改革开放以来,为吸引外资,在＿＿＿＿＿＿＿＿。(长足进步)

8. 由于外商的合法权益得到了切实的保障,不少外商投资企业,没有把利润汇回本国,＿＿＿＿＿＿＿＿＿＿。(开拓新业务)

四、想一想,谈一谈。

1. 外商在华投资主要有哪些形式? 请举例说明。

2. 就中国经济发展需要来看,中国更欢迎哪些方面的投资? 为什么?

3. 为了确保外商在华投资利益,中国政府制定和出台了哪些涉外经济法规? 这些法规能切实保障外商的合法权益吗?

4. 你认为中国投资环境怎样? 中国政府为改善投资环境作了哪些努力? 你认为还存在哪些问题?

五、阅读下面的短文,回答问题。

美好的误会

在合资企业里,中外老板、雇员之间,因为文化差异,常常会闹些误会。有些误会,就像生活中的润滑剂,使生活充满了快乐。

在合资企业里,工作效率高,节奏快,精神高度集中、紧张。突然,女秘书对公司总经理说:"先生,您太太来电话,说她今早起晚了,您来上班的时候,她没有同您吻别,现在,她要给您一个热烈的吻。"总经理连头也没有抬,说:"你先替我收着,等我忙完以后,你再给我。"

中国人同外国人的说话方式有很大不同,比如,外国人说话大多直来直去,中国人说话则比较委婉含蓄。一天,一个新来的女秘书,走到公司总裁面前,有些不安地说:"先生,我猜是您的电话。"总裁不解地反问:"猜? 我的就是我的,这还要猜吗?"女秘书面有难色,结结巴巴地说:"打电话的人好像很生气,说:'让……那个……老、老、老东西听电话!'"总裁一听,立即严肃起来,说:"啊,我知道了,你出去吧!"

1. 女秘书听到总经理说"你再给我"以后,会是什么反应? 事后,如果总经理醒悟过来,会怎么做?

2. 在第二个故事里,新来的女秘书是不熟悉打电话人的声音呢,还是清楚地知道是谁,但不便直说?

3. 你谈谈由于中外文化不同引起的"美好的误会"。

开放城市和经济特区 **39**

Open Cities and Special Economic Zones

一、开 放 城 市

爱德华：马先生，我这次来中国一个月，处处受到热情、友好的接待，完全改变了我来中国之前的印象。

马君仪：哦？来之前是什么印象？

爱德华：说来很可笑，不说也罢！

亨　特：他听一些人说，到了中国，人身没有自由，处处受限制，走到哪儿后边都跟着一大群人，就像看稀有动物一样。

马君仪：哈哈，说这种话的人，不是对中国有偏见，也是对中国缺乏最起码的了解。

爱德华：你说得很对，我来中国后，跑了很多地方，感受完全不一样。我还遇到许多来自世界各地的外国人，他们也都生活得很自由，很愉快。

亨　特：现在，中国已经对外开放了几百个城市，北京、上海、广州可以去，乌鲁木齐、拉萨也可以去。开放城市已经遍布全国各地。有些开放城市，对长住的外国人还实行国民待遇、市民待遇。

爱德华：开放城市是怎么选择的呢？

马君仪：一般来说，开放城市或者是经济比较发达，或者是历史、文化名城，或者是风景名胜，可供游览、休闲、参观、访问。

爱德华：不错，我这次到过几个城市，西安、青岛、杭州、苏州，既现代又古老，给我留下了难忘的印象。

马君仪：很高兴你去过这么多地方，可以说，每个开放城市，都是了
　　　　解中国经济、文化的一个窗口。你没有去上海吗？

爱德华：怎么没去？先去上海，再去的苏州、杭州。

亨　　特：我们一起去参观了浦东。上海，作为国际化大都会，中国
　　　　乃至亚洲的贸易、金融中心，让他赞不绝口。

爱德华：上海的小吃和甜点，总让我垂涎欲滴。还有上海话，实在
　　　　好听，可惜我学不来。

马君仪：这么说，我倒有一个建议，你不妨聘几位上海名点技师，在
　　　　贵国办一个上海食品厂，专门生产、经营上海风味糕点，这
　　　　样既做了生意，又学了上海话，岂不是一举两得？

爱德华：这个主意不错，可惜晚了，我的同行已经捷足先登了。

二、经济特区

爱德华：马先生，你能给我们介绍一下中国的经济特区吗？

马君仪：行啊。中国幅员辽阔，各地经济发展极不平衡，为了充分
　　　　发挥沿海城市和地区的优势，把沿海城市和地区作为吸引
　　　　外资和先进技术、发展进出口贸易的基地，带动全国经济
　　　　建设，我国政府对沿海某些地方采取了许多发展经济的优
　　　　惠政策，我们把这些地方叫做"经济特区"。

爱德华：噢，所谓"经济特区"，原来是指享有特殊优惠政策发展经
　　　　济的地区。

亨　　特：就是说，并不意味着，这些地区在政治、文化等方面有什么
　　　　特殊性。

马君仪：是的。你们知道，世界上许多国家现在都在进行改革，中
　　　　国改革开放的成功之路，之所以尤其引人瞩目，是因为中
　　　　国的改革进程充满了探索、试验、推广、调整。经济特区，
　　　　就是一个对外开放的"窗口"，一块探索建设社会主义市场
　　　　经济的"试验田"。

亨　特：这些试验田，确实相继产生了许多全中国的"第一"，比如第一家中外合资企业，第一家股票交易所，第一家外资银行，第一家产权拍卖市场，等等。

马君仪：经济特区率先并还在深入进行计划体制、价格体制、财政金融体制、流通体制、干部人事体制、社会保障体制等一系列改革，取得了宝贵的经验。

亨　特：很显然，全国各地都在效法他们的经验。

马君仪：这些试验田的成功，对外起了窗口作用，吸引了全世界企业家们的目光；对内起了示范作用，推动了全国的改革开放进程。

爱德华：那么，全中国目前有多少这样的经济特区呢？

马君仪：从1980年起，我国开辟了四个经济特区，即深圳、珠海、汕头、厦门经济特区，以后又有海南经济特区。除了经济特区，还有成百上千的经济技术开发区，遍布全国各地。

三、经济技术开发区

爱德华：请问马先生，开发区又是怎么回事儿？

马君仪：开发区同经济特区有许多相似之处，比如也是依托沿海地区相对发达的经济基础，专门划出一块地方，实行一些优惠政策，营造良好的投资环境，吸引外资和先进技术。

爱德华：那么，为什么不叫经济特区呢？

马君仪：主要是功能不同，这里已不再是"试验田"，这里是地区经济新的增长点，高科技和现代工业基地，还可以有效地调整城市产业结构和布局。同时，也借鉴了国外经济自由区的许多做法。

爱德华：那么，可以说开发区就是自由区吗？

马君仪：当然不能，我们只是借鉴了某些做法。比如，与国外经济自由区的出口加工区相比，开发区具有金融、服务、居住等配套功能;与保税区、保税仓库、自由贸易区相比,开发区的加工性更强、高科技水准更高,而贸易性就相对弱一些。

亨　特:如果与国外经济自由区的自由港相比,自由港不受海关监管,进出货物一律免税,而开发区处在海关监管之下,只能部分地享受减免关税的优惠。

马君仪:你说得很对。

爱德华:那么,开发区现在办得怎么样?

亨　特:都很成功,尤其是北京上地、上海浦东、天津、大连、烟台等经济技术开发区,在成百上千开发区中,可以说是首屈一指,闻名遐迩。

爱德华:我们去参观过上地开发区,在那里见到不少世界五百强中的知名企业。

亨　特:群雄争霸,抢滩登陆,谁也不甘落后!

马君仪:各地的开发区都有比较明显的优势,比如离市区近,交通方便,配套设施齐全,有智力、资金、信息、市场作依托。

亨　特:还有良好的服务体系,优惠的政策环境和法制相对完善的社会环境。开发区的这些独特优势,正是它的魅力所在。

马君仪:不少投资者,开始是怀着投石问路的心理进入开发区的,后来他们发现,他们的选择是明智的,可以甩开胳膊大步向前走。于是,纷纷追加投资,扩大规模,甚至把境外总部也迁来了。

爱德华:如此说来,还会有更多的后来者。

马君仪:这叫"家有梧桐树,自有凤凰来"嘛!

亨　特:所以,你们常说"筑巢引凤",是要构筑一个好的环境,把外资都吸引进来。这真是一个动人的比喻!

 **生　词**

1. 可笑	kěxiào	laughable, ridiculous

2. 也罢	yěbà	well;all right;no matter whether
3. 稀有	xīyǒu	rare,unusual
4. 偏见	piānjiàn	prejudice,bias
5. 待遇	dàiyù	treatment
6. 游览	yóulǎn	go sight-seeing,tour
7. 休闲	xiūxián	leisure
8. 作为	zuòwéi	regard as;in the capacity
9. 都会	dūhuì	a big city,metropolis
10. 垂涎欲滴	chuíxián yù dī	mouth drooling with greed
11. 技师	jìshī	technician
12. 捷足先登	jié zú xiān dēng	the swift-footed arrive first
13. 探索	tànsuǒ	explore,probe
14. 试验	shìyàn	experiment,test
15. 推广	tuīguǎng	spread,popularize
16. 相继	xiāngjì	in succession;one after another
17. 拍卖	pāimài	auction
18. 率先	shuàixiān	be the first to do something
19. 财政	cáizhèng	finance
20. 开辟	kāipì	open up,start
21. 依托	yītuō	rely on,depend on
22. 布局	bùjú	overall arrangement,layout
23. 保税区	bǎoshuìqū	bonded zone
24. 水准	shuǐzhǔn	level,standard
25. 自由港	zìyóugǎng	free port
26. 首屈一指	shǒu qū yì zhǐ	come first on the list
27. 闻名遐迩	wénmíng xiá'ěr	be known far and wide
28. 群雄争霸	qúnxióng zhēng bà	powers contending for hegemony
29. 抢滩登陆	qiǎngtān dēnglù	fighting for the beachhead for landing
30. 不甘落后	bùgān luòhòu	everybody hates to lag behind
31. 甩	shuǎi	swing,move backward and forward
32. 胳膊	gēbo	arm
33. 于是	yúshì	so,then,hence
34. 后来者	hòuláizhě	latecomer
35. 梧桐	wútóng	*Wutong*, Chinese parasol tree,

		phoenix tree
36. 凤凰	fènghuáng	phoenix
37. 构筑	gòuzhù	construct, build
38. 动人	dòngrén	moving, touching

专 名 Proper Nouns

1. 乌鲁木齐	Wūlǔmùqí	Urumchi
2. 拉萨	Lāsà	Lhasa
3. 浦东	Pǔ Dōng	Pudong

 练习

A

也罢

　　助词。①是"也就算了"的意思,表示作出某种处理、决断并不圆满,却只能如此。多用于否定句的末尾。②"也罢"连用(两个或更多),表示在所列举的情况下,结果都不变,常与上文的"不管、无论"等和下文的"都、也"等相呼应;有时还可以表示从中选择一个或一种,含有不计较、无所谓的意思。

　　Well; all right; whether... or... It is a particle. 1) It has the meaning of "well, let it pass", indicating the decision or disposal is not satisfactory, but can only be so. It is often used at the end of a negative sentence. 2) When used in reduplicated form, it means under all the conditions enumerated, the result remains the same. It is often used correlatively with 不管 or 无论 (no matter) in the previous text, and 都 or 也 (as well; either) coming afterwards. Sometimes it can be used to indicate a choice, implying a sense of "give no thought to" or "be indifferent".

一、熟读下列各句,体会并分别说明"也罢"的意义和用法。
　　1. 我不是急需这些东西,现在不买也罢。
　　2. 你同意也罢,不同意也罢,我都这么决定了。
　　3. 老板也罢,小职员也罢,都是人,都得吃饭、睡觉。

4. 拍卖也罢,承包出去也罢,由你好了。

5. 我们老板,不管赚钱也罢,亏损也罢,成功也罢,失败也罢,跟我们在一起总是乐呵呵的。

6. 你既然不肯请客、送礼、走后门,也罢了,我不勉强你,办不成事,你可别怨我!

二、请用"也罢"和下列短语造句。

1. 赚　赔　　平常心

2. 谈得成　　谈不成

3. 这件事他已经知道做错了

4. 认识不同

5. 找不到出租汽车

相继

副词,意思是"相互承继、一个跟着一个"。

In succession. It is an adverb meaning "in succession"; "one after another".

一、熟读下列各句,体会"相继"的意义和用法。

1. 大会上,部门经理、财务主管和经销部主任相继发言。

2. MP3、MP4 等播放器相继上市。

3. 在国家有力的宏观调控下,大批企业相继走出困境。

4. 几十家大型跨国公司相继落户浦东。

二、请用"相继"和下列短语造句。

1. 在 20 世纪最后一次全球金融危机中

2. 走出困境

3. 去开放城市或经济特区考察

4. 制定和出台了一系列有利于外商的优惠政策

5. 从温饱走上了小康

或者

连词,用在并列结构中。①表示两种或者两种以上的情况同时存在。②表示选择,提出两种或多种情况,结果必居其一。

It is a conjunction, used in compound structures. 1) It says that two or more situations exist at the same time. 2) It expresses choice, choosing one from two or more alternatives.

一、熟读下列句子,体会"或者"的意义和用法。

1. 或者严格履行合同,或者赔偿经济损失,二者必居其一。

2. 由于我国农村形势很好,大部分农产品价格与去年相同,或者相近。

3. 关于在贵国举办展销会的时间,或者在四五月,或者在九十月,不知对贵国是否合适?

4. 我国现设的经济特区,或者得地利,或者得人和,或者物产丰富,或者技术先进,都是外商投资的理想场所。

二、请用"或者"和下列短语造句。

1. 炒股　　投资房地产

2. 坐出租汽车(打的)　　骑自行车　　坐公共汽车

3. 参观访问　参加座谈会

4. 自己做老板　　给人打工

5. 出国留学　　应聘找工作

成千上万

这是一个固定格式,表示的不是一个确定的数,而是一个概数。"成"是表示数量多。"成千上万",也可以说成"成千成万"、"成千累万"。

Tens of thousands of. This is a set pattern, not referring to an exact figure, but an approximate number. 成 indicates a large number. 成千上万 can also be expressed as 成千成万 or 成千累万。

一、熟读下列各句,体会"成千上万"的意义和用法。

1. 每天上市的新产品成千上万。

2. 股价连日飙升,成千上万的股民涌向交易所。

3. 成功的企业并不多,成千上万的企业都只能勉强维持。

4. 英国著名经济学家凯恩斯的《就业、利息和货币通论》拥有成千上万的读者。

二、请用"成千上万"和下列短语造句。

1. 北京的自行车

2. 来中国学汉语的留学生
3. 农民企业家
4. 申请专利
5. 消费者权益

于是

连词,连接分句或句子,一般放在后一分句或句子的开头,表示后一事承接前一事,后一事往往是前一事引起的。

So;then. It is a conjunction to link up two clauses or sentences. It is normally placed at the beginning of the second clause or sentence, indicating that the latter carries on from the former and the latter is usually caused by the former.

一、熟读下列各句,体会"于是"的意义和用法。
1. 他们俩的意见不一样,又固执己见,于是争吵了起来。
2. 经济技术开发区具有各种优势,于是成了地区经济新的增长点。
3. 爱德华在中国考察了一个月,亲身经历了很多事,于是彻底改变了看法。
4. 他们有了筑巢引凤的思想,于是不断改善投资环境,终于引来了第一批外国客商。

二、请用"于是"和下列短语造句。
1. 破坏生态平衡
2. 彻底转变观念
3. 调整出口产品结构
4. 看好中国市场
5. 不得不给予极大关注

作为

动词。①当做,必带名词宾语。②就人的某种身份或事物的某种性质来说,必带名词宾语,没有否定形式。

Regard as;in the capacity. It is a verb. 1) It means "take as", and must take a nominal object. 2) It means "in the capacity, character or role of". It has to take a nominal object and does not have a negative form.

一、熟读下列各句,体会并分别说明"作为"的意义和用法。

1. 我现在是个商人,玩儿玩儿音乐只能作为业余爱好了。

2. 作为公司老板,我必须加强公司的财务管理。

3. 这个计划,就作为我们大家行动的依据吧!

4. 作为经济自由区的保税区,在区内可以从事仓储、加工、中转、贸易、金融等业务,国外货物进入区内不征关税,区内货物可以自由运往国外,如运往国内非保税区则要征关税,国内货物进入保税区,则视同出口。

二、请用"作为"和下列短语造句。

1. 发展中国家

2. 共同奋斗的目标

3. 经济特区

4. 合作伙伴

5. 崭新领域

B

一、请用下列词语组成短语。

稀有　提供　技师　水准　推广
待遇　游览　物质　率先　相继
拍卖　探索　试验　构筑　环境

二、熟读下列词语,并选择适当的词语填空。

垂涎欲滴　　首屈一指　　不甘落后
捷足先登　　闻名遐迩　　群雄争霸
抢滩登陆　　魅力所在　　动人的比喻
甩开胳膊大步向前走

1. 有些人自己不劳动,看到别人大把挣钱,吃好的,穿好的,又禁不住＿＿＿＿＿＿＿＿＿＿。

2. 改革开放后,中国农民从黄土地上解放出来,＿＿＿＿＿＿＿＿＿＿＿,他们或就地取材,办起了各种各样的乡镇企业,或走进城市寻找出路,农民企业家就这样应运而生了。

3. 随着中国不断扩大开放,实行"大经贸"战略,外商投资领域逐步扩大,形式也多种多样,有些＿＿＿＿＿＿＿＿的外商,已经尝到了甜头,获得了丰厚利润,正考虑在华扩大再生产和开拓新业务。

4. 中国旗袍能充分体现女性的曲线美,这正是它的＿＿＿＿＿＿＿＿。

5. 美国"硅谷"之所以在全世界享有盛誉,＿＿＿＿＿＿＿＿,主要因为它是美国信息产业的发祥地,是美国高科技人才云集的圣地。

6. 北京海淀中关村被誉为"中国的硅谷",这里人才济济,科研实力和成果同美国硅谷比,毫不逊色。为此,美国微软公司已在此＿＿＿＿＿＿＿＿＿＿＿＿＿＿,把中国公司的总部设在这里。

7. 汉语中形容女性美有很多＿＿＿＿＿＿＿＿,你学了这么长时间的汉语,能说出一两个来吗?

8. 发展中国家在21世纪＿＿＿＿＿＿＿＿,决心发挥各自优势,发展本国经济,积极参与国际经济的交流与合作。

9. 中国是＿＿＿＿＿＿＿＿的农业大国,一直把农业当做国民经济的基础。

10. 改革开放以来,经济特区、开发区和开放城市,以它独特的优势,引来外商纷纷投资,在那里很快出现了＿＿＿＿＿＿＿＿的局面。

三、请用括号里的词语完成下列句子。

1. 我第一次来中国旅行,带的行李差一点儿把我累死,＿＿＿＿＿＿＿＿＿＿＿＿＿＿＿＿＿＿＿＿＿＿＿＿。(缺乏最起码的了解)

2. 到广州旅行,＿＿＿＿＿＿＿＿＿＿＿＿＿＿＿＿。(留下了难忘的印象)

3. 经济特区率先实行了一系列改革,为全国＿＿＿＿＿＿＿＿＿＿＿＿＿＿＿＿＿＿＿＿＿＿＿。(取得了宝贵经验)

4. 经济特区和开发区是＿＿＿＿＿＿＿＿＿＿＿＿＿＿＿＿。(一个窗口)

5. 上海是一个国际化的大都会,是中国乃至亚洲的贸易、金融中心,＿＿＿＿＿＿＿＿＿＿＿＿＿＿＿＿＿＿＿＿＿＿。(明智的选择)

四、想一想,谈一谈:

1. 开放城市是怎么选择的? 经济特区是怎么选择的?

2. 目前中国有多少经济特区? 它们对中国改革开放起到了什么作用?

3. 开发区与经济特区有什么不同? 你去过哪些开发区? 请谈谈你的印象。

4. "家有梧桐树,自有凤凰来",对此你怎么看? "筑巢引凤"有必胜的把握吗?

五、阅读下面的短文,然后回答问题。

城 市 趣 闻

改革开放以后,中国彻底打破了封闭状态,特别是对外开放城市,社会生活日益现代化,你若到街上走走,会遇到许多有趣的事儿。

一大清早,城市里到处都是晨练的人,有年轻的姑娘小伙儿,有壮汉健妇,更有老头儿老太。看,那儿有三个老大妈,大概是晨练累了,正坐在树下一张椅子上聊天儿。一个说:"我现在的忘性特大,有时走进厨房,转了几圈,竟想不起来我去拿什么东西。"一个说:"我的忘性更大,有时站在楼梯上,竟不知道自己是要上楼还是要下楼。唉,真是老糊涂了!"第三个说:"谢天谢地,我还没这毛病。"说着,用手快乐地敲着木椅子,木椅子发出"咚咚"的响声。"啊,有人敲门!"她惊叫一声,立即站起身来。

城市公交车越来越多,越来越漂亮,也越来越先进。有些无人售票车,有一个规矩,就是一律前门上车,上车后自动刷卡或投币,到站从后门下车。一位乡下老大伯头一次进城,看见公共汽车来了,前门人多拥挤,就从后门上了车。上车后,也没见有卖票的,只有司机开车。他就走到前边问:"司机同志,要买票吗?"司机打量了他一下,"你是从哪儿上的?""从后门。""从后门? 从后门上车也要买票!"车上的乘客一听,都乐了。

1. 三位老大妈聊天儿谈忘性,第三位说,她还没有这个毛病,是真的吗?
2. 公交车上的乘客听司机说"从后门上车也要买票",就笑起来了,为什么?
3. 你在中国,也遇到过"城市趣闻"吗? 请说说。

跨国经营与全球经济一体化 40

Transnational Operation and
Integration of the World Economy

一、知识经济时代

爱德华：马先生，现在全世界都在谈论知识经济时代，贵国对这个话题也感兴趣吗？

马君仪：不是你感不感兴趣的问题，是不由得你不感兴趣。

爱德华：哦？为什么？

马君仪：很简单，全世界正在由工业经济向知识经济转变，这种转变势必对人类社会产生深远的影响。

亨　特：科学家们断言，知识经济时代的到来，必将使社会经济形态发生根本性变革，彻底改变世界面貌和人类社会生活。

马君仪：所以，或者随时代前进，或者被时代抛弃，形势逼人哪！

爱德华：看来，大家都感到了时代对我们的召唤。

马君仪：贵国对知识经济时代的觉悟最早，感受恐怕也最深。

爱德华：是的。近三十年来，随着高科技、特别是信息技术的发展，我们国家就在不断谈论知识经济。1990年，联合国研究机构正式提出了"知识经济"这个概念。

亨　特：1996年，经济合作与发展组织(OECD)首次给知识经济下了一个明确定义，即知识经济"是以知识为基础的经济"。

马君仪：这就是说，在工业经济时代，经济赖以发展的自然资源，资金、设备、原材料等，退居第二位，而知识、智力资源则成为资源配置的第一要素。

亨　特：科学技术的发展，成为经济发展的决定性因素。而且科学家们普遍认为,信息技术和生物技术,将成为 21 世纪关系国家命运和前途的关键因素。

爱德华:这个看法,事实上在我们国家已经得到了印证。

马君仪:据媒介记载,美国在 20 世纪 80 年代牵住了高科技开发的牛鼻子,到 90 年代基本形成了以高科技为龙头,以信息、服务为两翼的新的产业体系,同时带动其他产业的发展,于是使美国经济走向了稳定增长与繁荣。

爱德华:确实如此。美国信息产业的带头羊微软公司,从 1975 年初创到成功,仅用了二十年时间,它现在的总资产,与工业时代的典型代表、经过战后五十多年才发展起来的通用汽车公司几乎相等。

马君仪:这说明,当今世界竞争实力的较量,归根到底是知识的较量。谁在知识领域领先,谁就在未来的竞争格局中掌握了主动。

亨　特:当代高科技产业是典型的知识密集型产业。知识经济就是以高科技产业为支柱产业的。这个支柱树起来了,一个国家乃至世界经济的宏伟大厦才能高耸入云。

马君仪:所以,让我们顺应历史潮流,迎接知识经济的到来吧!

二、跨国公司的战略购并浪潮

爱德华:专家们预言,人类将在 21 世纪下半叶全面进入知识经济时代。

马君仪:我们暂时还不能证实这个预言,但我们已经清楚地看到,高科技,特别是信息技术、通讯技术和网络技术的发展,使世界变小了,国家与国家、地区与地区之间的联系更紧密了,国际分工的联结媒介——商品贸易、投资、技术、劳务等的流动加速了。

亨　特:是这样。全球经济一体化成了不可逆转的历史趋势和不可阻挡的世界潮流。

爱德华：当今世界已经出现了三大区域经济组织，即欧洲联盟、北美自由贸易区和亚太经济合作组织。世界经济区域化和集团化趋势，有力地推动着世界经济走向全球经济一体化。

马君仪：世界经济一体化，还有一个巨大的推动力，那就是大型跨国公司掀起的战略购并浪潮。

亨　特：是的。在新一轮企业购并高潮中，与其说是一家企业兼并另一家企业，不如说是两家企业为了各自未来的发展而在更高层次上缔结战略联盟，是更高水平上的产权战略合作。

爱德华：这是优势互补、风险共担、利益同享的"强强联合"，完全摈弃了人们早已司空见惯的"大鱼吃小鱼，小鱼吃虾米"的竞争模式。

马君仪：这种"强强联合"的战略目标十分明显，那就是放弃狭隘的民族观念，打破国界，着眼于全球竞争，充分利用全球人力、技术、资本和自然资源，占领全球的每一个市场，实现全球经营利益最大化。

爱德华：跨国界的"强强联合"，可以在海外建立生产加工基地，共同进行新产品的研制开发，满足企业对新技术、新产品快速反应的要求，形成全球性开发、生产、销售网络，实现一揽子生产要素和价值增值链条各个环节的跨国有效配置。

马君仪：种种迹象表明，大型跨国公司的战略购并浪潮，已经并将继续对世界经济格局产生深远的影响。

三、中国企业的跨国经营

爱德华：马先生，国际跨国公司战略购并浪潮，对中国也有冲击吗？

马君仪：为了公司系统利益最大化，跨国公司总是把价值增值链的不同环节，安排在最能发挥作用的世界各地。中国不可能不处在国际跨国公司价值增值链中。

亨　　特：是这样。事实上,中国已经成为跨国公司全球经营网络中理想的制造、加工基地,在这方面的直接投资已经相当可观。

爱德华：跨国公司在海外安排价值增值链环节,首选之地,当然是最贴近市场或资源的地方。

亨　　特：中国有世界上最大的市场,有丰富的自然资源和低廉、高质量的劳动力资源,当然是国际跨国公司安排生产、加工基地最理想的地方。

马君仪：随着跨国公司制造业进入中国,他们的开发中心,也陆续进入了中国,而且技术开发,也从适应中国市场项目,逐步转向创新开发项目。

亨　　特：近年来,中国的服务业,尤其是那些知识密集服务行业,如金融、保险、财会、法律、通讯、营销等行业,也有了长足发展。我相信,国际跨国公司海外营运中心,也将云集中国大陆。

爱德华：看来,中国在国际跨国公司全球战略中,处于十分重要而有利的地位。那么,中国的企业是否也在转向跨国化呢?

马君仪：全球经济一体化,不可能是单向的,而是双向的。中国的企业当然也要走出国门,建立自己的跨国公司,谋求在海外的发展。

亨　　特：我知道,像海尔、科龙等一些大型企业,在海外都有了生产基地。

马君仪：我国的联想集团,就已经在软件的最尖端技术区——美国硅谷建立了技术开发部门。

爱德华：哦? 这可了不起!

马君仪：世界经济的发展,为我国的改革开放和经济建设,创造了一个比较有利的国际环境。我们将抓住机遇,不断提高我们在跨国公司全球战略中的地位,以便更多、更充分地利用跨国公司投资带来的资金、技术和管理资源,促进我国的现代化建设和提高参与全球竞争的能力。

 生 词

1. 势必	shìbì	certainly will；be bound to
2. 断言	duànyán	state with certainty，affirm
3. 面貌	miànmào	face，features，appearance
4. 逼迫	bīpò	force，compel
5. 召唤	zhàohuàn	summon，call
6. 赖以	làiyǐ	rely on，depend on
7. 要素	yàosù	essential factor，key element
8. 命运	mìngyùn	fate，destiny
9. 印证	yìnzhèng	confirm，verify
10. 记载	jìzǎi	put down in writing，record
11. 牵	qiān	lead along，pull
12. 牛鼻子	niúbízi	the nose of an ox
13. 两翼	liǎngyì	both wings
14. 带头羊	dàitóu yáng	bellwether
15. 较量	jiàoliàng	have a trial of strength，measure one's strength with
16. 高耸入云	gāosǒng rù yún	reach to the sky，tower into the clouds
17. 收购(购)	shōugòu(gòu)	purchase，buy
18. 兼并(并)	jiānbìng (bìng)	annex
19. 预言	yùyán	predict；prophesy
20. 暂时	zànshí	temporary，transient
21. 紧密	jǐnmì	close together，inseparable
22. 联结	liánjié	join，connect，link
23. 媒介	méijiè	medium
24. 逆转	nìzhuǎn	deteriorate，take a turn for the worse
25. 阻挡	zǔdǎng	resist，obstruct
26. 缔结	dìjié	conclude，establish
27. 联盟	liánméng	alliance，coalition
28. 摈弃	bìnqì	abandon，discard

29. 司空见惯	sīkōng jiàn guàn	a common sight, a common occurrence
30. 目标	mùbiāo	objective, target, aim
31. 狭隘	xiá' ài	narrow-minded
32. 一揽子	yìlǎnzi	comprehensive, wholesale
33. 增值	zēngzhí	increase, proliferate
34. 迹象	jìxiàng	sign, indication
35. 贴近	tiējìn	press close to
36. 创新	chuàngxīn	bring forth new ideas; blaze new trails
37. 大陆	dàlù	continent
38. 单向	dānxiàng	one-way
39. 谋求	móuqiú	seek, strive for
40. 参与	cānyù	participate in, involve oneself in

专 名 Proper Nouns

1. 通用汽车公司	Tōngyòng Qìchē Gōngsī	General Motors
2. 北美自由贸易区	Běiměi Zìyóu Màoyì Qū	North American Free Trade Agreement (NAFTA)
3. 亚太经济合作组织	Yà-Tài Jīngjì Hézuò Zǔzhī	Asia-Pacific Economic Cooperation (APEC)

 练 习

A

不由得

"由",动词,"顺随、听从"。不由得:①不容。例如"不由得你不听"。②不禁、控制不住、不由自主。例如"听到这个消息,她不由得笑了"。"不由得"中的"得",可看做补语助词。相似的词还有"由不得",但和"不由得"的语法结构不同。

Can't help; cannot but. 由 is a verb. 1) It means "obey" or "yield to". For instance, 不由得你不听 means "You cannot choose not to listen according to your own will". 2) It means "cannot help", "not under control", "involuntarily". For instance, 听到这个消息, 她不由得笑了. 得 in 不由得 can be regarded as a complementary auxiliary. Similar expressions include 由不得 (be beyond the control of), but it has a different grammatical structure from 不由得.

一、熟读下列各句,体会"不由得"、"由不得"的意义和用法。

1. 这是我的公司,由不得你做主。

2. 知识更新如此迅速,不由得你不产生危机感。

3. 家有家规,国有国法,由不得你胡作非为。

4. 听他一席话,不由得想起了几十年前的旧事。

5. 微软公司依靠高科技,用二十年时间完成了通用汽车公司五十多年的积累,不由得你不信。

二、请用"不由得"或"由不得"和下列短语造句。

1. 情绪激动

2. 转变观念

3. 接受挑战

4. 出言谨慎

5. 打折出售

势必

副词,是"其形势发展必然结果是"的意思,用来强调事物发展中的因果必然性。意义和用法跟"必定"相当,总是用来判断未来。

Certainly will. It is an adverb, meaning "the development of the situation will certainly result in", used to emphasize the necessary cause-and-effect relationship in the development of matters. Its meaning and usage are similar to those of 必定, always used to give a judgment about the future.

一、熟读下列各句,体会"势必"的意义和用法。

1. 如果照原计划,势必要投入更多的人力、物力。

2. 高科技的发展,势必加速全球经济一体化进程。

3. 低价竞销,势必扰乱市场的正常秩序。

4. 随着跨国公司争夺国际市场的加剧,势必导致缔结战略联盟和契约合作。

二、请用"势必"和下列短语造句。

1. 失去机会
2. 扩大贸易逆差
3. 损害消费者权益
4. 投资资本市场
5. 埋伏下很多隐患

归根到底

"归"，动词，意思是"趋向或集中于一个地方"。"归根到底"，意思是"归结到根本上"；把许多问题集中到最根本点上，求得某种结论。在句子中常常用逗号隔开，作为一个独立成分，表示强调。

In the final analysis. 归 is a verb，meaning"converge or come together". 归根到底 means"coming back to the fundamentals"，converging many questions to the most fundamental point in order to come to a certain conclusion. It is often separated from the rest of the sentence by a comma as an independent element for emphasis.

一、熟读下列各句,体会"归根到底"的意义和用法。

1. 归根到底，我们还是朋友，让我们忘记过去那些不愉快的事儿吧！
2. 我讲了许多理由，归根到底一句话，我们还没到彻底破产的时候。
3. 目前，企业处于困境，有诸多问题，归根到底，是人的问题。
4. 我们发展经济的目的，归根到底是为了提高人民的生活水平。

二、请用"归根到底"和下列短语造句。

1. 保护人类生存的环境
2. 提高员工素质
3. 中国亿万农民走出贫困
4. 乡镇企业经受住了大风大浪的考验
5. 幸福家庭

着眼

动词。"（从某方面）观察、考虑"。常见用法有两种格式。①"从……着眼"，如果用否定式，否定词只能放在"从"的前边。②"着眼于"，"于"是介词，由"于"组成的介词结构，表示"着眼"涉及的对象。

Have something in mind; see from the angle of. It is a verb, meaning to view or see something (from a certain angle). It often takes either one of the following two forms. 1）The first is 从……着眼. If it used in the negative form, the negative word can only be placed before 从（from）. 2）In the form 着眼于, 于 is a preposition. The prepositional phrase introduced by 于 indicates the object of 着眼（seeing or viewing）.

一、熟读下列各句,体会"着眼"的意义和用法。

1. 我们做事情,要从大处着眼。
2. 我们不能只考虑眼前,还要着眼于未来。
3. 我们强调终身受教育,是着眼于提高公司员工素质,不是为了别的什么目的。
4. 作为公司总裁,我考虑问题,不从公司的前途着眼,难道要从某个人的私利着眼吗?

二、请用"着眼"和下列短语造句。

1. 中国实行计划生育
2. 规范不正当贸易
3. 农业产业化
4. 外商投资
5. 商业保险

B

一、请用下列词语组成短语。

谋求　暂时　召唤　目标　狭隘
联盟　联结　阻挡　兼并　参与
命运　较量　收购　缔结　创新

二、熟读下列词语,并选择适当的词语填空。

| 牵牛鼻子 | 带领 | 带头羊 | 不可逆转 |
| 高耸入云 | 司空见惯 | 长足发展 | 云集中国大陆 |

1. 上海浦东自定为开发区后,外商纷纷投资,一座座＿＿＿＿＿＿的大楼拔地而起,很快成为外商云集的地方。
2. 调整产品结构,关键是要＿＿＿＿＿＿,首先调整国有大中型企业的产品结构。

3. 全世界正在由工业经济向知识经济转变,这种转变势必对人类社会产生深远影响。这是＿＿＿＿＿＿＿的时代潮流,我们想发展就必须顺应这个潮流,跟上这个潮流。

4. 现在,消费者面对假冒伪劣商品,好像已是＿＿＿＿＿＿＿,见"假"不怪了!

5. 改革开放以来,外商＿＿＿＿＿＿＿,这也是 20 世纪末的一大景观。

6. 公司业务取得＿＿＿＿＿＿＿,这与公司决策层转变观念有直接关系。

7. 一个公司的董事会就是这个公司的＿＿＿＿＿＿＿。

三、请用括号里的词语完成下列句子。

1. 知识经济时代的到来,必将使社会经济形态发生根本性变革,＿＿＿＿＿＿＿
＿＿＿＿＿＿＿＿＿＿＿＿＿＿＿＿＿＿。(形势逼人)

2. 世界经济区域化和集团化趋势,有力地推动着世界经济走向全球经济一体化,＿＿＿＿＿＿＿＿＿＿＿＿＿＿＿＿。(不可阻挡)

3. 在新一轮企业购并浪潮中,出现了一种新的竞争模式,这是＿＿＿＿＿
＿＿＿＿＿＿＿＿＿＿＿＿＿＿＿＿＿＿。("强强联合")

4. 全球经济一体化,中国的企业也要走出国门,建立自己的跨国公司＿＿＿＿
＿＿＿＿＿＿＿＿＿＿＿＿＿＿＿＿＿＿。(谋求发展)

5. 世界经济的发展,为我国改革开放和经济建设,创造了有利的国际环境。我们要抓住机遇,＿＿＿＿＿＿＿＿＿＿＿＿＿。(提高参与竞争的能力)

四、想一想,谈一谈。

1. 知识经济是怎样的概念? 知识经济时代与工业经济时代有什么不同?

2. 在 20 世纪末的全球金融危机中,西方的一些经济强国风光不再,一派委靡不振的景象,连日本也出现了经济衰退,唯独美国经济稳定增长,为什么?

3. 为什么说全球经济一体化是不可逆转的历史趋势和不可阻挡的世界潮流?

4. 在全球经济一体化进程中,出现了大型跨国公司掀起的战略购并浪潮,请列举两三个实例略加说明。

5. 在国际跨国公司战略购并浪潮中,中国处在什么地位? 持什么态度?

五、阅读下面的短文,然后回答问题。

假如记忆能够移植

人类正在进入知识经济时代。高科技的发展,是知识经济时代赖以建立的基础。而科学发明,有时是始于一些新奇的、不可思议的、甚至是荒诞不经的假设。先有了这种假设,人们才去不停地探索,假设最终得到证实或修正,人类因此又前进一步。

假如记忆能够移植,就是这样一种假设,或许这又是人类一个新时代的起点。

假如记忆能够移植,我们把爱因斯坦的记忆移植给一个婴儿,婴儿就可能叼着奶嘴研究高等物理;把莎士比亚的记忆移植给一个文盲,他或许就会拿起笔写出《罗密欧与朱丽叶》的续集;啊,或许,我应该开一家记忆银行,把人类中最伟大的人物的记忆,都存入我的银行,谁想变得伟大,谁就到我那里来"借贷",暂时不需要了,再到我的银行寄存。噢,我可不打算寄存希特勒的记忆,如果有人移植去,人类就难逃第三次世界大战的劫难了;我也不寄存专门制造计算机病毒的那些家伙的记忆,谁要"借贷"去,岂不把全球的银行、股市搅得天翻地覆! 我当然还要特别警惕"黑客"闯入,它要是闯入了我的记忆银行,随便移植记忆,那可更要天下大乱了!

假如记忆能够移植,再加上克隆技术,人类不就可以完完全全复制自身了吗? 噢,可得注意优生优育!

1. 你听说过"记忆能够移植"的假设吗? 这种假设的基本内容是什么?
2. 你怎么看"记忆能够移植"的假设? 是可能的还是根本不可能的?
3. 你知道当代还有什么别的新奇的假设吗? 那种假设对未来可能产生什么影响?

英 译 课 文
English Translations of the Texts

Lesson 21
OPENING PATTERN OF CHINA'S FOREIGN TRADE

(1) The Present and Future of China's Foreign Trade and Economic Relations

Hunter: Mr. Edward, let me introduce you to my Chinese friend, Mr. Jiang Qi, who works for the Ministry of Commerce.

Jiang Qi: Very glad to meet you, Mr. Edward.

Edward: Very glad to meet you too, Mr. Jiang.

Hunter: Mr. Jiang, our company makes all the arrangements for Mr. Edward's business trip to China this time. And the first item on his program today is to invite you for a meeting.

Edward: Mr. Jiang, it is really amazing that during the last global financial crisis in the 20th century, China's economy, instead of having a recession, made magnificent achievements. And that's the reason why I have made this business trip to China. I want to see it with my own eyes.

Hunter: The company of Mr. Edward's is a large-scale multinational corporation. They would like to further expand their cooperation with China under such a good situation.

Jiang Qi: That's great and you are most welcome.

Edward: I have noticed that China's foreign trade have made remarkable progress in the past few years.

Jiang Qi: That's right. China's foreign trade ranks the third in the world now, second only to America and Germany.

Hunter: The achievements of China's economic construction and its blue print for future development show boundless opportunities for trade and economic cooperation to the world.

Edward: Yes, that's right, and we don't want to miss the opportunity.

Jiang Qi：　What is your plan then, Mr. Edward?

Edward：　I need to have a better understanding of the orientation of China's future development.

Jiang Qi：　Do you still have doubts?

Edward：　Not exactly. I greatly admire the large number of foreign firms that have achieved great successes in China.

Hunter：　Mr. Edward wants to know more clearly about the new measures China is to take for the future.

Jiang Qi：　Oh, we will usher in the future with an even more open posture. We will take an active part in the global and regional economic and technological cooperation, develop vigorously bilateral and multilateral trade relations and speed up the diversification of markets.

Hunter：　This goes with the trend of globalization of the world economy.

Edward：　The world is becoming smaller and smaller. People from different countries can overcome their own weak points by learning from each other's strong points through communication so as to achieve common development.

Jiang Qi：　The Chinese people are willing to make greater contributions towards this end.

(2) The Strategy of "Broadly Based Economy and Trade"

Edward：　Mr. Jiang, I am most interested in what you called "the all-round opening". Can you elaborate on it?

Jiang Qi：　You might know that before the opening up, China's foreign trade was simply the import and export of goods.

Hunter：　And the volume seemed to be quite small too.

Jiang Qi：　We ranked the 32nd in world trade then.

Edward：　It does not match the status of such a large country as China.

Jiang Qi. ：　More importantly, it hindered the communication and cooperation between China and other countries of the world, and restricted the development of China's national economy.

Edward：　So you are going in for an "all-round opening"?

Jiang Qi：　That's right. The first thing we do is to change old modes of thinking thoroughly and go in for "broadly based economy and trade".

Edward: How broad?

Jiang Qi: Oh, what we mean by "broadly based economy and trade" refers to import and export trade in goods, import and export trade of technologies, and international trade in services.

Edward: This means that China will shift from trade in goods only to an all-round communication and cooperation with various countries of the world.

Hunter: Not "will". China has already done that, and have achieved rapid developments in the past few years.

Edward: Such all-round opening is most attractive to large multinational groups like ours.

Jiang Qi: This is only the opening in the aspect of trade. Our "all-round opening" also includes the regional opening and the active and effective introduction and utilization of foreign investment. Apart from "introducing in", we also "go out", in order to vigorously open up the domestic and the international markets so as to realize two-way communication and cooperation.

Edward: That's all-round opening in its true sense. May I ask which regions have been opened to the outside world?

Jiang Qi: The open areas have been extended from special economic zones and the coastal open cities to such inland areas as those along the borders and the rivers, and provincial capitals.

Hunter: China is actively leading foreign capital to the middle and western parts of China.

Jiang Qi: In a word, we have formed a pattern of opening up, which is all-round, multi-level and multi-channel in character.

Edward: This is really exciting.

Hunter: There is a Chinese saying that goes: The sea is wide enough for all fish to leap and the sky is high enough for all birds to fly. It is up to you now, Mr. Edward.

Edward: You just wait and see.

Lesson 22
TECHNOLOGY TRADE

(1) The Business of Technology Trade

Edward: Mr. Jiang, I'd like to consult you on some questions concerning technology trade today.

Jiang Qi: Please don't stand on ceremony. Let's discuss together.

Edward: Can you give me a brief introduction to the situation of technology trade in your country?

Jiang Qi: Technology trade only accounted for a very small proportion of China's foreign trade before the reform and opening up to the outside world.

Hunter: So there was an opinion that China's foreign trade at that time was solely in the form of import and export trade.

Jiang Qi: There is a grain of truth in it.

Edward: Then, China's technology trade only got developed since its reform and opening up, right?

Jiang Qi: That's right. Particularly, China's trade in technology export only got started in the 1980s. After 20 years' development, it was expanded to over 100 countries and regions.

Edward: It has been developing at an astonishing speed.

Jiang Qi: China's technology trade started from a low level, and there is a big difference between what China has achieved and that of the developed countries. So it has a great potential.

Edward: Despite all that, there has been an amazing progress after all.

Jiang Qi: In recent years, our country has made great efforts to adjust the structure of the export products, having gradually realized the shift from the resource-intensive to the labor-intensive and then to the technology-intensive type. We have gained some advantages in technology trade in the international market.

Hunter: I know that China's technology trade is quite competitive in terms of hardware trade as well as software trade.

Edward: Can you say it again? I didn't quite understand the meaning of this sentence.

Hunter: Oh, software trade refers to the buying and selling of knowledge and hardware trade refers to the buying and selling of complete sets of machinery and equipment.

Jiang Qi: To put it more concretely, it includes license trade, technical consultancy, training of professional personnel, engineering design, installation and commissioning of equipment, trade in complete sets of equipment and transfer of patented and exclusively-owned technology.

Edward: Does China have advantage in all these respects?

Jiang Qi: Yes, we have exported such software technology as crossbreeding of rice to Japan, Germany and some other developing countries. And a considerable scale has been attained in trade in complete sets of equipment and knowledge in such fields as mechanical and electrical equipment, petrol-chemistry, cement, building materials, communications, shipbuilding, and aviation and aeronautics.

Hunter: The time has gone when China had to rely on its export of agricultural products, raw materials, and low value-added goods.

Edward: I am very glad to hear that. I believe that we will become the closest partners in technology trade and cooperation.

(2) Contract Negotiation in Technology Trade

Edward: Mr. Jiang, you know that technology trade is a compensated transfer of technology, and in technology trade negotiations, the contract price is often a knotty problem.

Jiang Qi: Yes, technology trade involves a transfer of knowledge, wisdom and spirit. The negotiating partners often have difficulty in reaching a common understanding as to the evaluation of these intangible assets.

Hunter: For ordinary trade in goods, determination of the price is comparatively easy as there is a relatively stable market price and comparison with similar goods. As for knowledge products, they are usually intangible. How should the price be set then?

Jiang Qi: This, to a large extent, depends on the will of the transferring party and that of the recipient and thus is rather indeterminate.

Edward: Mr. Jiang, a patent technology involves a formidable process from its development to its production and operation, which requires large amounts of labor and funds. The fee for technology transfer should be a reasonable compensation for these inputs.

Jiang Qi: But there are great differences between the costs for the technologies developed under different conditions and by utilizing different means of R & D. They can hardly be taken as the basis for negotiation.

Edward: But the "different conditions and different means" you referred to were achieved only after previous input and did not drop from heaven. They justify compensation as well.

Jiang Qi: Apart from the special technology that is developed at the request of the recipient, other transferred technologies have been realized in the process of producing the products of the transferring party, and the R & D expenses have been included in the production cost and recovered or apportioned in the sale of the products.

Hunter: Mr. Jiang, do you mean to say that such technologies should be transferred free?

Jiang Qi: Of course not. I only said that the transferring fee thus calculated couldn't be taken as the basis for negotiation.

Edward: What's your brilliant idea then?

Jiang Qi: It may not be brilliant, but I think that a more reasonable and easy to handle method is for the transferring party and the recipient to share the extra profit made after the utilization of the technology.

Edward: That is another method for calculation, but it is troublesome to check the extra profit and so it is difficult to practice.

Jiang Qi: Therefore, the method often used is to take the sales volume of the products produced by using the technology concerned as the basis for the calculation of the fee for the transfer of technology.

Edward: Good. We can have an in-depth study of this method in our future negotiations on technical trade.

Hunter: Has China adopted some special methods concerning other terms and conditions that are essential in a technology trade contract?

Jiang Qi: Of course. And we are concerned about some other issues too.

Edward: Such as ...

Jiang Qi: Such as the clause about the definition of key terms, the clause about the scope of licensing agreement, and clauses concerning the improvement and development of the technology, technical information and security, technology service and assistance.

Hunter: Yes, concerning these clauses, the two parties involved in the technology transfer may have discrepancies in the legal aspect and in their interpretation.

Edward: As long as both sides have the sincerity, these discrepancies can be removed.

Jiang Qi: We do have the sincerity and the patience as well.

Edward: That's great. I am expecting a successful cooperation.

Lesson 23
SERVICE TRADE

(1) New Concept and New Field

Edward: Mr. Jiang, today I would like to acquaint myself with service trade in your country.

Jiang Qi: Oh, that is also a topic I'm interested in.

Edward: As far as I know that your country has great advantages in sea transportation and tourism. But many service trades such as telecommunication, finance, insurance, I'm afraid, are still new domains and new subjects for your country.

Jiang Qi: You are right, but not completely.

Edward: What do you mean?

Jiang Qi: Sea transportation and tourism are China's advantaged industries. But our international competitiveness in such service trades as telecommunication, finance, insurance, is rather low. That is what you are right about.

Edward: Then what am I wrong about?

Jiang Qi: The international service trade of our country is now being upgraded. All modern service trade forms are not new subjects for us. Moreover, our country's modern service trade has made great progress in recent years.

Edward: Nowadays, international service trade of developed countries accounts for 75% of the total volume of import and export in global service trade. Service trade has become the pillar industry of national economy and an important measure to balance international income and expenditure. What is the status quo of your country?

Jiang Qi: We know that there is a big gap between us and developed countries in service industry. The export of service industry of our country accounts for only 9% of the total volume of export trade, noticeably lower than the world average level 19%. Our service trade has a nearly 10 billion US dollars deficit.

Edward: Of course it is understandable. Everything has to run its course.

Hunter: Actually, China is a country which attaches great importance to business service. We can see the slogan "customers first, service foremost" everywhere in China.

Jiang Qi: It is true. But traditional service industry takes the forms of household and individual service, while modern international service trade is a newly-emerging industry based on modern scientific and technological development and industry upgrade.

Edward: You are right. According to the definition in *General Agreement on Trade in Services*, trade in services almost covers all fields except direct trade in goods.

Jiang Qi: Exactly. Such as telecommunication, finance, insurance, architecture, computer and information service. Moreover, services like satellite navigation, E-commerce, E-bank and E-currency, not only increase service efficiency and quality, but also the value-added rate of service.

Hunter: Service trade has become a new growing point of each country's economy, and a new engine driving the global economic development.

Jiang Qi: We have adopted the concept of service trade. Chinese government has made opening up the market of service trade one of the basic national policies. We are building a novel industry which is competitive in international trade.

Edward: So excited to hear that! What measures has the Chinese government adopted?

Jiang Qi: Shall we talk about it after a break?

(2) New Challenges and New Opportunities

Jiang Qi: Mr. Edward asked me just now about what measures the Chinese government would take, and I can assure you that China is opening up its market for service trade step by step and in a planned way.

Edward: Could you give more details?

Jiang Qi: While our domestic service trade is developing fast, the scope of our international service trade is being expanded step by step.

Hunter: China has advantages in many aspects of service trade, such as supplementary services to trade in goods (transportation and international clearing), international tourism, contracting foreign projects and labor cooperation, etc.

Jiang Qi: Oh, we can only say that we are narrowing the gap in these aspects.

Hunter: The annual growth rate of China's service trade is more than 15%, not only higher than that of its national economy, but also higher than that of the world's service trade. Mr. Jiang, you are too modest.

Jiang Qi: I am not being modest. There is still great potential in our traditional service trade, many more newly-emerging industries have just got started, and there are still blanks in certain industries.

Edward: That is not your problem. The world's trade in services takes hi-tech as its foundation. Science and technology develop with each passing day, and some service trades are being separated from manufacturing continuously. Every country has blanks.

Jiang Qi: And that's exactly the reason why we have a strong sense of crisis.

Hunter: But let me quote a popular saying in China: Challenges coexist with opportunities.

Jiang Qi: Challenges in this respect are extremely severe. You know that towards the end of the 20th century, the WTO signed two documents on services in telecommunications and IT.

Edward: Yes, and that means the countries which signed the above-mentioned documents account for more than 90% of the market in IT products and telecommunications.

Jiang Qi: And the liberalization of service trade in this area requires the formulation of a global standard for computers and telecommunications. Can you imagine China being excluded? What other choices does China have?

Hunter: I'll quote another Chinese saying: Meet the challenges and grasp the development opportunities.

Jiang Qi: That's our only choice. In the negotiation of China's accession to the WTO, we made commitments in other domains including scores of areas such as finance, insurance, and retail trade.

Edward: Which means that your country will open up service trade in these areas?

Jiang Qi: We have already done that. There already have been joint-ventured foreign trade companies, branches of foreign banks which have been authorized to deal in RMB business, and foreign-invested outlets of retailing chain stores established in China. Steps of opening have been taken in such areas as tourism, civil aviation, accounting and legal counseling, etc.

Edward: Oh, that's a very good opportunity for us as well. We hope that China can realize full liberalization of trade in services.

Jiang Qi: The control and protection of trade in services mainly rely on domestic policies and regulations. They cannot depend on tariffs or other measures along the border as in the case of trade in goods. Therefore, a great deal remains to be done in national treatment, market access, transparency, and the collection of statistical data and other information. China's opening up in service trade can only proceed step by step.

Edward: We can understand that.

Lesson 24
PROJECT CONTRACTING AND LABOR COOPERATION

(1) Boundless Commercial Opportunities

Edward: I am lucky that I have the opportunity to attend this grand international conference.

Jiang Qi: I have benefited a great deal from this international conference on project contracting which is attended by representatives from hundreds of enterprises in more than 20 countries who gather together under the same roof to have a thorough study on many questions.

Hunter: Project contracting and labor cooperation is a comprehensive kind of service trade, which involves broad areas and is a really promising industry.

Jiang Qi: That's true. It not only earns foreign exchange by direct export of labor, but also leads to export of large quantities of goods, technologies and complete sets of equipment.

Edward: And more importantly the export of services involving high intellectual ability.

Jiang Qi: It is a major trend in the development of international trade for the center of gravity to move from the export of goods to the export of capital, intellectual ability and technology. One of its marked characteristics is the unprecedented flourish of project contracting and labor cooperation.

Hunter: Which implies boundless commercial opportunities.

Jiang Qi: But opportunities here also coexist with challenges.

Edward: I have noticed that the involvement of the developing countries is altering the market pattern of international project contracting and labor cooperation.

Hunter: They have cheap labor. So they have advantage in the competition for labor-intensive projects, especially in those developing countries where extremely high technology is not required.

Edward: Advantage is not an accurate term as they already constitute no small threats to the contractors in the developed countries, and have brought the profit margin down to a great extent in project contracting.

Jiang Qi: But the developed countries still have absolute advantage in funds and technology.

Edward: That is a fact too. Therefore, most of them would only like to be responsible for the project design, counseling, technical instruction, monitoring, supervision and the supply of equipment, and are more than willing to contract out the civil engineering and the labor service related to it.

Hunter: Just because the profit margin for such kinds of services involving high intelligence is tens or even hundreds of times that of normal labor service.

Jiang Qi: Especially at present when there are increasing numbers of comprehensive, extra-large projects demanding high technology. The gap and inequality in competition between the developing and the developed countries are all the more obvious.

Hunter: That's true. The contract value for such projects as airport, harbor, industrial city, nuclear power plant, highway and large-scale reservoir is usually in the billions.

Jiang Qi: At present, the situation in which developed countries are monopolizing such projects remains unchanged basically. But the monopoly is being broken. Out of the fierce competition, a new pattern is taking shape in the division of labor and cooperation between the developing and the developed countries.

Hunter: I think that is an encouraging change.

Edward: Both the developed and the developing countries can bring into playing their respective advantages.

Jiang Qi: Mr. Edward, you are not afraid that your business is being taken away, are you?

Edward: Ha ha, meals and business can be shared alike.

(2) The Market of Project Contracting and Labor Cooperation

Edward: Mr. Jiang, can you talk about project contracting and labor cooperation in China?

Jiang Qi: Our foreign project contracting and labor cooperation is developing rapidly, undergoing a shift from dispatching mainly construction workers to sending out technical personnel who are engaged in services involving high intellectual ability. We are competitive in such areas as construction, ocean transportation, satellite launch, and computer software, etc.

Edward: Oh, how amazing! What about China's market for labor service, then?

Jiang Qi: China has a most brisk market for labor service that is the richest in labor resources.

Hunter: I think that the quality of Chinese engineers, technicians and workers are among the best in the world. They love their work, have good abilities and are proficient in their skills. Foreign-invested companies in China are happy to employ them.

Edward: Do foreign contracting firms have good business opportunities in China?

Jiang Qi: Just as the market for goods, the Chinese market for project contracting has extremely broad prospects.

Hunter: The Xiaolangdi water conservancy project on the Yellow River that attracts the world's attention is contracted by Germany, France and Italy. Taking part in the design and construction are high-level technical and management personnel from various countries. The contract value reaches 1.1 billion US dollars.

Edward: Oh, that's a wonderful business.

Jiang Qi: China has opened its gate, and Chinese contractors are entering different countries all over the world. China also provides ample opportunities for foreign contractors. That's what we mean by complementing each other with their own advantages and being reciprocal.

Hunter: So far as I know, just take the building industry as an example, famous architect companies from the United States, France, Japan, South Korea, Malaysia etc. have all contracted projects in China.

Jiang Qi: Infrastructure is still a weak link in China and on its vast expanse of land many major projects that are vital to the country's sustained development are waiting to be constructed.

Hunter: China has invited public bidding internationally for many projects, and they have attracted numerous bidders from abroad.

Jiang Qi: There has been fierce competition.

Edward: We are not afraid of open and fair competition.

Hunter: In project contracting, it is not infrequent that the firms giving out contracts for projects have "black-box handling" or do it in other rule-violating ways.

Edward: It is not uncommon that contractors engage in improper conducts, go against the rules or laws to subcontract or transfer the contract for many times.

Jiang Qi: All this may lead to unimaginable consequence or hidden danger. Therefore, we must first oppose such conducts and secondly ban them resolutely.

Edward: I hope China will have a very good environment for competition.

Hunter: There is recently a big project in Beijing inviting bidding. Does Mr. Edward have the interest to join in?

Edward: Oh, I am quite willing to join in the fun, to have a look at the scene of competition in tendering.

Lesson 25
PROCESSING TRADE

(1) Forms of Processing Trade

Edward: Mr. Jiang, I'd like to know something about processing trade in your country.

Jiang Qi: Mr. Edward, so you are interested in processing trade?

Hunter: Ha, not just interested, we can say that's the only thing he is in love with. This is one of the main reasons why he is in China this time.

Jiang Qi: That's good. We have many opportunities of cooperation in this respect.

Edward: I hope so. Then what is the situation of processing trade in your country?

Jiang Qi: It is one of the important forms of trade in services. It already accounts for half of our country's foreign trade.

Edward: What does that mean?

Jiang Qi: I was saying that the total value of import and export of our processing trade already accounts for more than half of the total value of the country's import and export of goods.

Edward: Oh, that is beneficial both to China and to foreign countries.

Hunter: The high wages and high level of energy consumption in our country lead to high production costs, which have weakened our relative competitiveness on the market.

Edward: Therefore, many large firms in the world have established their processing bases abroad.

Jiang Qi: That's true. The most typical among them may be Nike. Every pair of the world-famous Nike shoes are produced abroad.

Hunter: That's an example we can learn from. Processing trade has brought handsome profits to both sides.

Edward: To be frank, China has a broad labor market with skilled workers at low wages, and it is the most ideal place in the world for processing trade.

Jiang Qi: By developing processing trade, we can increase job opportunities, learn advanced production technology and management experiences, and promote the sale of some supplementary materials. We would be only too glad to go with it.

Edward: Then, Mr. Jiang, could you tell me about the forms of processing trade in China?

Jiang Qi: There are mainly three forms, namely, processing with materials provided, processing with materials imported, and assembling with parts provided.

Edward: What are the obligations on your side?

Jiang Qi: According to the contract signed by the two parties, to process the materials or supplementary materials provided by the foreign partner into finished goods, and send them to the foreign partner in order to be sold abroad.

Edward: How are the fees calculated then?

Jiang Qi: Processing fee is collected for processing with materials provided or imported. Processing and assembling fees are collected for assembling with parts provided.

Hunter: What if we request you to provide supplementary materials, or assemble parts and components?

Edward: The foreign party of course has to pay for the corresponding costs.

Jiang Qi: That goes without saying.

Edward: Mr. Jiang, if the goods made by processing with materials imported, for some reasons or other, cannot be sold abroad, either partly or totally, can they be turned into domestic sale?

Jiang Qi: Yes, but you have to make up for the customs duty for the imported materials and parts. If they belong to license-controlled goods, you have to submit your import license to the customs for inspection.

Edward: That is a flexible policy.

(2) Supervision on Processing Trade

Edward: Mr. Jiang, many countries in the world exercise regional control over processing trade. Is it the same with your country?

Jiang Qi: No, we practice an open model, and so it springs up all over the place. China's policy for processing trade and its management model is the least tight in the world.

Hunter: Mr. Edward, that is to say, you can find cooperative partners for processing trade everywhere in China.

Edward: That means I can have ample freedom in making choices.

Jiang Qi: The European and American countries have a mechanism of tax preservation. For the import of materials and the export of finished goods, they levy duties before giving drawbacks, or require guarantee by banks. We just have formalities for registration and cancellation after verification. We don't even practice the system of having a guarantee account set up at the bank counter.

Edward: Oh, that's really attractive.

Hunter: China has relatively few restrictions on the variety and quantity of processing trade.

Jiang Qi: At present, we only exercise a total quantity control over a few items such as wool, and cotton.

Edward: Such easy policies of China's are most beneficial to the development of processing trade.

Jiang Qi: In a word, our country provides many preferential policies in the respect of processing trade, which have created a very good environment for foreign businessmen.

Edward: That's true. But after hearing your entire introduction, I start to have some doubts. Are you not worried that processing trade will go out of your control?

Hunter:	Ha, there are always lawbreaking merchants. They want to avail themselves of loopholes in the policies even in their dreams.
Jiang Qi:	Even some law-abiding merchants hope that our control over processing trade is loose and lenient to the maximum.
Edward:	But there is a limit to everything. Even market economy has an intangible hand. The market will become chaotic without this hand, will it not?
Jiang Qi:	So we exercise strict control and supervision while adopting preferential and relaxed open policies.
Edward:	That goes without saying. How do you exercise supervision and control then?
Jiang Qi:	Take the completion and transfer in deep-processing for example. We insist on transfer to another factory only after the completion of customs formalities.
Hunter:	The parts and materials for processing are goods that require customs supervision. The customs can exercise effective control only by allowing transfer after the completion of customs formalities.
Jiang Qi:	But some enterprises want the transfer before the completion of customs formalities, and they act without obtaining approval from the customs. We regard such acts invariably as breaching the relevant regulations in our checking.
Edward:	Are there other problems?
Hunter:	So far as I know, as China does not exercise regional management, the worst problem is parts and materials entering the border but not the factory, and finished goods going out of the factory but not the border.
Edward:	Aren't these acts of evading tariffs, smuggling or trafficking in smuggled goods?
Jiang Qi:	What's more, some magnify the unit consumption in order to have larger figures of cancellation, or resell bonded parts, materials, or finished goods illegally. All this goes against the basic principles of processing trade.
Hunter:	China has a resolute attitude in strengthening the customs control and punishing smuggling severely.

Jiang Qi: Towards those law-breaking cases, we deal with them resolutely in accordance with the stipulations in our Customs Act concerning the penalty and the tracing back period.

Edward: Such measures can guarantee the normal economic order under the more lenient policies and they will win support and respect.

Jiang Qi: And that's the reason why China's processing trade has been able to develop very fast and make great achievements.

Lesson 26
OPENING OF RETAIL TRADE

(1) Strolling Around the Market

Hunter: Mr. Edward, we roamed from the east to the west and from the south to the north of the city, and have looked at seven to eight stores already. Shouldn't we have a rest now?

Edward: I heard that Good Luck Shopping Center does extremely good business. Let's go and have a look.

Hunter: There are over two hundred super stores in Beijing, each with a space of over 10,000 square meters. If you want to see all of them, do you think we can manage?

Edward: I guarantee that this would be the last one.

Hunter: You really are a workaholic. You have to invite me to dinner tonight so that we can relax.

Edward: No problem, let's go.

Hunter: Look, here is Good Luck Shopping Center. It is quite ordinary.

Edward: Didn't you say just now that it is a chain supermarket?

Hunter: Yes, it is similar to chain stores or warehouse stores in foreign countries, unlike walking into Scitech, Wangfujing, Oriental Plaza, or the International Trade Center, which is just like strolling in the first-class posh stores in the world.

Edward: But I would like to have a feel of a different kind of store.

Hunter: And that's the reason why you would like to see an ordinary supermarket like Good Luck Shopping Center?

Edward:	Being ordinary is exactly its special feature. It serves the ordinary people, with a complete range of goods at low prices. Look, there is a big parking lot outside, and there are shopping carts here. It seems that it is very convenient for ordinary people to shop here.
Hunter:	You sing its praise even before entering it. Let's go inside.
Edward:	O. K. Oh, it's spacious, with many customers too.
Hunter:	Do you want to make some purchases to test their management level?
Edward:	That won't be necessary. We are in the same trade. Look, open shelves, electronic means for the settling of accounts, very few attendants, and timely replenishment of the shelves. All these point to a smooth flow of goods and scientific management. It has attained a high-level of operation.
Hunter:	This is a real case in which laymen watch the fun while experts see the knack. Can we go back now?
Edward:	Not yet. I would like to have a chat with their general manager. After one day's visit, I have got many questions to ask.
Hunter:	Oh? We might as well do that so that we won't need to spend time to ask others.

(2) Retail Trade after the Ban Is Lifted

Ding Yibo:	I am sorry our general manager is not in today. Can I help you?
Hunter:	We are unexpected guests. We came without an appointment.
Edward:	We may have committed a breach of etiquette.
Ding Yibo :	Please don't stand on ceremony. What can I do for you?
Edward:	Today we have been wandering from one store to another, and we wish to consult you on a few questions.
Ding Yibo:	Consult me? I am overwhelmed. I'll try my best.
Edward:	Can you talk a little bit about the development of retail trade in your country?
Ding Yibo:	Like the retail trade in the world, ours has also taken three big steps.
Hunter:	That is to say, it has gone through department stores and supermarkets, and is now going towards chain management.
Ding Yibo:	Yes, we have realized the transfer from retail trade being organized

by lines to being organized by business styles.

Hunter: In the early days, retail shops were established according to product lines, such as green grocery, cloth shop, grain and oil shop, grocery, etc.

Edward: Retail shops being divided according to product line was the outcome of an immature market economy which was characterized as the seller's market.

Ding Yibo: China's retail trade before reform and opening up was like that. Now things have changed a great deal.

Edward: This we have noticed. Today we have visited many different types of stores.

Ding Yibo: What I mean by retail trade being organized by business styles is that the market is divided and the retail enterprises and stores are set up according to consumers and consumer groups of different social strata. Therefore, apart from large-scale posh department stores, there are also stores of various styles, such as ordinary, warehouse-style supermarket, chain stores, convenience shops, ten-yuan shops, staple food kitchen, etc.

Hunter: So today we have seen a scene of prosperity in the retail trade.

Edward: What has brought about such tremendous changes in the retail trade of your country?

Hunter: Of course it is the result of reform and opening up.

Ding Yibo: That's right. At the beginning stage of reform and opening up, retail trade in China could be regarded as a forbidden zone, which did not allow foreign capital to enter.

Edward: Mr. Ding, do you mean to say that the ban has been lifted now?

Ding Yilo: Yes, the ban has been lifted, and the scope for opening is being expanded gradually.

Edward: Can you be a bit more specific?

Ding Yibo: Now there are joint-venture retail enterprises approved of by the State Council, or by the local governments, and foreign invested retail enterprises in such forms as through leasing, invitation of foreign investment by real estate developers, or special shops affiliated to hotels.

Hunter:	I know that super transnational chain stores such as Walmart from the United States, Carrefour from France, Metro from Germany and Makro from Holland have entered China.
Ding Yibo:	They are backed up by abundant funds, and have squeezed into China's retail market by adopting the strategy of low prices, which has constituted a strong charge at China's retail trade.
Edward:	Are you not worried about opening up your retail trade in this way?
Ding Yibo:	We regard it as a kind of competition and stimulation.
Edward:	May I take the liberty of asking you the following question? It is said that there are now nearly 100 huge posh stores in Beijing each exceeding 10,000 square meters, and the same number of stores of similar sizes are under construction. Does China have such high consumption demand and power?
Hunter:	According to some relevant materials, Beijing's consumption power is one eighth of that of Tokyo or New York City, but the number of high grade stores in Beijing is eight times as many as that in each of these two cities.
Edward:	If the domestic demand is slack due to the impact of world's financial crisis, what will be the situation of competition like in the retail trade?
Ding Yibo:	That's a good question. The key issue is to continuously expand the domestic demand. A great domestic demand will make life easy for everybody, and there won't be vicious competition among retailers by drastically slashing their prices, is that right?
Edward:	It seems that you are fully confident about your opening in the retail trade.
Ding Yiho:	We strengthen macro-control and encourage famous international commercial conglomerates to enter our domestic market on the one hand, and at the same time enhance the ability of our retail enterprises to compete with foreign enterprises so that we can join efforts to develop China's retail market. Such being the case, should we still have any doubts about the future?

Lesson 27
FIFTEENTH OF MARCH

(1) Whose Festival

Hunter: Mr. Edward, what day is today?

Edward: What day? It is quite an ordinary day.

Hunter: No, today is quite special. What do you say is the date today?

Edward: March 15th. Oh, I remember, today is the World Consumer Rights Day.

Hunter: That's right. Look at both sides of the street. They are fully decorated with color flags and banners with slogans on them. And there are drums and gongs, singers and dancers.

Edward: That's true, just like a festival. March 15th here is a lot more fun than in our country.

Hunter: But it was first initiated by President Kennedy.

Edward: I remember that when delivering his State of the Union Address on March 15th, 1962, he first put forward the idea that consumers should have the four basic rights of safety guarantee, free choice, obtaining information and expressing opinions.

Hunter: Later he added one more, which is that consumers are entitled to indemnification.

Edward: In 1983, Consumers International designated March 15th every year as International Consumers' Day.

Hunter: It seems that China attaches more importance to this day than any other country.

Edward: How do you know?

Hunter: Every year on this day, China publicizes in a big way the rights of the consumers. The Central TV Station and local TV stations hold special performances with "March 15th" as the theme. Counseling is provided everywhere on the streets. It can be said that March 15th has become a national holiday in China.

Edward: I didn't expect that China would attach so much importance to consumer rights.

Hunter: The Chinese authorities have made the Law for the Protection of

Consumer Rights, which is being resolutely implemented.

Edward: How resolute? Can you elaborate?

Hunter: I'll give you an example. There are often shoddy goods being sold in stores, is that right?

Edward: Yes, there are lawbreaking merchants everywhere.

Hunter: In China, there are people specialized in fighting against shoddy goods. They go to stores to buy shoddy goods and then make complaints to the Consumers' Association or even bring the matter to court.

Edward: What is the purpose then?

Hunter: To teach those lawbreaking merchants a lesson, and to protect consumer rights.

Edward: Can he achieve his goal?

Hunter: He has in his hand the Law for the Protection of Consumer Rights as his weapon, and so he can always win support from departments concerned in China. They are being referred to as "heroes combating shoddy goods".

Edward: It sounds novel to me.

Hunter: Look, on-the-spot counseling is provided in front of that store. Let's go and have a chat with the people there and we can hear more novel things.

Edward: Good. Let's go.

(2) March 15th Counseling on the Street

Edward: Are you here for on-the-spot counseling, Miss?

Fangfang: Yes, I bought an on-sale dress from a store, and discovered that it had quality problems after I went home. I went to ask for a return, but the store said that there was no refund for discount goods.

Edward: Was the dress expensive?

Fangfang: No, and therefore my mother told me to let it pass, saying: "Why were you so eager to get things on the cheap?"

Edward: But you did not listen to her and came here.

Fangfang: That's right. I want to take it seriously with the store and have it straightened up.

239

Edward:	Have you had your counseling and what did they say?
Fangfang:	A gentleman from the State Bureau of Quality and Technology Supervision told me that discount goods are not the same as shop-worn goods sold at reduced prices. According to the law of product quality, same as for other goods, when there is a quality problem, the store should be responsible for repair, change, or refund, and there should be no less after-sale service.
Edward:	Oh, fantastic. Miss, I congratulate you on getting things straightened up.
Fangfang:	Thank you. But I still have to talk to that store.
Edward:	And they should have nothing more to say.
Fangfang:	Not necessarily. They always have excuses and ways to deal with you.
Hunter:	And what would you do then?
Fangfang:	It is nothing but throwing in more time and energy. If they don't pay attention, I'll find some news media to have the matter exposed.
Hunter:	What if they are not afraid?
Fangfang:	If that doesn't work, I'll go to the Consumers' Association or take the matter to court.
Edward:	Oh, Miss, I really admire your spirit of never giving up until you reach your goal.
Fangfang:	Thank you, I'll have to go. Good-bye.
Edward:	Sir, you are from the Municipal Consumers' Association. May I ask you a couple of questions?
Wu Kaiji:	Most welcome! What are your questions then?
Edward:	Do you do this kind of on-the-spot counseling on March 15th every year?
Wu Kaiji:	Yes, but there is a different theme each year.
Edward:	What's the theme for March 15th this year then?
Hunter:	Is it what's written on the banner, "Safe and Healthy Consumption"?
Wu Kaiji:	Yes, "Safe and Healthy Consumption".
Edward:	Are there big problems in this respect?
Wu Kaiji:	In consumption there are from time to time cases of damage to human body, health or property.

Edward:	Can you give me a couple of examples?
Wu Kaiji:	For instance, serious infection was caused to a lady after her using the cosmetics bought; gas poisoning or even death was caused by using a gas water heater; or one's dignity gets insulted and physical and mental health impaired by illegal body search when shopping at a supermarket, etc.
Edward:	Oh, these are serious cases. Don't consumers know how to protect themselves? Is your publicity campaign really necessary?
Wu Kaiji:	The majority can take the initiative to seek legal protection, but quite a few do not know how to seek protection after being harmed because they are not clear about the laws and regulations concerning indemnity request, and the safety period of a product.
Edward:	I have noticed that there are large numbers of smokers in China. Are there cases in which smokers suit tobacco producers?
Wu Kaiji:	Not yet. According to some authoritative statistics, only 10% of the victims make complaints after the harm is done in consumption.
Hunter:	Oh, that proportion is too small.
Wu Kaiji:	Some consumers swallow the insult and resign themselves to bad luck when they know perfectly well that the responsibility rests with the store, or even when they choke with resentment after being maltreated by the store because they are not confident enough about making complaints.
Edward:	Then, apart from such publicity campaign as you are doing, what is the real situation of resolving disputes and complaints in consumption?
Wu Kaiji:	Most of the complaints are satisfactorily and properly resolved. Each year we retrieve one to two billion *yuan* of the economic losses suffered by consumers.
Hunter:	That's no small success.
Wu Kaiji:	In certain areas, the complaint rate stays high, and some disputes remain unsolved because there was not enough evidence collected. We will continuously strengthen our publicity campaign and law enforcement.

Lesson 28
FINANCIAL SERVICES

（1）Touring Beijing's Financial Street

Hunter： Taxi!

Driver： Please get in. Where are you two going?

Hunter： Financial Street. Do you know Beijing's Financial Street?

Driver： How can I not know? I often take foreign friends there. They say that is China's "Wall Street".

Edward： Oh, China's "Wall Street"?

Driver： I don't know what the Wall Street in the United States looks like. But I know that this financial street is really imposing. The buildings there contend for beauty and height.

Edward： And you feel very proud of it, don't you?

Driver： Sure. That is a bright and beautiful scene in Beijing.

Hunter： Do you know why foreigners call it China's "Wall Street"?

Driver： Probably because of the number of banks there. The People's Bank of China, the Bank of China, the Industrial and Commercial Bank of China, the China Construction Bank, the China Bank of Communications, the People's Insurance Corporation of China, the China Securities Corporation. Anyway, the headquarters of national banks and non-bank financial institutions are all located on this street.

Edward： Please go faster. We can't wait to see this "Wall Street" in China.

Driver： That is a piece of treasure land. As a financial street, it might well have a longer history than the Wall Street in the United States.

Edward： Do you mean that the street was completed long ago?

Driver： No, the construction of the financial street you are going to see got started only in the early 1990's.

Hunter： Then you meant that it was China's financial center long ago?

Driver： That's right. As early as in the Ming and the Qing dynasties, that place was called "the Gold Street", which means "the financial street" in modern terms. Apart from the national "silver shops", big businessmen and rich families started to make their way and become rich there.

Hunter: There must be many stories about that place.

Driver: I can go on for three days and nights without stopping.

Edward: Then tell us one or two.

Driver: Ah, in those days, it was no other than some families being happy and others sad. Oh, here we are. I will tell you the stories next time when I take you.

Hunter: I like chatting with taxi drivers in Beijing. I get to know many things.

Driver: I like chatting with my customers too, especially foreign friends. They all want to know more about Beijing, and we should play good hosts.

Edward: Thank you very much. It is a nice experience to be in your cab.

Driver: You are welcome. If we have the luck, see you next time.

(2) A Visit to the People's Bank of China

Edward: Mr. Zhu, we have just visited the Financial Street. It was really magnificent.

Zhu B. S.: This is an area where the main business is that of the financial institutions. It has many types of financial markets such as stocks, securities, funds, gold, foreign exchange readjustment, financial mortgage, leasing, futures, etc., and law firms and accounting firms with financial characteristics.

Edward: It is a financial center worthy of its name.

Zhu B. S.: That's true. It will become a national center for financial management, financing and clearance, and an information center as well, which is characterized by its complete functions, advanced facilities, and complete auxiliary installations. It will gradually develop into an international financial center.

Hunter: Then financiers can feel the pulse of the rapidly developing Chinese economy, and watch the fast changing financial movements of the world.

Edward: At present, have foreign financial institutions come and set up their operations on the Financial Street?

Zhu B. S.: This place enjoys exceptional advantages, and a large number of foreign-invested operational and intermediary financial institutions have taken a fancy to this piece of treasure land.

Hunter： The Chinese government has continuously broadened its steps in opening the financial market and this suits their convenience.

Zhu B. S.： Yes, we are actively and steadily pushing forward with our opening of the financial market, and have removed the geographical restrictions for foreign-invested banks to set up their operational branches in China.

Edward： Were there such geographical restrictions before?

Hunter： At the beginning, foreign-invested financial institutions were only allowed in Beijing, Shanghai and Shenzhen.

Zhu B. S： Now the regions for foreign-invested banks to set up operational branches have been expanded from more than 20 cities including Beijing to all the key cities of the country.

Edward： Then, have the restrictions on the operational scope of foreign-invested banks in China been removed as well?

Zhu B. S.： That has to be done step by step. But some representative offices of foreign-invested banks in China have obtained permission to be upgraded to branches.

Edward： Do they include banks from the United States?

Hunter： Yes. The representative office of Chase Manhattan Bank in Beijing has been upgraded into a branch, and the Citibank has long been permitted to engage in interbank lending and borrowing.

Zhu B. S.： Since December, 2006, the branches of foreign banks in China can apply to convert into foreign legal-person banks registered in China to develop RMB business to citizens within the territory of China. RMB business has been completely opened to foreign-invested banks.

Hunter： Since April, 2007, some foreign-invested banks have completed such conversion and allowed to do business officially.

Zhu B. S.： Yes. The business scope of these banks is being rapidly expanded as well, from RMB savings, loans, short-term loans, house mortgage to guaranty, acceptance of bills, discount, financing large projects and deals in national bonds.

Edward： Oh, this opening situation is really fascinating. Such operations activate the capital flow, which will inject large amounts of funds into enterprises both domestic and foreign, bringing new opportunities for development.

Hunter: China has all along been implementing a steady monetary policy, keeping the RMB from depreciation and maintaining a low inflation rate, thus making a big contribution to the stability of the world's financial situation, which has won wide praises from all over the world. We are fully confident of the prospect of China's economic development.

Zhu B. S: Our macro-economy functions healthily, with a surplus in international payments, an abundant foreign exchange reserve, and the economy developing at a sustained high growth rate. With an even more open posture, we will attract more foreign entrepreneurs to make investments in China.

Edward: It goes without saying that further opening in the financial industry is included, right?

Zhu B. S: Yes. Of course, in order to prevent and eliminate financial risks, such opening can only be steady and carried out step by step.

Hunter: That's understandable. To put it in a Chinese saying: Hot gruel cannot be eaten without patience, and one cannot get fat on one mouthful.

Lesson 29
CAPITAL MARKET

(1) The Driving Force of Economic Growth

Edward: Mr. Zhu, we have just had a very good conversation. Now I have another question and I hope you will not spare your comments.

Zhu B. S. : Mr. Edward, you are being too polite. Let's discuss together.

Edward: Is there a fully liberalized capital market in China?

Zhu B. S. : Oh, I think that the so-called liberalization of capital is a relative concept. Even the degree of liberalization of capital in the United States is in a continuing process of development. Do you agree?

Edward: You are quite right in saying so, Mr. Zhu. Now, will you please talk about the capital market in your country?

Zhu B. S. : The capital market in our country is still in a process of being culti-vated and developed.

Hunter: China seems to have adopted a very cautious attitude towards the de-velopment of the capital market.

Zhu B. S. : We are both cautious and active. We are to build a liberalized capital market which is standardized, can be supervised and controlled, and has self-discipline.

Edward: That requires an extremely complete legal system and regulations of market games.

Hunter: I am afraid that is a headache for the entire world.

Zhu B. S. : Yes. Since mankind entered the 1990s, the international capital has been expanding rapidly. The quantity and speed of the capital flow has reached an unprecedented scale and market transactions are more brisk than ever before.

Hunter: According to some statistics, the capital financed by enterprises through capital markets in the world exceeds US $5 billion a day, and the daily transaction volume of foreign exchange markets and the flow of short-term funds is over US $10 trillion. Such huge amounts of funds and their flow are difficult for any country or any internation-al force to control.

Zhu B. S. : That's the reason behind the frequent occurrences of regional or glob-al financial crises. But countries in the world are not in a state of in-ertia.

Edward: As a matter of fact, each financial crisis is a lesson for everybody, and the legislation for the capital market becomes sounder.

Zhu B. S: This proves that we can accomplish something, and we have ways to prevent and resolve financial risks.

Hunter: It seems that Mr. Zhu is very optimistic about the liberalization of the capital market in China.

Zhu B. S: Because we have many excellent teachers.

Edward: Who are they?

Zhu B. S. : You.

Edward: We?

Zhu B. S. : Exactly. There is an old Chinese saying that goes: "Past experience, if not forgotten, is a guide for the future." Your capital market has had a history of over 200 years. How many experiences and lessons would you say are there in this course?

Hunter: Now I understand. China is extremely good at learning from other people's experiences and lessons.

Edward: Our image as teachers doesn't seem to be too good. Sometimes we may have set a bad example. That's what you call "teacher by negative example", is that right?

Zhu B. S. : Bad things can be turned into good ones. Experiences and lessons are both precious.

(2) A Capital Market That Is Both Loved and Hated

Edward: Mr. Zhu, what you said just now made me think a lot.

Zhu B. S. : Oh?

Edward: When you think carefully about the history and the present situation of the international capital market, it makes you love and hate it at the same time.

Zhu B. S. : How can my words give you such a thinking?

Edward: Just think about it. How many countries and how many people have got rich through the capital market? How can you not love it?

Hunter: But one financial crisis after another also made countless people go bankrupt and commit suicide, and put the economy of many countries into a hopeless situation.

Edward: And this makes people hate it.

Zhu B. S. : Your thoughts do make sense, Mr. Edward. But love and hate in the world is very complicated and it is very difficult to make clear.

Edward Oh? You seem to have a lot to say too.

Zhu B. S. Yes. I thought that you also noticed the present situation and the development trend of the international capital market.

Hunter On the international capital market, several currencies such as the US dollars, euros, and the Japanese yen, are still occupying the absolute dominant position.

Zhu B. S. The position of the US dollars is especially strong. Investors always prefer to buy assets valued in US dollars. On the international capital market, the demand for financial assets in US dollars is especially strong.

Edward: Your RMB will become a hard currency on the international market sooner or later.

Zhu B. S.: We have no doubt about that either, but it takes time. At the present, when developing countries are doing business or borrowing money abroad, they have to bear not only interest rate and exchange rate risks, but also the influence of the political and economic policies of a few countries.

Edward: That cannot be helped.

Zhu B. S.: That creates the actual inequality on the international capital market.

Hunter: Oh, now I understand. On the international capital market, some people are happy while some others are worried. It is really beyond a few words whether it is loved or hated.

Zhu B. S.: To be sure, we don't feel sad because of this, let alone pessimistic.

Hunter: The self-confidence and the ability China displayed and the role China played in the financial crisis towards the end of the 20th century swept away the global pessimistic atmosphere, which has remained fresh in people's memory until now.

Zhu B. S.: The international capital market, with its great momentum, does have its weak side. That financial crisis, which affected the entire world, taught us many things.

Edward: Many people became wiser after that catastrophe.

Zhu B. S.: The excessive speculation of a handful of people, especially the conduct of manipulating the market, often leads to violent shakes of the international capital market.

Hunter: In order to realize maximal profit, it is inevitable for a moderate degree of speculation to exist on the market.

Zhu B. S.: But it is also absolutely necessary to contain excessive speculation.

Edward: Yes, though the free flow of huge amounts of short-term funds without supervision and control makes the international capital market extremely brisk, the unbridled and vicious speculation of a handful of people is an important factor that leads to financial crisis.

Zhu B. S. : It is the developing countries that suffer the most. These countries are extremely short of construction funds and need to absorb large amounts of foreign capital. Once violent shakes occur on the capital market, the investment confidence is weakened and foreign capital is suddenly withdrawn. This would leave an impact that is unthinkably devastating.

Edward: You are right. The developing countries should strengthen their management, supervision and control of the free flow of short-term funds.

Zhu B. S. : Experience tells us that appropriate restriction on short-term investment, and encouragement of long-term investment, especially that on infrastructure, may effectively prevent and resolve financial risks.

Edward: The whole world has noticed that China has great potential in attracting foreign capital.

Zhu B. S. : We are actively cultivating and developing the capital market, expanding the market scope, introducing various financial instruments and derivatives, perfecting legislation and strengthening supervision and control, so as to guarantee the healthy operation of the capital market.

Edward: In that case, funds will flow into China in an endless stream from all over the world.

Lesson 30
MARKETS OF SECURITIES AND STOCKS

(1) Shareholders Talk about the Stock Market

Hunter: Hey, are you all here to exchange stocks?

SH. A. : We have come to play. (SH. = Shareholder)

Edward: Play?

Hunter: The common Chinese people call adventure "playing with one's life", and they call exchange of stocks "playing with stocks".

Edward: Oh, how interesting! But the stock market is no fun.

SH. B. It is fun! When the stock prices go up, the irresistible temptation excites you like crazy. When the prices drop, it makes you shiver with fright.

SH. A: How exciting! When many people dawdle the whole day away on the stock market, they are playing with this kind of heartbeat.

SH. C: This kind of people are money-burnt, and they have the experience of speculating in shares. Therefore they can play like that. I have neither the economic strength, nor the psychological capacity to stand strain.

Edward: You have just entered the stock market?

SH. C: Yes. I can't even tell what is a bull market and what is a bear market.

SH. B: Hey, a bull market is also called a long market, with the stock prices going up, and people in high spirits. A bear market is short-sellers' market, driving the stock prices down, resulting in a slack stock market.

SH. A: From now on, you can play with stocks by following me. When you see me look bullish, you just rush into the market and keep a full stock.

SH. B: When you see him wearing a bearish look, you should clear the stock by selling everything, and then flee.

SH. A: Please don't make such cutting remarks about me. But the feeling of slashing or jumping from the top of a building is no fun. As I have had such bitter experience, I have developed the psychological capacity to bear strain.

SH. C: You are a big player, and win or lose, you keep a poker face that does not change color and your heart never beats a bit faster. How can I follow you?

SH. B: To invest in the stock market, you get dividend and extra bonus, yielding a greater profit margin. When you see other people rake in large amounts of money, you cannot help casting covetous eyes at it, and pushing yourself into the stock market.

SH. C: Yes. Who can help feeling envious? Who would complain of having too much money? But the risks on the stock market are great, which scares me.

SH. A: In my opinion, risks go with the wind. Only when you follow the wind, will you have risks. If you follow the wind, you are bound to meet with risks.

Hunter: And that's your explanation of "risks"?

SH. A: Those who have newly entered the stock market lack the knowledge and experience about the market, and they easily follow blindly, buying in when prices go up, and selling when prices fall, resulting in either large amounts being tightly bound up, or themselves being smashed to pieces and their bones ground to powder. Are these not risks of following the wind blindly?

SH. C: Therefore, I'd better not act upon the happiness, anger, grief or joy of others. But how can we not follow the wind blindly?

Edward: There is a sculpture in the club of New York Stock Exchange, a bull and a bear fighting each other. From the front angle, it looks as if the bull has won over the polar bear. But from another angle, what you see is the polar bear giving a fatal blow to the bull.

Hunter: The stock market is just like that. There is no eternal bull market, nor eternal bear market. It is undergoing myriad changes from one to the other in the twinkling of an eye. That is the advice given to the stock-players by this sculpture.

SH. A: Therefore, to play with stocks is a branch of learning. One should not merely try one's luck, but have to rely on one's knowledge, to be good at analyzing the basic situation and future trend of the composite index, grasp at all times different indices, such as the Dow Jones industrial average, the Hang Seng index, the Shanghai index, the Shenzhen index and the index of China's Economic Daily. Only in this way, can one increase the probability of success.

Edward: A Wall Street stock exchange prophet once said that the stock market abides by the law of universal gravitation. It takes you two and a half hours to get to the top of the Imperial Tower by climbing the stairs one by one, but it only takes eight and a half seconds for you to get to the ground if you jump from the top.

SH. A: That's absolutely true. I now know that the frenzied speculation on the stock exchange, with the prices soaring and slumping, can turn a millionaire into a pauper overnight.

Edward: That is what economists refer to as "the tulip phenomenon". In the Netherlands, the price of tulip, which is the national flower, as a result of frenzied speculation, once went up by 5900% in a couple of years. But an avalanche overnight made the priceless tulip worth almost the same as an onion.

SH. A: So my secret of success lies in the correct choice of the timing of entering and withdrawing. When the stock prices keep going up violently, it is the time to sell. When the stock prices go down, the atmosphere is at a low ebb of a cycle, and the public opinion is generally pessimistic, in eight or nine cases out of ten there is going to be a bounce back. And it is the best time to buy in.

Edward: You sound like a skillful mature shareholder.

SH. A: You flatter me. Oh, the transaction has begun.

SH. B: Now the stock market is weird. The composite index keeps going down, and there is a lot of speculation on shares of firms that are losing money. The opening prices today for these shares are 53 points higher than the closing price yesterday. After I have completed this transaction, I'll also go to speculate on these junk shares.

SH. A: Excuse me, Sirs. I'll have to go to the chamber for big shareholders. Good-bye.

(2) Economists Talk about the Stock Market

Hunter: Mr. Yu, you are a renowned economist in China, and we wish to consult you on a few questions.

Edward: Could you please tell me what financial instruments there are in China?

Yu R. Z.: There are mainly three kinds, including bonds (State Treasury bond, financial bond, and corporate bond), stocks (A shares, B shares, and H shares), and funds.

Hunter: Are B shares those of Chinese enterprises listed within China but bought by foreigners?

Yu R. Z.: Yes, and H shares are those of Chinese enterprises listed in Hong Kong. The issuances of B shares and H shares have raised large amounts of foreign capital for the construction of key projects in our country. They also play an important role in the integration of China's securities market with the international capital market.

Edward: Apart from the three major types that you have just mentioned, are there futures, options, transferable corporate securities and other financial derivatives?

Yu R. Z.: The variety of our securities is increasing continually.

Edward: Who are the people that go to the Chinese securities market then?

Yu R. Z.: Basically the same as the structure of the international securities market, they include legal persons, institutions, stock salesmen, brokers, and natural persons.

Hunter: China is a country with a large population. If someone from every household is engaged in the speculation of shares, like the situation in the United States, how many shareholders will there be then?

Yu R. Z.: It can be calculated theoretically, but not practically.

Edward: In any case, China is always a big market, which the international capital looks upon with favor.

Yu R. Z.: China is a developing country and needs large amounts of construction funds. A healthy, orderly and safe securities market plays an important role in the optimal allocation of resources, the readjustment of economic structure, the accumulation of more social funds, and the promotion of national economy.

Hunter: The famous economist Keynes once said that the greatest and most exquisite invention during the several thousand years of human commercial civilization is stocks.

Yu R. Z.: Yes, its tremendous role in modern and contemporary world economy has given ample proof to this point.

Hunter: The frenzied expansion and fast flow of capital in modern and contemporary international capital market has injected immeasurable vitality into the development of the world economy, but it has also made the world economy more and more difficult to control.

Edward: Therefore, how to take precautions against and alleviate to the minimum the potential risks on the capital market is an important issue facing all countries in the world.

Yu R. Z.： Yes, China has promulgated a series of laws including the Law on Securities. The China Securities Regulatory Commission is effectively
exercising its functions, strengthening its supervision and control over
securities and futures, improving the market transparency and the
quality of information disclosure, taking precautions against and re-
moving risks, and safeguarding market stability and its healthy development.

Lesson 31
MARKET OF COMMERCIAL INSURANCE

（1）**The Difficult Start of Commercial Insurance**

Edward： Mr. Lu, how's your firm's business this year?

Lu Ming： Now competition is fierce in insurance, and business is difficult.

Hunter： I often see various insurance companies solicit clients on the street,
and it seems that business is OK with them.

Lu Ming： That's only a nice facade. As a matter of fact, that's just like the
barber's shoulder pole, only one end is warm.

Edward： What does that mean?

Lu Ming： The insurance companies are anxious to get clients, but the other side
does not have the enthusiasm yet.

Edward： Why not?

Lu Ming： That's hard to explain in a few words. I think the late start is an important factor.

Hunter： A late start is not necessarily bad, getting everything started from
scratch, with few competitors, lots of business opportunities, and a
large potential market.

Lu Ming： There are both advantages and disadvantages. You only mentioned
the advantageous side of it.

Hunter： What's the disadvantageous side then?

Lu Ming： I think the first thing lies in the insurance industry itself. For instance, the quality of the employees is generally speaking not high
enough.

Hunter: To work in the insurance industry requires not only experience, but also special knowledge. When the insurance companies are anxious to expand their business, it's hard for them to avoid such a conduct as eating whatever is available like a hungry person, hiring anyone available as their employee.

Lu Ming: This may imply many hidden hazards.

Edward: It is very difficult to explain the insurance terms clearly without special knowledge about the insurance industry. If the policy holder takes out an insurance policy in a daze, and could not get the full amount of compensation because of a violation of the notification obligation, it is hard to avoid disputes.

Lu Ming: That's true. Let's take the indemnity for the accidentally wounded or disabled for example. According to the insurance policy, there is a time limit for the policy holder to notify the insurance company and apply for compensation. If the insurer has not fulfilled his obligation of notification, disputes are hard to avoid between the insurance company, the policy holder, the insured and the beneficiary.

Hunter: If the damages are not paid in full, the insurance company will be given the bad name of a cheat.

Lu Ming: What is worse, some employees of insurance companies go so far as to solicit clients by hook or by crook.

Hunter: Be it white or black, a cat that catches rats is a good cat.

Lu Ming: But clients are not rats.

Hunter: Oh, I was joking. Customers are gods, and insurance companies should be their guardians.

Edward: To win over clients is the main business of insurance companies. In fierce competition, insurance companies encourage each employee to show his or her special prowess like the Eight Immortals crossing the sea. He who can win over clients is a good one.

Lu Ming: But he should not boast and talk big, making empty promises or promising impossible terms so as to misguide or cheat the clients to take out an insurance policy.

Edward: That is the most basic business ethics of a businessman. There should be a demarcation line between what is legal and what is illegal even when each shows his or her special prowess like the Eight Immortals crossing the sea.

Hunter: Unlawful conducts by businessmen can be found in all countries of the world. Some even go so far as to obtain cash by illegal means or do money laundry for the insured companies or persons, thus seriously disrupting the financial and insurance markets.

Lu Ming: That is a serious problem.

Edward: I think the poor quality of the employees is just one of the problems at the initial stage.

Lu Ming: Yes. The public still does not have a good understanding of commercial insurance and they lack the awareness of insurance. The high insurance premium is also a threshold that is difficult for the low-and middle-income social strata to step over. Difficulty in obtaining compensation after taking insurance leads to the public's distrust of insurance companies. All these are disadvantageous factors that restrict the development of commercial insurance.

Edward: However, China is a populous country, and insurance links every family. Foreign insurance companies are still very optimistic about the Chinese market.

(2) Commercial Insurance Is Getting Warmed Up

Lu Ming: Mr. Edward, since you just mentioned the concern of foreign insurance companies about the Chinese market, I have some new information for you.

Edward: Excellent!

Lu Ming: Along with the deepening of our reform and opening up, the scale of our insurance market is expanding continuously. As our opening is accelerated, the insurance industry is entering a period of rapid development.

Edward: Can you be a bit more specific?

Lu Ming: Do you have a good understanding of the traditional Chinese social security system?

Hunter: I know a little. All the medical expenses of staff and workers are reimbursed by the enterprise or the work unit. Expenses concerning birth, aging, sickness and death are all borne by the enterprise or work unit.

Edward: I see. In that case, does the public need commercial insurance?

Hunter: As staff and workers have welfare security from the state, they of course do not have the awareness of insurance, nor the need for commercial insurance.

Lu Ming: Things are different now. We are having a thorough reform of the old welfare systems, such as those in medical treatment, provision for the aged, and distribution of accommodation, so as to establish a social security system in the real sense.

Edward: Such reform measures will surely bring opportunities to the development of commercial insurance.

Hunter: In Japan, whose insurance revenue is among the world's top ten, the insurance rate of city and town residents is as high as 560 %; in the United States, it is 148 %; while in China it is only 5% at the present. As China possesses large amounts of material wealth and a large population, it has an insurance market that cannot be matched by Japan or the US.

Lu Ming: That's true. Just take pension funds as an example. Supposing that 4 hundred million people in China joined pension funds, and the average monthly pay-in per capita is 80 *yuan*, pension funds thus collected will amount to 400 billion *yuan* a year and the peak for payment will arrive only 20 years later. By that time, the accumulated pension funds will have surpassed 8 trillion *yuan*.

Edward: In the United States, pension funds have always been the biggest investors in the capital market. Such large amounts of pension funds have special significance for China, whose construction funds are relatively scarce.

Lu Ming: Apart from insurance to provide for aging, there is still property insurance, health insurance, insurance for the growing up of children, unemployment insurance, auto insurance, insurance against accidental disasters, etc. All the commercial insurance products have large potential markets, which are to be tapped in a big way.

Edward: That's an extremely attractive prospect. As insurance is a branch of international trade in services, what plan does China have in the opening up of its domestic insurance market?

Lu Ming: It is not just a "plan". Actually, insurance companies from the United States, Canada, Britain, and Japan have been permitted to enter the Chinese market, either in the form of solely foreign-invested companies, joint-stock companies, or Sino-foreign joint ventures.

Edward: What kind of business are these companies engaged in?

Lu Ming: Mainly in property insurance, life insurance, insurance against accidents, flood and fire insurance, insurance against accidental injury to air passengers, etc.

Hunter: So far as I know, the main targets of their service are foreigners and foreign enterprises.

Lu Ming: The opening of the insurance market to the outside world can only be done step by step. Nevertheless, you can see several thousand employees of American International Group, Inc. (AIG) active at Shanghai's street corners and lane ends dealing in life insurance and property insurance.

Edward: Such an opening situation in China is really encouraging.

Lu Ming: Now, a market structure is taking shape, in which Chinese state-owned commercial insurance companies are the main force, Chinese and foreign insurance companies coexist, and many insurance companies compete with each other.

Edward: Well begun is half done. China's insurance market will rank among the world's most advanced.

Lu Ming: We are quite sober. We got started late, have a weak basis, and lack experience. We are still short of veteran personnel, with only a small variety of coverage, and the intermediary role of the notaries and agents has not been fully developed. In a word, we still have a great deal to accomplish.

Edward: The ship has set sail. Would it be long before its triumphant arrival at the opposite shore?

Lesson 32
MARKET OF ENVIRONMENTAL PROTECTION INDUSTRY

(1) Awareness of Environmental Protection

Hunter: Oh, here we are.

Sun Y. M.: Welcome, Mr. Hunter and Mr. Edward.

Hunter: Sorry to have kept you waiting.

Sun Y. M.: It's all right. Dad, Mum, our guests are here.

Sun B. J.: Oh, welcome.

Ning X. L.: Come on in, please.

Hunter: Thank you.

Edward: Your courtyard is beautiful, filled with greenness and fragrant flowers.

Hunter: And birds humming as well. Oh, on this tree hangs a birdcage.

Sun Y. M.: That's my father's pet.

Sun B. J.: My pet is not a kitten or puppy, but a singing skylark.

Edward: Mr. Sun, your home isn't like one in a big city.

Sun Y. M.: My father likes flowers, plants and birds. Now that everybody talks about environmental protection and returning to nature, he is in higher spirits.

Sun B. J.: Humans have only one globe, which is our common home, the environment we live in. If we do not take care of it, who will?

Ning X. L.: It is a shame that there are still too many people who do not care for our homeland. They shoot wild animals as game, cut down trees in forests indiscriminately, and dump waste water and rubbish everywhere, with no awareness of environmental protection at all. They know to go to parks for physical exercises, but some of them use branches for boxing practice or use them as swings ....

Sun Y. M.: Those are minor things. Beijing alone discharges more than 2 million tons of industrial and domestic waste water a day. And over 90% of the sewage and waste water in the country are discharged into rivers, lakes, and seas, big or small. Out of the 532 main rivers in the country, 436 are polluted. The Bohai Sea, which faces Dalian and Tianjin, may become a dead and foul sea because of the industrial pollution from its periphery.

Hunter： Is the situation that serious?

Sun Y. M. ： That is not all. What is more, there is soil erosion, desertification of farmland and grasslands, air pollution in cities, garbage pollution, and "white pollution" caused by plastic wrappings and agricultural plastics, etc. According to the newspaper, the direct economic loss in China caused by pollution reaches 2 trillion *yuan* in 2006.

Edward： The situation is serious, but I am not shocked. After the world entered the era of industrialization, environmental pollution and damage is getting worse every day.

Hunter： The willful plunder and uncontrolled exploitation of natural resources have resulted in the rapid deterioration of ecological environment, and human beings have felt that a crisis in their own existence is drawing nearer day by day.

Sun B. J. ： Therefore, environment and development are common questions facing the whole mankind.

Hunter： What is encouraging is that there is an awakening of the awareness of environmental protection in the whole world.

Edward： Everybody has their responsibility in environmental protection, and governments and decision-makers of each country have an even more important and decisive role to play.

Sun B. J. ： That's right. Our government has drawn up a National Construction Plan for Ecological Environment, which makes the protection and construction of a good ecological environment and the realization of sustainable development a basic policy of our modernization drive. It has also promulgated a series of laws including the Forest Law, Law on Water and Soil Conservation, Law on the Protection of Wild Animals.

Sun Y. M. ： Ah, Mother Earth, I'll bring back to you the blue sky and white clouds, the green mountains and clear waters, the singing of birds and fragrance of flowers!

Edward： Oh, Miss Sun is a poet.

(2) A Morning Sun That Is Rising

Edward: Mr. Shi, we have noticed that the State Environmental Protection Bureau has exercised a recognition system for environmental protection products. Can you give us a briefing about it?

Shi Kaiji: Yes, but what in particular do you want to know?

Edward: For instance, why does your country exercise the recognition system for environmental protection products?

Shi Kaiji: You know that the environmental protection industry is developing fast. Now, the global market value of environmental protection products has reached US$600 billion, and a similar amount is going to be invested in this industry.

Edward: It has far surpassed such newly emerging industries as tourism and software.

Hunter: Just like a bright morning sun that is rising.

Shi Kaiji: Yes, it is a rising-sun industry with bright prospects. It is not only a new point of growth for the domestic economies of various countries, but also a new point of growth for international trade.

Edward: That's absolutely true. For instance, the "surge of green consumption" which is sweeping the world has led to a profound industrial revolution in various countries, having developed and cultivated many newly emerging industries.

Hunter: Just take the harnessing of pollution from the exhaust of motor-driven vehicles for example. The monitoring and survey of the exhaust need special meters and instruments. And it involves the development and use of solar energy and other new alternative energy resources, the R & D of electricity-driven vehicles, etc.

Shi Kaiji: For household appliances, we need computers and TVs that can shelter radioactivity and electromagnetic radiation, non-freon refrigeration technology that can protect the ozone layer, and low-noise washing machines that can sterilize and disinfect.

Hunter: Ha, if we go on to "green foods", their production, processing, packing, transportation, and storage, each and every link of them, would need the support from the environmental protection industry.

What's more, there is the recycling and utilization of rubbish, waste water, drainage, and waste and used solid matters.

Edward： Numerous newly emerging industries and service sectors have been and will continue to be derived from the environmental protection industry, which has also given impetus to the development of high-technologies of many disciplines.

Hunter： There is boundless prospect in their domain of development, application and potential market.

Shi Kaiji： Yes, to develop the environmental protection industry has become a fundamental strategy and important means for various countries in readjusting their economic structure, invigorating old industries, fostering newly emerging industries so as to realize a sustainable economic development.

Hunter： What is most attractive is that the environmental industry has brought along the rapid development of international trade in environmental protection products.

Edward： Ever since the day of its establishment, the WTO established a trade and environment committee. The international standardization organization has put forward the ISO14000 series of international standards for environmental control. With or without the green mark, the environment mark, and the ecological mark, and whether a product can pass through the ISO14000 attestation, has become or is becoming an important condition in international trade.

Shi Kaiji： As the environmental protection standards become more and more strict, some countries use environmental protection as an excuse to push their "green" trade protectionism, setting up new non-tariff barriers in international trade.

Edward： Trade disputes caused by environmental protection barriers constitute an important characteristic in international trade in recent years. This is probably the reason why China exercises a recognition system for the environmental protection products entering China from abroad.

Shi Kaiji： We should integrate with the outside world, and at the same time protect the interests of our consumers and develop our own environmental protection industry, shouldn't we?

Hunter: The vigorous development of the environmental protection industry and the trade in products therefrom have led to a new competitive situation.

Shi Kaiji: The development of the environmental protection industry is extremely uneven in the world. In countries where the environmental protection industry is more developed, the market for some environmental protection products is approaching saturation. Their environmental protection enterprises are marching into foreign markets, which constitutes a new challenge for the developing countries whose environmental protection industry is relatively underdeveloped.

Edward: To put it in your words, it is at the same time a new opportunity for development, right?

Shi Kaiji: Yes, and we will seize this opportunity of development as well.

Lesson 33
MARKET OF INFORMATION INDUSTRY

(1) **China's Silicon Valley**

Edward: Hunter, did you say that we are going to pay a visit to China's Silicon Valley?

Hunter: Yes, Miss Sun is a very good guide. You will enjoy it so much that you do not want to come back.

Sun Y. M.: That is a very special district.

Hunter: Didn't you feel strange when you heard the name of "Silicon Valley" in China?

Edward: I was wondering about it. We have a "Silicon Valley" in San Francisco in the US, but I did not know that there is also a place called "Silicon Valley" in Beijing.

Hunter: The original name of the "Silicon Valley" in San Francisco is Santa Clara. Do you know why people call it the "Silicon Valley"?

Edward:	Are you making fun of me on purpose or what? This is common sense, which is known even to a three-year old.
Hunter:	Out with it then.
Edward:	Everybody knows that the microelectronic industry of the United States is concentrated in that place, and the key material for the microelectronic industry is the silicon chip. So Santa Clara is also known as the "Silicon Valley".
Hunter:	Absolutely correct. 10 points to your credit.
Edward:	Are you giving an intelligence test?
Sun Y. M.:	As a matter of fact, the reason why the "Silicon Valley" has enjoyed a good reputation in the world is that it is the birthplace of the US information industry, a sacred place where US high-tech talents are gathered.
Edward:	Miss Sun has given a very good explanation. Are we going to visit a place like that now?
Hunter:	You got it right. It was originally a place in Beijing's Haidian District. Radiating from the center of Zhongguancun. Now it covers an area of 100 square kilometers where thousands of high-tech enterprises are gathered.
Edward:	It is the birthplace of China's information industry, and a place where high-tech talents are gathered, isn't it?
Hunter:	It fully deserves the name of "China's Silicon Valley".
Sun Y. M.:	The world-renowned Peking University, Qinghua University, Chinese People's University, and a dozen other institutions of higher learning, and the research institutes of high-tech and frontiers of science of the Chinese Academy of Sciences are all situated here.
Hunter:	This place has gathered numerous talented people, and its scientific research capabilities and achievements are no inferior to those of the Silicon Valley in the US.
Sun Y. M.:	Such newly emerging information industries as laser photolithography technology, large-scale integrated circuit, mainframe computer and software that are located here are either in the leading position or in step with developments in the world. Same as the Silicon Valley in the United States, the development of the information

industry in the Zhongguancun District has reflected the development orbit of the information industry of China.

Hunter: At first it was called the computer street, each facade on both sides of the street was a computer store.

Sun Y. M.: They also sold peripheral computer products such as software, printers, cables, etc. But in a word, they were small shops with a small shop front, most being commission agents for famous foreign brand computers.

Edward: Such being the case, it was no match for our Silicon Valley.

Sun Y. M.: Everything has a process of development. Now the situation is totally different.

Hunter: Modern buildings rise steeply from level ground one after another.

Sun Y. M.: What is more important, such large-scale information industry groups as Lenovo, and Founder, etc. have their own business and production base for their own brands.

Hunter: They have combined research, development, production and marketing into an organic whole.

Edward: Oh, have there been such great changes?

Sun Y. M.: Not only that. Microsoft from the United States has set up the headquarters of its China company here, and they are providing extremely favorable conditions to attract talented people, getting ready to compete with their Chinese counterparts.

Edward: As the saying goes, what you hear may be false, but what you see is true. Now I'd like to go and have a good look at China's Silicon Valley and see what it is like.

Hunter: I have experienced your seriousness. I am afraid that we'll make Miss Sun extremely tired.

(2) Ushering in the Information Era

Sun Y. M.: Mr. Edward, here is the PC department of the Lenovo Group. Please come on in.

He Y. L.: Welcome, welcome. Please take a seat.

Edward: Mr. He, Miss Sun is accompanying us on our visit today. She was full of praise of your company all the way, which ignited my boundless respect for your company.

He Y. L.： I am afraid that Miss Sun flattered us.

Hunter： The Lenovo Group is indeed the leading enterprise of China's information industry.

He Y. L.： The information industry has become the leading industry in the contemporary economy. In the world's process of advancing from the industrial era to the information era, such developed countries as the United States have taken the early opportunies and we have to accelerate the development of the electronic information industry so as to push forward the transformation of our national economy with information technology.

Sun Y. M.： In the global financial crisis at the end of the 20th century, some economic powers in the West lost their grandeur and momentum, with only the US economy being always vigorous without a decline. It is because it is supported by the information industry which has been developing vigorously.

Edward： Miss Sun put it well. Among the new job opportunities in the US, 37 % are provided by the information and its related industries.

He Y. L.： Not only that. First of all, the information industry itself is a product that is knowledge- and technology-intensive with a high value added. Both the manufacture of information equipment and the information services with the computer as the main platform such as the exploring, gathering, storing and transmitting of information resources can create tremendous economic benefit.

Sun Y. M： The value created in such IT products as the optical fiber, computer, multi-media, mobile communication, program-controlled exchange, satellite navigation, and TV reception accounts for a big proportion in the total income of the national economy.

He Y. L.： With the contribution from information products taken away, the US national economy would have had a negative growth.

Hunter： That's true. It is because the information industry can create such huge amounts of economic benefit that, on the US stock market, what is most sought after is hi-tech stocks and the stocks of the information industry are sold at the highest prices.

Sun Y. M. :　Enormous capital resources have made the electronic information industry the quickest in upgrading, updating and regenerating its products.

Edward:　Bill Gates once said that Microsoft was just 18 months away from bankruptcy. That indicates the fierce competition in the information industry.

He Y. L. :　Whoever has the most advanced technology has the market. The surge of digitalization has brought about a fundamental breakthrough in the information industry. Our times are accelerating the transition to digitalization characterized by networks and intellectual power.

Hunter:　At present, household electric appliances with IT are rising to prominence, from intelligence card to videophone, from portable palmtop to internet access at home . . . .

He Y. L. :　All aspects of daily life need some gadgets that are simple and convenient, such as a digital intelligent product that can make speech sounds, a module as small as a piece of chewing gum, or a box on top of the TV as small as the palm.

Hunter:　You can surf on the Internet in your kitchen or bedroom to see whether tickets are still available for the baseball game that very day or in which restaurant free wine can be obtained. When you come through the door, the TV or hi-fi recognizes you and starts playing your favorite music or show.

Sun Y. M. :　They sound like stories in *the Arabian Nights*!

Hunter:　Not at all. These products have already come out. A person who does not know computer at all can enjoy all this only by one touch, one click or simply picking up the telephone receiver.

He Y. L. :　Who can predict how many novel inventions the information industry will produce and how many vivid and colorful life dramas will be performed in the future!

Edward:　It is really hard to predict. But we are certain that it will not only enhance social economic prosperity unprecedentedly, but also change our life to a great extent.

Lesson 34

INTELLECTUAL PROPERTY RIGHTS AND FRANCHISE TRADE

（1）**Protection of Intellectual Property Rights**

Edward: Mr. He, the information era is based on knowledge and high technology, and intellectual property rights are the most important property rights of an enterprise, do you agree?

He Y. L.: Absolutely. Intellectual property rights form an intangible asset of an enterprise, and maybe a huge sum at that.

Sun Y. L.: According to the calculation of economists, the brand value of Coca Cola and Marlboro reaches 40 to 50 billion US dollars.

Hunter: The prerequisite is their protection. If fake goods that infringe others' rights flood the market and form a wide-ranging attack on the certified products, the losses thus caused will also be very considerable.

He Y. L.: That is the reason why in international trade, the protection of intellectual property rights has been taken more and more seriously, and often becomes the fuse that ignites trade wars.

Edward: Many small frictions occurred between our two countries concerning computer software, laser CD and VCDs.

Hunter: I still remember that the infringement on the 19 films made by eight film makers including the 20th Century Fox caused a lot of bubbling and gurgling.

Edward: What was that?

Hunter: Two stores copied and sold laser VCDs of those 19 films without obtaining the authorization from the copyright holders.

Sun Y. M.: Our government protected the lawful rights of the copyright holders in accordance with law. After careful investigation and hearing, the court pronounced that the plaintiff won the case, and the defendant should stop the infringement immediately and indemnify the plaintiff for economic losses.

He Y. L.: In the area of intellectual property rights, neither the infringement nor the protection is unilateral. Some of our famous brand products have also been infringed upon in your country. Mutual cooperation and understanding on the basis of equality and mutual benefit is necessary in the international arena.

Sun Y. M. : If one side uses the pretext that the other side has not protected intellectual property rights adequately to exercise trade retaliation, and the other side is forced to counteract, it is not just one side that suffers.

Edward: I think we have done our bit.

He Y. L. : Though our differences of opinion in the area of intellectual property rights have not been solved entirely, we have, through patient negotiations, signed a Memorandum of Understanding, and have eventually avoided trade wars more than once.

Sun Y. M. : We want peace and not trade wars.

Edward: Oh, I think we have promoted mutual understanding today.

Hunter: We can come to a common understanding in the area of the protection of intellectual property rights.

He Y. L. : Not just a common understanding. The legislation, administration of justice, and the actual achievements of our country in the protection of intellectual property rights are universally recognized.

Hunter: We have noticed this fact too.

(2) Agreements and Conventions on Intellectual Property Rights

Edward: When Miss Sun said, "we want peace" just now, you seemed to be shouting a slogan.

Sun Y. M. : That was not a slogan. That is our sincere hope. We don't want trade frictions. We want fair and proper competition based on equality and mutual benefit.

Edward: However, good wishes cannot replace reality. After all, clear ownership and regionalism characterize intellectual property rights. Infringement and anti-infringement are inevitable, independent of human will.

Hunter: Some people always drool with envy over some new technology and new products that have won the favor of customers. They make and sell fake goods without authorization, jeopardizing the interests of both customers and holders of the intellectual property rights.

He Y. L. : But this should not necessarily become the cause for trade frictions or wars. On the contrary, it should become the driving force to push forward the international cooperation in the area of intellectual property rights.

Sun Y. M. : And that's the fact as well. Didn' t the international multi-lateral conventions in the area of intellectual property rights come into being just because of this?

Edward : I admit that what the two of you said was right. But the level of protection provided by various countries is usually in conformity with the development level of their economy, science and technology.

Hunter : It is difficult for intellectual property rights of the developed countries to be protected in some countries.

Sun Y. M. : Each country has a different situation and so they have different positions. When opinions are different, the standards set are naturally different. And no country should impose its own will or standards on another.

He Y. L. : And so in the area of protecting intellectual property rights, not only are multi-lateral international conventions necessary, bilateral agreements between countries are also needed.

Edward : Then, what multi-lateral international conventions has your country signed?

He Y. L. : So far as I know, we have joined all the important ones. Our country is a member of WIPO and has successively signed *Paris Convention on the Protection of Industrial Property*, *Madrid Agreement for International Registration of Trade Marks*, *Bern Convention for the Protection of Literary and Artistic* Works, *Geneva Convention on Universal Copyright*, and *TRIPS* of the WTO, etc.

Hunter : China has indeed made remarkable progress.

He Y. L. : That's universally recognized. The international obligations we have undertaken in the protection of intellectual property rights have covered nearly all the fields such as patents, trademarks, computer software, specialized techniques, hi-tech, copyrights, and commercial secrets.

Sun Y. M. :   Our government has also signed memoranda on the protection of intellectual property rights with the United States, the European Union, Switzerland, and Japan, mutually promised to protect the lawful rights of natural and legal persons of the other party in accordance with their laws and with reference to international conventions.

Edward: I would also like to know about the situation in your country concerning law enforcement. If laws are not followed or their enforcement not strict, it will still give lawless persons opportunities that can be exploited.

He Y. L. :   Our attitude to the protection of intellectual property rights is determined, and the dynamics in law enforcement is being continuously strengthened. For intellectual property rights, our country has a leading body for coordination, such law-enforcing departments as the Industry and Commerce Administration, and judicial court within the People's Court for cases concerning intellectual property rights.

Sun Y. M. :   Once such infringement acts as pilferage, imitation or fraud are found, we will resolutely take over the goods, destroy them and stop such acts, and will give necessary civil or legal punishment.

He Y. L. :   The rights of Marlboro cigarettes and films made by Fox and other companies are forcefully protected in our country.

Edward: It seems that we have already had a firm basis to develop franchise trade in the area of intellectual property rights.

Sun Y. M. :   Convincing facts have proved that our country has got into the advanced ranks in the protection of intellectual property rights.

He Y. L: In the era of knowledge-based economy, franchise trade has become the most important and fundamental form in international trade. The mutual understanding and cooperation in the protection of intellectual property rights will surely and greatly promote the economic development of various countries in the world.

Lesson 35
DUMPING AND ANTIDUMPING

(1) **Regulating Improper Trade**

Edward: Mr. Shi, thank you very much for inviting me to this seminar on commercial laws.

Shi Kailai: You are welcome. Through discussion, we can enhance mutual understanding and iron out differences.

Hunter: Dumping and antidumping is really a very complicated question of law, but it is also a question that cannot be avoided.

Shi Kailai: To be frank, many human factors are involved here.

Edward: Of course, all things are done by humans.

Shi Kailai: That is not what I meant. For instance, subsidy and dumping are two unfair acts in trade which distort the conditions for competition. The antisubsidy and antidumping laws in international trade are for the regulation of these acts.

Edward: This aim allows of no doubt.

Shi Kailai: But in fact, there are plenty of people who abuse the antidumping law.

Hunter: That's what you meant by human factors.

Shi Kailai: That's right. You two know that dumping in international trade refers to the act of manufacturers or exporters of one country (region) who push into the market of another country (region) by selling at a lower price than that on the domestic market or the cost.

Edward: Such dumping at low prices causes significant losses to the related industry in the importing country.

Shi Kailai: And substantive damage as well.

Edward: Yes, or it constitutes threat of significant losses or severe hindrance to the establishment of this industry.

Shi Kailai: It has to be proved as well that there is a direct cause and effect relationship between the act of dumping and the substantive damage.

Edward: Yes, all these conditions are necessary to the determination of dumping.

Shi Kailai: The complete process of dumping is exporting by reducing prices, squeezing in and occupying the market, causing the industry of the other party to collapse, monopolizing the market, and obtaining monopoly profit.

Hunter: Therefore, dumping violates the principle of fair competition and fair trade, disturbs the normal order of trade, and is naturally resisted by the importing country.

Shi Kailai: But the retaliation against dumping should be reasonable. If it surpasses the reasonable scope or extent, antidumping itself will become a kind of trade discrimination and new protectionism.

Edward: What do you think is the reasonable scope or extent then, Mr. Shi?

Shi Kailai: For instance, to arbitrarily determine a case of dumping when dumping as a matter of fact does not exist, or to exaggerate the extent of dumping at will so as to exercise antidumping measures without reason, or to raise the antidumping tariff inappropriately. These are examples of exceeding the rational scope and extent.

Hunter: Ha, it is hard to avoid the situation in which both parties claim to be in the right.

Shi Kailai: But facts are facts after all.

Edward: Fortunately, now we have the antidumping law, and we can handle affairs in accordance with the law and set the facts straight.

Hunter: The party that suffers can lodge an antidumping appeal, and based on this the government can place the case on file for investigation and make a ruling.

Shi Kailai: Yes, according to the antidumping law, the accused should also have the opportunity of response and defense. However, this still cannot eliminate many human factors.

Edward: Mr. Shi, I have noticed that you attach a lot of importance to what you call "human factors". Can you tell me why?

Shi Kailai: Let's have a break. Shall we go and have a drink?

Edward: That's a good idea.

(2) Normal Value and "Substitute Country"

Shi Kailai: Do you two know that unreasonable antidumping has constituted a serious threat to our export commodities, and we have to show great concern.

Edward:	Some of our US products have also been listed in the antidumping investigation.
Hunter:	Your first antidumping case is against the news print from the United States, Canada and South Korea.
Shi Kailai:	That's correct. But up to now, among the thousands of antidumping cases between WTO members, most were initiated by Western developed countries. And quite a number of them involve price discrimination.
Hunter:	The basis on which to determine the existence of dumping is the normal value of an export product and its export price. If the export price is lower than the normal value, it should be regarded as dumping.
Edward:	It can be measured by the comparable price of the same goods for consumption in the normal trade of the exporting country, or calculated by cost plus reasonable expenses for management, sales, etc. and the profit.
Hunter:	If the normal value can in no way be determined, it can be calculated by using the same goods of a substitute country.
Shi Kailai:	And that's the source of problem.
Edward:	Is that so?
Shi Kailai:	Just take some "antidumping cases" against our export products for example. Some countries insist on arbitrarily using the price of the same goods of a substitute country to measure whether the Chinese products constitute dumping, calculate the extent of dumping and levy very high antidumping tariffs.
Edward:	But that's recognized by the WTO's antidumping law.
Shi kailai:	However, when choosing the "substitute country", they seem to be holding an elastic ruler that can be lengthened or shortened at will.
Edward:	I don't quite understand.
Shi Kailai:	The situation in each country is different. Many "substitutions" are extremely unreasonable. For instance, once in an antidumping case, the substitute countries chosen for us were Switzerland and Japan. Wasn't that ridiculous?
Hunter:	That might be a very special case.
Shi Kailai:	No. There was something even more ridiculous. In the same "anti-

dumping case", they used the labor force of Malaysia, the coal of India and the transportation expenses of the Ganges River to calculate the normal value of the Chinese product.

Edward: The resources and labor costs of different countries are different and sometimes it is really hard to compare.

Shi Kailai: Some people don't want to admit the following fact: cheap labor and raw materials give Chinese products incomparable advantage in comparative cost.

Hunter: And in choosing a "substitute country", this important factor should not be neglected.

Shi Kailai: What's more important, some countries turn a blind eye to the influence of our economic reform on market policies and price mechanism.

Hunter: China used to practice a planned economy and now it is really working hard to establish a new market economic system.

Shi Kailai: But some countries are not willing to look squarely at this fact. They don't want to admit that the prices of our goods are actually market prices, which reflect the normal value of the goods. Neither looking for a "fair price" from a "substitute country", nor calculating the so-called "fair price" by using methods that are totally divorced from China's real situation is desirable.

Hunter: Now the situation has changed a great deal. Many countries have noticed the great changes that have taken place in China's economic system. Some countries have recognized China as a country that is transforming its economy. The EU and some other countries have removed China from the list of nonmarket economy countries.

Edward: After the Uruguay Round negotiations of the GATT, the tariffs of various countries have continually been cut down, and the non-tariff barriers have gradually been reduced. Antidumping and antisubsidy have become important component parts in the foreign trade policies and laws of most member economies of the WTO.

Shi Kailai: We agree to promote exports in accordance with the international trade standards. We are opposed to expanding export by using methods of dumping; but we are also opposed to practicing new trade protectionism by using antidumping as an excuse.

Edward: I very much appreciate your stand.

Lesson 36
INDUSTRIALIZATION OF AGRICULTURE AND TRADE OPPORTU-NITIES

(1) The History and Present Situation of China's Agriculture

Xiao Yulan: Mr. Edward, let's chat while we make the tour, shall we?

Edward: Thank you, Ms. Xiao, for accompanying us today.

Xiao Yulan: We work in the Ministry of Agriculture and serve people in the countryside. When we accompany our foreign friends to the countryside, we can on the one hand get to know the situation there, and on the other, we can hear your suggestions, thus killing two birds with one stone.

Hunter: China is a big agricultural country, with seven hundred and forty million people, or about 57% of its population, living in the countryside. The economic situation in the countryside has a pivotal influence on the entire national economy.

Xiao Yulan: Yes, we have always taken agriculture as the basis for our national economy, giving it the top priority of consideration and development.

Edward: We can see that. It is obvious that highly mechanized operation has been realized on this piece of farmland that stretches to the horizon. You have had a fairly advanced agricultural economy.

Xiao Yulan: Not yet. In most places of our country, it is still the traditional agricultural economy, with the household being the basic unit, and hoe and plough as the basic tools, using simple primitive labor for the production of plants and domestic animals. The purpose of operation has not entirely broken away from the restrictions of self-sufficiency.

Edward: That's natural. Even the country with the highest extent of industrialization for agriculture also took this road once.

Hunter: This is the legacy left by our ancestors.

Xiao Yulan: But this kind of traditional extensive operation should have long been placed in the historical museum.

Hunter: It's just a matter of time. Sooner for one place, and later for another.

Edward: Since 1990s, the tide of hi-tech has not only promoted the global transition from the industrial economy to a knowledge-based economy, but also vigorously pushed the traditional agriculture into an era of industrialization.

Hunter: The foreign exchange earning agriculture has rapidly risen to prominence on a global scale and the traditional agricultural production is moving towards industrialization and into factories.

Xiao Yulan: Our agricultural economy must follow this historical trend.

Hunter: I think this is what you have done and are doing.

Xiao Yulan: Yes. In recent years, fundamental changes have taken place in China's agriculture. In the past, the different stages of agricultural operation such as pre-production, in-production, post-production, and production, processing and sales were completely separated. The peasants' income was only the value created in the production of materials and primary products.

Hunter: And the profit made in processing, transportation and sales were several times, or even scores of times that of the income of the peasants.

Edward: Do you know about our almonds?

Xiao Yulan: Yes. American almonds are very popular on the Chinese market, sold at high prices.

Edward: The planting, harvesting, processing and sales of our almonds have formed a connected sequence. They are exported to more than 90 countries and regions. 80 % of the almonds sold in the world come from California, and the foreign exchange they earn accounts for 1% ~ 1.5 % of the over 60 billion US dollars of the total US export of agricultural products.

Hunter: The planters also have a considerable share of the profits made from the sales of the products.

Xiao Yulan:	And that is the benefit from the industrialization of agriculture. The economically developed areas of our country have taken the road of combining agriculture with industry and commerce, and a large number of enterprises integrating agriculture with industry and commerce have emerged.
Edward:	It seems that the Chinese traditional agriculture is marching towards industrialization. Can you take us to see an enterprise of this kind?
Xiao Yulan:	Of course. But let's first go and visit a good hand at farming.

(2) Industrialization Has Helped Create a Huge Potential Market

Fang X. N.:	Oh, Director Xiao, you are here.
Xiao Yulan:	Let me introduce you to each other. Mr. Edward, Mr. Hunter, and this is Mr. Fang Xingnong.
Fang X. N.:	Welcome, welcome. Please come on in.
Edward:	Thank you. This is your home?
Fang X. N:	Yes, please feel at home.
Edward:	Oh, such a big house and such a large garden, even more imposing than those of the American plantation owners.
Fang X. N.:	I owe this to the reform and opening up.
Hunter:	How did you get rich then?
Fang X. N.:	When the household contracting system was practiced in the countryside, I contracted 50 *mu* of land and 100 *mu* of barren hill. I planted both crops and fruit trees. In a few years' time, I went from simply having enough food and clothing to leading a well-off life.
Xiao Yulan:	He is among the new generation of peasants who were awakened first.
Fang X. N.:	In the past, the only thing we knew was intensive and meticulous farming so as to get higher yields of grain production.
Xiao Yulan:	In order to maximize crop yields, we did not hesitate to reclaim land from a lake, open up wasteland by destroying forests, and graze sheep and cattle excessively, resulting in serious soil erosion and frequent natural disasters.

Fang X. N. : The blind pursuit of maximal yields has sabotaged the ecological environment and cannot but be punished by nature.

Xiao Yulan: He is educated, well-informed and understands science and technology. He didn't follow the beaten track that had been followed by Chinese peasants for thousands of years.

Edward: Oh, how terrific!

Fang X. N. : I only took the market as the guide, and implement my production plan on the basis of the market demand, paying attention to the deep processing of agricultural and its side products. As for the circulation of the products, I tried my best to break away from the regional restrictions, going from the town and the village to the whole country and the world.

Xiao Yulan: The green foods and fruits he produces have been sold to as far as Europe and the United States.

Edward: You are not an ordinary peasant. You are a wise entrepreneur.

Hunter: You have marched from the individual and manorial style of farming onto industrialization and run an enterprise on a commercial basis.

Fang X. N. : Not yet. I have still a long way to go. I have not yet realized scale economy, intensified operation, and the extent of mechanization and science and technology content are still not high.

Edward: You want to solve the problem of perfecting and extending the chain of agriculture production?

Fang X. N. : Exactly.

Xiao Yulan: Mr. Edward, he has provided you with a very important piece of information.

Edward: You mean to say that he told me there exist great commercial opportunities in the process of industrialization of China's agriculture?

Xiao Yulan: Isn't it so? All the links in our agriculture, from planting, harvesting, desiccating, storage, freshness preservation, grading to processing, packaging, transportation and sales are still weak. How much input of funds, equipment, science and technology does it need in order to realize high level industrialization?

Fang X. N. :   We need various kinds of machinery for agricultural production and processing, genetic engineering for both plants and domestic animals, and modern information technology so that a completely new channel of circulation can be established between production, management and customers through the information highway.

Xiao Yulan: Ours is a vast country, with unbalanced levels of economic development. We still need to make great efforts to strengthen the agricultural infrastructure, and establish a socialized service system so as to accelerate the development of the middle and western regions that are still relatively backward economically.

Edward: Yes, there does exist a huge potential market in the process of industrialization of China's agriculture!

Hunter: It seems that foreign entrepreneurs still lack sharp vision and sufficient interest in this respect.

Fang X. N. :   But our forward strides do not wait for the latecomers.

Lesson 37
VILLAGE AND TOWNSHIP ENTERPRISES

(1) A New Force Suddenly Emerging

Edward: Ms. Xiao, we just mentioned that a large number of enterprises integrating agriculture with industry and commerce have emerged in China.

Hunter: In China these enterprises are referred to as village and township enterprises.

Edward: Village and township enterprises? What are their characteristics then?

Xiao Yulan: Let's ask Mr. Fang to answer this question. He is now a village and township entrepreneur who is known nationwide.

Fang X. N. :   Village and township enterprises represent a new phenomenon, which emerged after China's economic reform. After the household contract responsibility system in association with production was put into practice, idle work force needed new outlets and peasant entrepreneurs came into being as the times required.

Xiao Yulan: In 1980s, as a new force suddenly coming to the fore, village and township enterprises, in a few years' time, reached an annual production value of hundreds of billions of *yuan*, nearly a quarter of the GNP.

Edward: Oh, that was a very big proportion. What were the main items that these enterprises dealt in then?

Xiao Yulan: Having been liberated from the yellow earth, the peasants ran various small factories by obtaining materials from local sources and utilizing local resources and idle work force.

Fang X. N.: Some were engaged in hand weaving, some went in for the processing of agricultural products and its side products, some made spare parts which the urban big factories were reluctant to produce, and others simply formed contracting teams to go into cities to canvass business.

Xiao Yulan: It was the seller's market at that time. There was a serious shortage of goods, with many blanks on the market and a relatively big space for maneuver there. Anything produced could be sold.

Hunter: That was a heaven-bestowed opportunity, which provided the village and township enterprises a good chance for development. Is that right?

Fang X. N.: Exactly. We seized the opportunity and made up omissions and deficiencies, producing what the market needed, selling what the market was short of, and doing what the city residents were unwilling to do.

Xiao Yulan: They brought the advantages of village and township enterprises into full play, being flexible and able to achieve success one way or another.

Fang X. N.: To use our own words, a small boat can make a rapid turn. We keep our eyes on the market. If the products are salable today, we produce them. When they are not salable tomorrow, we make a shift to produce new goods that are popular and needed.

Edward: It seems that Chinese village and township enterprises have their unique model of management. But small boats may not be able to stand heavy storms either.

Fang X. N.：You put it right, Mr. Edward. When the market was saturated, with an increasingly narrow space for maneuver, and when supply and demand were balanced or supply exceeded demand, it was like the sudden strike of a storm in which the village and township enterprises in general felt the threat to their existence.

Xiao Yulan：At that time, Chinese village and township enterprises went through several years of hesitation, reorganization and improvement, with large numbers closing down, ceasing production, merging or changing their production lines.

Fang X. N.：But quite a number of village and township enterprises stood the test of great storms. They completely cast aside the small-scale household manual workshop style, vigorously introduced foreign capital, technology, advanced equipment and management models, and ran large-scale modern enterprises, embarking on the road of an export-oriented economy.

Hunter：Such enterprise groups as Kelong, Chunlan, and Little Swan in China are actually village and township enterprises. They are not just big enterprises in China, but are among the top ranks in the world, being very competitive on the international market.

Xiao Yulan：In 1990s, Chinese village and township enterprises entered into a period of extraordinary development. In 1995 their total production reached a total of 6350 billion *yuan*, holding up half the country's industry, accounting for nearly one third of the GDP.

Fang X. N.：Now there are thousands of village and township enterprise groups of national scale in China, apart from 10,000 large- and medium-sized ones. They are among the main organizations that turn over profits and pay taxes to the state and local authorities, having become the main body of China's rural economy and an important component of the national economy.

Edward：In the history of the world's economic development, there were many examples of enterprises which were once brilliant but ended up as brief as a flash in the pan.

Hunter: Statistics showed that in Japan, counting from the establishment of the enterprise, only 18.3% could pass 10 years smoothly, only 8.5% could celebrate the 20th anniversary in a happy manner, and only less than 5% could hold a grand 30th birthday party.

Edward: How did the Chinese village and township enterprises keep their youthful vigor then?

(2) A New Chapter in the Development of Village and Township Enterprises

Fang X. N.: Mr. Edward just now raised a very sharp question. It is really very difficult for an enterprise to be prosperous forever without a decline.

Xiao Yulan: After the village and township enterprises entered the period of extraordinary development, great changes took place on the Chinese market. The seller's market became the buyer's market.

Edward: This change meant that enterprises and businessmen who used to dominate the market at will had to place themselves at the mercy of the laws of the market.

Fang X. N.: Yes. In a fleeting moment, the state-owned enterprises, the village and township enterprises and all other enterprises were faced with severe challenges.

Hunter: For the market situation, the first problem was that the domestic demand was not strong enough and the consumption lacked momentum, with products piling up, resulting in overstock. Even foreign-invested enterprises were affected to different degrees, and the village and township enterprises felt the difficulty all the more.

Fang X. N.: Quite a number of enterprises saw their benefits sliding, with losses increased. They either continued production with great difficulties, or were faced with a situation of stopping or half-stopping production. Even those enterprises who had good returns found their development slowing down, with inadequate stamina.

Xiao Yulan: At that moment, the key to the existence and development of the village and township enterprises was to realize the optimization and upgrading of the industrial structure to adapt to the already changed market situation.

Edward: What did you do then?

Xiao Yulan: While trying to improve management, we made great efforts to adjust the industrial structure.

Fang X. N.: The biggest barrier to the development of village and township enterprises was the tendency to have the same industrial structure. Most village and township enterprises belonged to the secondary industry in the main. They took such industries as machinery, textiles, chemicals, and foods as their main business.

Hunter: In that case, weren't village and township enterprises the synonym of village and township industry?

Edward: Redundant construction at a low level inevitably led to saturation of the market. Sameness of industrial structure would trigger off a scramble for materials, for the market, and lead to price wars, resulting in a situation of simultaneous prosperity and decline.

Xiao Yulan: That's true. Therefore, we have to increase the dynamics in structure adjustment, bring into full play the resource advantages of different localities, vigorously develop the processing industry of agricultural and its side products, set up enterprises that integrate agriculture with industry and commerce, and combine the development of village and township enterprises with the industrialized management of agriculture.

Fang X. N.: Especially, we'll have to enlarge the input to develop high and new technologies for agriculture, such as functional genomics for important crops, combating plant diseases and pests, the development and utilization of important biological resources, etc.

Xiao Yulan: In a word, we'll take village and township enterprises as the lead to push forward the transition of the entire agriculture towards intensified, scaled economy and mature market mechanism so as to finally realize the high-level industrialization and modernization of agricultural industry.

Edward: Oh, that's a brand-new road of development.

Xiao Yulan: The village and township enterprises have blood relationship with agriculture that can never be cut off. Taking the industrialization

of agriculture as its foothold, the village and township enterprises
have advantages that are richly endowed by nature. If we follow
this road unswervingly, we will surely create a new situation for
the development of village and township enterprises.

Fang X. N.: And compose a new chapter that is even more brilliant and glorious.

Edward: Excellent! I sincerely wish you success.

Lesson 38
FOREIGN-INVESTED ENTERPRISES

(1) Modes of Investment

Edward: Assistant Minister, this time I have spent about a month in your country making an on-the-spot investigation. Before I go back, I would like to acquaint myself with the policies of your government concerning foreign-invested enterprises.

Hunter: Mr. Edward has learned a great deal in his investigation this time. He is fully confident in the Chinese market, and is determined to go all out in China.

Ma Junyi: Most welcome. Since you have been making your investigation in China for a month, I think you are already familiar with the situation of foreign businessmen investing in China.

Edward: That was just like looking at flowers while riding a horse, only having scanty knowledge of it. I still have many questions. For instance, what are the modes of foreign-investment in China at the present?

Ma Junyi: The main forms are solely foreign-invested enterprises, Sino-foreign joint ventures and Sino-foreign cooperative enterprises.

Hunter: They are what people usually refer to as the three types of foreign invested enterprises.

Ma Junyi: Along with the continuous expansion of China's opening up and the implementation of the "broadly-based economy and trade" strategy, the scope of foreign investment has been gradually expanded, with various forms of joint ventures and cooperation.

Edward：I know that your country is gradually opening up the retail trade and finance and insurance industries and other services. Joint ventures can take the form of joint stock system. They can form joint ventures or cooperate with state-owned enterprises. They can also choose to form joint ventures or cooperate with individual, private or non-governmental enterprises.

Ma Junyi：Yes, joint ventures set up by the Founder Group with American Digital Equipment, and by the Haier Group with Sanyo Electric of Japan are examples that have attracted wide attention.

Edward：May I ask what kind of investment is most welcome by China at the moment?

Ma Junyi：In order to accelerate the development of our national economy, we welcome foreign businessmen to make various kinds of investment in China. So far as the needs of the development of our national economy at present is concerned, we most welcome foreign businessmen to make long-term investments in such areas as mines, transportation, communications, energy resources and high-tech.

Edward：I fully understand.

Ma Junyi：China has a vast territory with unbalanced economic developments. The eastern and coastal areas are economically more developed, and the middle, western and remote areas are relatively backward. Therefore, we encourage foreign businessmen to invest in China's middle and western areas.

Edward：Those places need funds, with broader prospects for investment. To make investments in the middle and western areas may also be regarded as a good choice.

Ma Junyi：We welcome Mr. Edward to go there to make an all-out effort.

Edward：I will consider Mr. Ma's suggestion seriously. We are more than willing to do what we can for the development of China's economy.

(2) The Rights, Obligations and Benefits of Investors

Edward：Mr. Ma, there is no denying the fact that the ultimate aim of commercial activities is to make money. I cannot avoid earthly concerns and hold myself aloof from the vulgar either. May I ask whether the investment interests of foreign businessmen can be safeguarded in China?

Ma Junyi: You can set your mind at rest. In order to protect the interests of foreign investment in China, our country has made and promulgated a series of laws and regulations governing business relations with foreigners. These laws and regulations stipulate clearly and in detail the rights enjoyed by foreign businessmen.

Hunter: So far as I know, they include Law on Foreign-Invested Enterprises and detailed rules for its implementation, Law on China-Foreign Joint Ventures and rules and regulations for its implementation, Law on Income Tax of Foreign-Invested and Foreign-Owned Enterprises, etc.

Ma Junyi: We not only earnestly implement all policies for absorbing foreign investment that have been promulgated, but also, while keeping the stability of these policies, continuously replenish and perfect the system of laws and regulations governing foreign investment. Our government has consistently protected the lawful rights of all foreign-invested enterprises in China according to law, including intellectual property rights.

Edward: Can you be more specific?

Ma Junyi: That's fairly complicated. To put it briefly, the properties of foreign businessmen enjoy the right of protection and free disposal; foreign investors have the right of planning the production, independent management, and the right to hire and fire employees.

Edward: What about their obligations?

Ma Junyi: To put it simply, they have to operate in conformity with the law. At the same time, they have to pay attention to the improvement of the quality of Chinese employees and protect their lawful rights.

Edward: Judging from what I hear, the laws and regulations of your country governing relations with foreigners are in conformity with international conventions. But can you guarantee that they are not just scraps of paper?

Ma Junyi: It seems that Mr. Edward still has some doubts. Your one-month investigation is much too short. Let me tell you a simple fact.

Edward: What fact?

Ma Junyi: Now China has more than 550,000 foreign-invested enterprises, with more than 650 billion US dollars actually put in. What's more, most of these enterprises are running well with good profits. A large number of them are in no hurry to remit their profits back home, but to use them in China for the expansion of production and for new projects. Some large-scale transnational corporations have even moved their regional headquarters, research institutes and development centers from other places to China.

Hunter: All this proves that their lawful rights and benefits have been effectively safeguarded, and that they are fully confident in making investment in China.

Edward: I am reassured as well.

(3) **Investment Environment**

Edward: Mr. Ma, I would also like to know about your investment environment.

Ma Junyi: Hard environment or soft environment?

Hunter: It has been 30 years since China adopted the reform and opening-up policy, and its infrastructure such as transportation and communication have made rapid progress, which has laid a solid material foundation for the absorption of foreign investment.

Edward: I don't see a lot of problems with the hard environment. Would you please say something about the soft environment?

Ma Junyi: All right. Our country is politically stable, secure in social life with a fast growing economy and a huge potential market. Our government has promulgated a series of investment policies beneficial to foreign businessmen. I think all this constitutes the most important soft environment.

Edward: What Mr. Ma said is absolutely correct.

Ma Junyi: Of course, we still need to make great efforts to improve various aspects of the soft environment.

Hunter: Some functional departments have very low efficiency, with different units passing the buck to each other, and the documents travelling incessantly. And there is also bureaucracy, formalism, etc., which is a headache for many foreigners.

Ma Junyi: We have been making continuous efforts to perfect our service system for foreign investment and to improve our quality and efficiency of service. For instance, we provide service with "a coordinated process" "one-station style" handling of business, computer networking, and customs management of enterprises by classifications, etc. The phenomena you mentioned have been changed to a great extent.

Hunter: These are perfectly obvious. But in some places, the phenomena of "four improprieties" have not stopped despite repeated prohibitions.

Edward: What are these "four improprieties"?

Ma Junyi: Oh, they are: "improper inspections", "improper collection of fees", "improper apportions", and "improper fines". Our attitude is to stop them resolutely, bring them under control earnestly, and investigate and prosecute them seriously. We will improve the operability of our policies, increase the transparency of our work and protect the normal operations of law-abiding enterprises.

Edward: Thank you Mr. Ma for your sincerity and frankness. As a matter of fact, unsatisfactory things exist everywhere in the world, and we will not make excessive demands on China.

Ma Junyi: But we won't excuse ourselves because of that. We know perfectly well that the improvement of investment environment, especially the soft environment, is a long and arduous task. We will, as always, make our best efforts to build a more stable and favorable policy environment and a more equal and more transparent environment for competition. Foreign businessmen will find that China is the most ideal place for them to do business and make investment.

Edward: I fully believe in it.

Ma Junyi: Our goal for utilizing foreign investment is to promote the economic growth of our country. But at the same time, we have to safeguard the lawful rights of foreign businessmen in China, and enable them to make profits.

Edward: Ah, we do hope we have a good prospect of profit, but we are not bent solely on profit.

Ma Junyi: You are a good businessman.

Lesson 39
OPEN CITIES AND SPECIAL ECONOMIC ZONES

(1) Open Cities

Edward: Mr. Ma, during the month of my visit to China, I have received warm and friendly reception everywhere, which has totally changed my impression of China before I came.

Ma Junyi: Oh? What was your impression before you came?

Edward: It was laughable, and I'd rather not say it.

Hunter: He heard someone saying that after coming to China he would have no personal freedom and would be submitted to confinement everywhere. Wherever he went, he would be followed by a large crowd watching him as if he was a rare animal.

Ma Junyi: Ha, ha, whoever said all this was either prejudiced against China, or lacked a basic understanding of China.

Edward: You put it right. After coming to China, I have been to many places, and my impression is totally different. I have also met many foreigners who have come from all over the world and they all enjoy freedom and lead a happy life here.

Hunter: Now China has opened up hundreds of cities. You can go not only to Beijing, Shanghai and Guangzhou, but also to Urumqi and Lhasa. Open cities are spread out all over China. Some open cities have given residential foreigners national treatment and the treatment of city residents.

Edward: How are open cities selected?

Ma Junyi: Generally speaking, these cities either have a comparatively well-developed economy or are themselves scenic spots or historically and culturally famous places, which attract foreigners to come for visits, leisure, or tourism.

Edward: Oh, yes. I have been to quite a few cities this time, such as Xi'an, Qingdao, Hangzhou and Suzhou, which are both ancient and modern, leaving an unforgettable impression upon me.

Ma Junyi: I am very pleased to know that you have been to so many places. We may say that each open city is a window to the understanding of China's economy and culture. Didn't you go to Shanghai?

Edward: How could I miss it? I went to Shanghai before going to Hangzhou and Suzhou.

Hunter: We went to visit Pudong together. He was profuse in praise of Shanghai, as it is an international metropolis and the trade and financial center of China and even Asia.

Edward: The snacks and desserts of Shanghai always make my mouth water, and the Shanghai dialect is so pleasant to the ear, but I can't get the pronunciation right.

Ma Junyi: Such being the case, I have a suggestion for you. Why not invite several famous refreshment makers from Shanghai to run a Shanghai-style food products factory in your country and deal in Shanghai-flavored snacks? While doing business, you can learn the Shanghai dialect as well, thus killing two birds with one stone.

Edward: That's a good idea, but I am a bit too late. Some people in the same trade are swifter footed and have arrived before me.

(2) Special Economic Zones

Edward: Mr. Ma, can you tell me something about China's special economic zones?

Ma Junyi: Yes, of course. China has a large expanse of territory and unbalanced economic developments in various places. In order to bring into full play the advantages of the coastal cities and regions, and to build them into bases for developing import and export business and for attracting foreign capital and advanced technology so as to give impetus to the national economic construction, the Chinese government has adopted a series of privileged policies to be practiced in certain coastal places. These places are called "special economic zones".

Edward: Oh, "special economic zones" are so called because they enjoy privileged policies for economic development.

Hunter：　That is to say, it does not mean they are special in political or cultural aspects.

Ma Junyi：　That's right. You know that many countries in the world are engaged in reform. The reason why the successful road of China's reform and opening up attracts the world's attention is that China's reform process is filled with exploration, experiment, "popularization", and "adjustment". "Special economic zones" serve as "windows" open to the outside world, "experimental plots" to explore the construction of a socialist market economy.

Hunter：　These experimental plots have produced many "number ones" in China, such as the first Sino-foreign joint venture, the first stock exchange, the first foreign-invested bank, the first auction market for property rights, etc.

Ma Junyi：　The special economic zones have been leading in and are still carrying out, a series of profound reform in the planning system, price system, fiscal and monetary system, circulation system, personnel management system and social security system, and have obtained precious experiences.

Hunter：　Obviously, various places in the country are learning from their experiences.

Ma Junyi：　The success of these experimental plots has played the role of "windows" to the outside world, having attracted the eyesight of the entrepreneurs of the whole world, and the role of an "example" within the country, pushing forward the process of reform and opening up of the whole country.

Edward：　How many such special economic zones are there in China then?

Ma Junyi：　Starting from 1980, four special economic zones were established. They were Shenzhen, Zhuhai, Shantou and Xiamen. Later Hainan special economic zone was set up. Apart from special economic zones, there are hundreds of economic and technological development zones which are spread all over China.

(3) Economic and Technological Development Zones

Edward：　Mr. Ma, may I ask what development zones are?

Ma Junyi: There are many similarities between development zones and special economic zones. For instance, they are established, with the backing of relatively well-developed economy in the coastal areas, by designating a place for the practice of some preferential policies to build a good investment environment so as to attract foreign capital and advanced technology.

Edward: Why aren't they called special economic zones then?

Ma Junyi: Mainly because they have different functions. They are no longer "experimental plots", but new growth points of local economy, bases for high technology and modern industries. They can also effectively adjust the city's industrial structure and its distribution. At the same time they have drawn on the experience of free zones abroad.

Edward: Such being the case, can we say that development zones are free zones?

Ma Junyi: Of course not. We have merely used them for reference. For instance, compared with the export processing zones in free economic regions abroad, our development zones have such complementary functions as finance, service and accommodation. Compared with bonded areas, bonded warehouses or free trade zones, our development zones have a stronger function of processing and a higher level of high technology, but a weaker function of trading.

Hunter: If compared with free ports in free economic zones abroad, the free ports are not under the customs supervision and control, with all imports and exports exempted from customs duties, but development zones are under the supervision and control of the customs. They can only enjoy partial reduction or exemption of customs duties.

Ma Junyi: Exactly.

Edward: How are the development zones operating now?

Hunter: They are all very successful. Among the hundreds of development zones, especially the ones in Shangdi of Beijing, Pudong of Shanghai, Tianjin, Dalian, Yantai, etc. come first on the list and are famous far and near.

Edward: We have visited the development zone in Shangdi, seeing quite a number of well-known enterprises that are among the world's top 500 there.

Hunter: Just like powers contending for hegemony or fighting for the beachhead for landing, everybody hates to lag behind.

Ma Junyi: The development zones in various places all have their own comparative advantages, such as being near to the city proper, with convenient transportation, a complete set of supporting systems, being backed up by intelligence, funds, information and market.

Hunter: And also a good service system, a preferential policy environment, and a social environment whose legal system is relatively complete. All these unique advantages constitute their glamour.

Ma Junyi: Quite a number of investors had a mentality of throwing a stone to explore the way when they first came into the development zones. Later they found that they had made a wise decision, and they could go ahead in big strides with full steam. Therefore, they put in more investments, expanded the scale, or even moved their headquarters here from abroad.

Edward: Such being the case, there must be many followers to come.

Ma Junyi: This is called: "When there is a *Wutong* tree in your yard, the phoenix will come voluntarily."

Hunter: So you often say "building a nest to attract the phoenix", which means to build a good environment to attract foreign investment. That is really a lively metaphor.

Lesson 40
TRANSNATIONAL OPERATION AND INTEGRATION OF THE WORLD ECONOMY

(1) The Era of Knowledge-Based Economy

Edward: Mr. Ma, now the whole world is talking about the era of knowledge-based economy. Is your country also interested in this topic?

Ma Junyi: It is not whether one is interested, but that one has to be interested.

Edward: Oh, why?

Ma Junyi: That's simple. The whole world is undergoing a transition from the industrial economy to the knowledge-based economy, which will surely exert a profound influence on the human society.

Hunter: Scientists assert that the advent of the era of knowledge-based economy will surely bring about fundamental changes to the social economic formation, and completely change the face of the world and the social life of human beings.

Ma Junyi: Therefore, one either goes ahead with the times or is cast aside. The situation spurs us on!

Edward: It seems that everybody feels the call of the times.

Ma Junji: Your country is the first that is aware of the era of knowledge-based economy, and you may have the deepest feelings.

Edward: Yes, in the recent 30 years, along with the development of high technology, especially the information technology, our country has been talking about knowledge-based economy. In 1990, a UN research institute officially put forward the concept of "knowledge-based economy".

Hunter: In 1996, OECD gave a clear definition to knowledge-based economy, that is, it is an economy based on knowledge.

Ma Junyi: That is to say, natural resources, funds, equipment and raw materials, on which the development of economy depended in the era of industrial economy, have receded to the second place, and knowledge and intellectual resources have become the most important factor in the allocation of resources.

Hunter: The development of science and technology has become the decisive factor for economic development. And scientists generally hold that information and biological technologies will become the key factors related to the destiny and future of a country in the 21st century.

Edward: This view is already confirmed by the facts in our country.

Ma Junyi: According to news media, the United States grasped the key link of R & D of high technology in the 1980s just like leading the cow by its nose. In the 1990s, it has formed a new industrial system with high technology as the core, and information and services as its two wings that lead the development of other industries. Therefore, the

US economy went through a period of steady growth and prosperity.

Edward: That's true. Microsoft, the bellwether of the American information industry, only used 20 years from its start-up in 1975 to its success. Its present total assets are almost as large as those of GM, which was the typical representative of the industrial era and spent more than 50 years after the war for its development.

Ma Junyi: All this proves that the contest of competitive strength in the world today is after all a contest of knowledge. Whoever takes the lead in the realm of knowledge gains the initiative in the future competitive pattern.

Hunter: Modern high-tech industry is a typical knowledge-intensive industry. A knowledge-based economy takes the high-tech industry as its pillar. Only with this pillar erected, can the grand economic tower of a country or of the world reach the sky.

Ma Junyi: Therefore, let's follow the historical trend of the times and welcome the advent of knowledge-based economy.

(2) The Tide of Strategic Mergers by Transnational Corporations

Edward: Experts predict that mankind will fully enter the era of knowledge-based economy in the second half of the 21st century.

Ma Junyi: At the moment we cannot prove this prediction yet. However, we have clearly seen that the development of high technology, especially the information technology, telecommunication technology and networking technology, has made the world smaller. Countries and regions have become more closely connected, and the flow of the media linking the international division of labor, such as trade in goods, investment, technology and labor service has accelerated.

Hunter: That's true. The integration of the world economy has become an irreversible historical trend and an irresistible global tide.

Edward: There have emerged three regional economic organizations in the present-day world, i. e. , EU, NAFTA and APEC. The regionalization and group forming trend of the world economy has vigorously pushed the economy of the entire world towards integration.

Ma Junyi: Another powerful driving force of the integration of the world economy is the tide of strategic mergers by transnational corporations.

Hunter: Yes, in this new round of merger tide of enterprises, it is not so much one enterprise annexing another as two enterprises forming a strategic alliance on a higher plane for their respective future development, a strategic equity cooperation on a higher level.

Edward: This kind of alliance between two powerful enterprises, which is characterized by complementing each other with their advantages, sharing risks and interests, has completely cast aside the mode of competition that was a common occurrence and characterized by big fish eating the small fish and the small fish eating the shrimps.

Ma Junyi: The strategic aim of such alliance between powerful enterprises is extremely obvious. That is to give up the narrow concept of nationality, break the country borders, keep one's eyes on the global competition, bring into full play the human resources, technology, capital and natural resources of the whole world and occupy every market of the world, so as to realize the maximization of the interest by global management.

Edward: Alliance between powerful enterprises across the country borders enables them to establish production and processing bases abroad, jointly conduct R & D of new products, satisfy the demand of the enterprises on the quick response to new technology and new products, form a global network of development, production and marketing, and realize the effective transnational allocation of the whole package of key production factors and various links in the chain for the appreciation of value.

Ma Junyi: There is every indication that the tide of strategic mergers by transnational corporations has produced and will continue to produce profound influence on the world economic structure.

(3) Transnational Operations of Chinese Enterprises

Edward: Mr. Ma, has the tide of strategic mergers by transnational corporations had any impact on China?

Ma Junyi: In order to maximize the interest of the corporate system, transnational corporations allocate different links in the value appreciation chain to different places in the world where they can be brought into full play. China cannot but be placed in the value appreciation chain of international transnational corporations.

Hunter: That's true. As a matter of fact, China has become an ideal manufacturing and processing base in the global operating network of transnational corporations. Direct investment in this respect is considerable.

Edward: When allocating links in the value appreciation chain overseas, the transnational corporations first choose places that are near either to the market or to the resources.

Hunter: As China has the world's largest market, rich natural resources and cheap and high-quality work force, it certainly is an ideal place for international transnational corporations to allocate their manufacturing and processing bases.

Ma Junyi: Along with transnational corporations allocating their manufacturing centers in China, their development centers gradually arrive. And their technological development projects are gradually shifted from projects that suit the Chinese market to projects that blaze new trails.

Hunter: In recent years, the service industries in China, especially those knowledge-intensive ones such as finance, insurance, accounting, law, telecommunications and marketing, have made rapid progress. I believe that the overseas operating centers of international transnational corporations will come together in crowds to the Chinese mainland.

Edward: It seems that China is situated in an important and advantageous position in the global strategy of international transnational corporations. Then, are Chinese enterprises turning towards globalization?

Ma Junyi: The integration of the world economy is not one-way traffic, but goes two ways. Chinese enterprises will surely go out of the country border, establish their own transnational companies and seek overseas development.

Hunter: I know that such large-scale enterprises as Haier and Kelong have established their production bases abroad.

Ma Junyi: The Lenovo Group of China has established its technological development department in the area where the most advanced software technology is located — the Silicon Valley in the United States.

Edward: Oh, that's really amazing.

Ma Junyi: The development of the world economy has created a relatively advantageous international environment for the reform, opening up and economic construction of our country. We will seize the opportunity, constantly raise our position in the global strategy of transnational corporations, so that we will be able to utilize the capital, technology and management resources brought about by the investment from transnational corporations, with a view to promoting our modernization drive and improving our ability in joining in the global competition.

生词总表

Vocabulary List

生词	拼音	课号

A

爱护	àihù	32
安定	āndìng	38
安家落户	ān jiā luò hù	28
安稳	ānwěn	37
暗箱	ànxiāng	24

B

八仙过海，各显其能	bāxiān guò hǎi, gè xiǎn qí néng	31
巴掌	bāzhang	33
拔地而起	bá dì ér qǐ	33
把握	bǎwò	28
罢了	bàle	36
摆布	bǎibù	37
摆脱	bǎituō	36
曝光	bàoguāng	27
颁布	bānbù	32
榜样	bǎngyàng	25
棒球	bàngqiú	33
包工队	bāogōng duì	37

饱和	bǎohé	32
宝贵	bǎoguì	29
保护神	bǎohù shén	31
《保护工业产权巴黎公约》	Bǎohù Gōngyè Chǎnquán Bālí Gōngyuē	34
《保护文学艺术作品伯尔尼公约》	Bǎohù Wénxué Yìshù Zuòpǐn Bó'ěrní Gōngyuē	34
保密	bǎomì	22
保全	bǎoquán	25
保税区	bǎoshuìqū	39
报复	bàofù	34
报销	bàoxiāo	31
爆发	bàofā	34
悲观	bēiguān	29
北大方正	Běidà Fāngzhèng	33
北美自由贸易区	Běiměi Zìyóu Màoyì Qū	40
被告	bèigào	34
被迫	bèipò	34
逼近	bījìn	37
逼迫	bīpò	40
比尔·盖茨	Bǐ'ěr·Gàicí	33
比重	bǐzhòng	22
彼岸	bǐ'àn	31
毕竟	bìjìng	22
边境	biānjìng	23
编织	biānzhī	37
贬值	biǎnzhí	28
变革	biàngé	35
变换	biànhuàn	30
遍地	biàndì	25

辩护	biànhù	35	层面	céngmiàn	26
标语	biāoyǔ	23	差异	chāyì	22
标志	biāozhì	32	插	chā	27
飙升	biāoshēng	30	查处	cháchǔ	38
摈弃	bìnqì	40	产权	chǎnquán	34
并	bìng	37	产物	chǎnwù	26
并存	bìngcún	31	产业	chǎnyè	23
波及	bōjí	29	长盛不衰	cháng shèng	
博物馆	bówùguǎn	36		bù shuāi	33
渤海	Bó Hǎi	32	长足	chángzú	21
薄弱	bóruò	24	徜徉	chángyáng	26
补贴	bǔtiē	35	场面	chǎngmiàn	24
不甘落后	bùgān luòhòu	39	敞开	chǎngkāi	24
不堪	bùkān	24	畅通	chàngtōng	26
不容置疑	bù róng zhìyí	35	倡导	chàngdǎo	27
不失为	bùshīwéi	38	超常	chāocháng	37
不速之客	bú sù zhī kè	26	超凡脱俗	chāofán tuōsú	38
布局	bùjú	39	炒作	chǎozuò	29
步伐	bùfá	23	扯皮	chěpí	38
步骤	bùzhòu	23	彻底	chèdǐ	31
部长	bùzhǎng	38	撤回	chèhuí	29
			成长	chéngzhǎng	31
C			成果	chéngguǒ	33
			成就	chéngjiù	21
财政	cáizhèng	39	承包	chéngbāo	23
采集	cǎijí	33	程控	chéngkòng	33
彩旗	cǎiqí	27	惩罚	chéngfá	36
参考	cānkǎo	34	充斥	chōngchì	34
参与	cānyù	40	充实	chōngshí	38
惨痛	cǎntòng	30	充裕	chōngyù	28
灿烂	cànlàn	32	重复	chóngfù	37
仓储	cāngchǔ	26	宠物	chǒngwù	32
操纵	cāozòng	29	抽逃	chōutáo	29
草原	cǎoyuán	32	筹集	chóují	30
测验	cèyàn	33			

臭氧	chòuyǎng	32	大气	dàqì	32
出台	chūtái	38	大通银行	Dàtōng Yínháng	28
初步	chūbù	31	大有人在	dà yǒu rén zài	35
锄头	chútou	36	大张旗鼓	dà zhāng qí gǔ	27
储备	chǔbèi	28	逮住	dǎizhù	31
储存	chǔcún	33	代替	dàitì	34
处罚	chǔfá	25	带动	dàidòng	23
触摸	chùmō	33	带头羊	dàitóu yáng	40
传输	chuánshū	33	待遇	dàiyù	39
创汇	chuànghuì	36	单调	dāndiào	31
创新	chuàngxīn	40	单向	dānxiàng	40
吹牛皮	chuī niúpí	31	诞生	dànshēng	32
垂青	chuíqīng	30	当局	dāngjú	27
垂涎三尺	chuíxián sān chǐ	34	当之无愧	dāng zhī wúkuì	33
垂涎欲滴	chuíxián yù dī	39	荡	dàng	32
赐教	cìjiào	29	档次	dàngcì	26
从而	cóngér	35	导航	dǎoháng	23
从事	cóngshì	24	导火线	dǎohuǒxiàn	34
凑	còu	24	导向	dǎoxiàng	36
粗放型	cūfàngxíng	36	导致	dǎozhì	24
促使	cùshǐ	36	倒卖	dǎomài	25
脆弱	cuìruò	29	盗窃	dàoqiè	34
存亡	cúnwáng	37	道·琼斯 工业指数	Dào · Qióngsī Gōngyè Zhǐshù	30
D			得天独厚	dé tiān dú hòu	28
			抵制	dǐzhì	35
搭上	dāshàng	27	地球	dìqiú	30
打击	dǎjī	25	地域	dìyù	21
打假	dǎjiǎ	27	帝国大厦	Dìguó Dàshà	30
打破	dǎpò	24	缔结	dìjié	40
打印机	dǎyìnjī	33	典型	diǎnxíng	25
打折	dǎzhé	27	点击	diǎnjī	33
大陆	dàlù	40	电磁	diàncí	32
大难临头	dà nàn líntóu	30	刁难	diāonàn	27
大盘	dàpán	30			

雕像	diāoxiàng	30		发行	fāxíng	30
盯	dīng	37		法人	fǎrén	30
定律	dìnglǜ	30		法制	fǎzhì	29
定心丸	dìngxīnwán	38		烦琐	fánsuǒ	22
定义	dìngyì	22		反弹	fǎntán	30
动人	dòngrén	39		反对	fǎnduì	24
动态	dòngtài	28		反而	fǎn'ér	21
都会	dūhuì	39		反面	fǎnmiàn	29
杜绝	dùjué	38		反映	fǎnyìng	33
断言	duànyán	40		贩私	fànsī	25
多头	duōtóu	30		坊	fāng	28
夺	duó	36		防范	fángfàn	28
				仿佛	fǎngfú	26

E

				仿冒	fǎngmào	34
额外	éwài	22		放牧	fàngmù	36
恶化	èhuà	32		放射性	fàngshèxìng	32
恶性	èxìng	26		放松	fàngsōng	26
遏制	èzhì	29		非但	fēidàn	23
而已	éryǐ	38		废水	fèishuǐ	32
耳听为虚，	ěr tīng wéi xū,			沸沸扬扬	fèifèiyángyáng	34
眼见为实	yǎn jiàn wéi shí	33		分包	fēnbāo	24
20 世纪	Èrshí Shì jì			分割	fēngē	36
福克斯	Fúkèsī	34		分离	fēnlí	23
				分配	fēnpèi	31

F

				分歧	fēnqí	22
				分摊	fēntān	22
发包	fābāo	24		分享	fēnxiǎng	22
发挥	fāhuī	24		分支	fēnzhī	28
发迹	fājì	28		粉身碎骨	fěn shēn suì gǔ	30
发掘	fājué	33		丰厚	fēnghòu	25
发狂	fākuáng	30		风光	fēngguāng	37
发明	fāmíng	30		风景线	fēngjǐngxiàn	28
发起	fāqǐ	35		疯狂	fēngkuáng	29
发射	fāshè	24		凤凰	fènghuáng	39
发祥地	fāxiángdì	33				

服从	fúcóng	30
氟	fú	32
幅员	fúyuán	36
辐射	fúshè	32
福利	fúlì	31
辅助	fǔzhù	25
负	fù	33
附设	fùshè	26
复制	fùzhì	34
富豪	fùháo	28
覆盖	fùgài	33

G

改观	gǎiguān	38
概括	gàikuò	38
感慨	gǎnkǎi	29
感染	gǎnrǎn	27
感伤	gǎnshāng	29
岗位	gǎngwèi	33
高峰	gāofēng	31
高耸入云	gāosǒng rù yún	40
高速公路	gāosù gōnglù	36
告知	gàozhī	31
胳膊	gēbo	39
割	gē	37
格局	géjú	21
更新换代	gēngxīn huàndài	33
更有甚者	gèng yǒu shèn zhě	31
工程	gōngchéng	22
工缴费	gōngjiǎofèi	25
工资	gōngzī	25
工作狂	gōngzuò kuáng	26
公说公有理,婆说婆有理	gōng shuō gōng yǒulǐ, pó shuō pó yǒulǐ	35

公文	gōngwén	38
供应	gōngyìng	24
共识	gòngshí	22
贡献	gòngxiàn	21
构成	gòuchéng	24
构筑	gòuzhù	39
股份	gǔfèn	31
股票	gǔpiào	28
股息	gǔxī	30
鼓励	gǔlì	26
固然	gùrán	22
固体	gùtǐ	32
挂牌	guàpái	30
关乎	guānhū	24
关注	guānzhù	31
观察	guānchá	28
观念	guānniàn	21
官僚主义	guānliáo zhǔyì	38
管制	guǎnzhì	23
光缆	guānglǎn	33
广阔	guǎngkuò	24
归属	guīshǔ	34
规范	guīfàn	29
规划	guīhuà	32
硅谷	Guīgǔ	33
硅片	guīpiàn	33
轨迹	guǐjī	33
国际消费者联盟组织	Guójì xiāofèizhě Liánméng Zǔzhī	27
国情咨文	guóqíng zīwén	27
过度	guòdù	29

H

海淀	Hǎidiàn	33

海阔凭鱼跃， 天高任鸟飞	hǎi kuò píng yú yuè, tiān gāo rèn niǎo fēi	21
涵盖	hángài	23
航空	hángkōng	22
航天	hángtiān	22
豪华	háohuá	26
好样儿的	hǎoyàngrde	31
何乐而不为	hé lè ér bù wéi	25
和平	hépíng	34
荷兰	Hélán	30
核查	héchá	22
核电站	hédiànzhàn	24
核销	héxiāo	25
恒河	Héng Hé	35
恒生指数	Héngshēng Zhǐshù	30
横幅	héngfú	27
衡量	héngliáng	35
红利	hónglì	30
宏观	hóngguān	28
宏伟	hóngwěi	28
后盾	hòudùn	26
后劲	hòujìn	37
后来者	hòuláizhě	39
沪指(上海 证券交易 所指数)	Hùzhǐ(Shànghǎi Zhèngquàn Jiāoyì- suǒ Zhǐshù)	30
花旗银行	Huāqí Yínháng	28
华尔街	Huá'ěr Jiē	28
滑坡	huápō	37
化解	huàjiě	28
划掉	huàdiào	35
话题	huàtí	23
欢乐	huānlè	28
缓慢	huǎnmàn	37

荒谬	huāngmiù	35
荒漠化	huāngmòhuà	32
荒山	huāngshān	36
荒唐	huāngtáng	35
黄金	huángjīn	28
辉煌	huīhuáng	21
回避	huíbì	35
回归	huíguī	32
回收	huíshōu	22
毁	huǐ	36
活力	huólì	30
火灾	huǒzāi	31
获悉	huòxī	27
获准	huòzhǔn	23

J

饥不择食	jī bù zé shí	31
机顶盒	jīdǐnghé	33
机动车	jīdòngchē	32
机械化	jīxièhuà	36
机制	jīzhì	25
积压	jīyā	37
基地	jīdì	25
基金	jījīn	30
基因	jīyīn	36
跻身	jīshēn	23
稽查	jīchá	25
激动	jīdòng	30
激光	jīguāng	33
激活	jīhuó	28
激励	jīlì	26
亟待	jídài	24
急剧	jíjù	29
棘手	jíshǒu	22

集成电路	jíchéng-diànlù	33	角度	jiǎodù	30
集约化	jíyuēhuà	36	较量	jiàoliàng	40
挤占	jǐzhàn	26	较真	jiàozhēn	27
济济一堂	jǐjǐ yì táng	24	阶层	jiēcéng	31
给付	jǐfù	31	接轨	jiēguǐ	30
记忆犹新	jìyì yóu xīn	29	接收	jiēshōu	33
记载	jìzǎi	40	街头巷尾	jiē tóu xiàng wěi	31
技师	jìshī	39	节制	jiézhì	32
迹象	jìxiàng	40	结构	jiégòu	22
加工	jiāgōng	25	结束	jiéshù	22
加州（加利福利亚州）	Jiā Zhōu（Jiālìfúlìyà Zhōu）	36	结算	jiésuàn	23
			结转	jiézhuǎn	25
家乐福	Jiālèfú	26	捷足先登	jié zú xiān dēng	39
家园	jiāyuán	32	截至	jiézhì	35
家族	jiāzú	37	解放	jiěfàng	37
价位	jiàwèi	26	解雇	jiěgù	38
价值连城	jiàzhí lián chéng	30	解禁	jiějìn	26
驾驭	jiàyù	29	介入	jièrù	24
尖端	jiānduān	33	界限	jièxiàn	31
尖锐	jiānruì	37	借鉴	jièjiàn	29
坚定不移	jiāndìng bù yí	37	禁不住	jīnbuzhù	28
坚决	jiānjué	24	紧密	jǐnmì	40
坚实	jiānshí	34	谨慎	jǐnshèn	29
坚挺	jiāntǐng	29	尽如人意	jìn rú rényì	38
艰巨	jiānjù	22	进军	jìnjūn	32
艰难	jiānnán	31	禁区	jìnqū	26
监理	jiānlǐ	24	经济特区	jīngjì tèqū	21
兼并（并）	jiānbìng（bìng）	40	经受	jīngshòu	37
简要	jiǎnyào	22	精耕细作	jīng gēng xì zuò	36
建材	jiàncái	22	精巧	jīngqiǎo	30
建设	jiànshè	26	景象	jǐngxiàng	33
建筑	jiànzhù	23	竞标	jìngbiāo	24
江山	jiāngshān	25	敬业	jìngyè	24
交割	jiāogē	30	敬意	jìngyì	33

境外	jìngwài	38	科龙	kēlóng	37
旧金山	Jiùjīnshān	33	可喜	kěxǐ	24
就地取材	jiùdì qǔcái	37	可笑	kěxiào	39
就业	jiùyè	25	肯定	kěndìng	33
居高不下	jū gāo bú xià	27	肯尼迪	Kěnnídí	27
局限	júxiàn	36	空间	kōngjiān	37
举措	jǔcuò	21	空头	kōngtóu	30
举世公认	jǔshì gōngrèn	34	空白	kòngbái	23
举世瞩目	jǔshì zhǔmù	24	空子	kōngzi	25
举债	jǔzhài	29	控告	kònggào	27
举足轻重	jǔ zú qīng zhòng	36	口号	kǒuhào	34
俱乐部	jùlèbù	30	口香糖	kǒuxiāngtáng	33
剧烈	jùliè	29	夸大	kuādà	35
距离	jùlí	36	夸海口	kuā hǎikǒu	31
聚集	jùjí	31	垮	kuǎ	35
觉悟	juéwù	36	会计	kuàijì	23
觉醒	juéxǐng	32	宽敞	kuānchang	26
绝境	juéjìng	29	宽恕	kuānshù	38
崛起	juéqǐ	33	矿山	kuàngshān	38
			亏损	kūisǔn	37
K			匮乏	kuìfá	31
开辟	kāipì	39	**L**		
开采	kāicǎi	32			
开创	kāichuàng	37	垃圾股	lājī gǔ	30
开荒	kāihuāng	36	拉萨	Lāsà	39
开架	kāijià	26	赖以	làiyǐ	40
开盘	kāipán	30	蓝图	lántú	21
凯恩斯	Kǎi'ēnsī	30	缆线	lǎnxiàn	33
砍伐	kǎnfá	32	滥	làn	32
抗	kàng	37	浪潮	làngcháo	32
抗衡	kànghéng	26	劳务	láowù	23
考察	kǎochá	38	老鼠	lǎoshǔ	31
考验	kǎoyàn	37	乐得	lèdé	24
苛求	kēqiú	38	乐而忘返	lè ér wàng fǎn	33

雷同	léitóng	37	掠夺	lüèduó	32
类型	lèixíng	26	落得	luòde	31
犁	lí	36			
理睬	lǐcǎi	27	**M**		
理论	lǐlùn	30	马来西亚	Mǎláixīyà	35
理所当然	lǐ suǒ dāng rán	35	骂名	màmíng	31
力度	lìdù	27	埋伏	máifú	31
立案	lì'àn	35	迈开	màikāi	23
立场	lìchǎng	34	麦德龙	Màidélóng	26
立法	lìfǎ	29	脉搏	màibó	28
立足点	lìzúdiǎn	37	满仓	mǎncāng	30
利弊	lìbì	31	盲从	mángcóng	30
联结	liánjié	40	盲目	mángmù	30
联盟	liánméng	40	冒昧	màomèi	26
联想集团	Liánxiǎng Jítuán	33	冒险	màoxiǎn	30
链条	liàntiáo	36	贸然	màorán	26
两翼	liǎngyì	40	媒介	méijiè	40
亮丽	liànglì	28	媒体	méitǐ	27
辽阔	liáokuò	24	煤气	méiqì	27
列为	lièwéi	23	美国数字	Měiguó Shùzì	
吝惜	lìnxī	29	设备公司	Shèbèi Gōngsī	38
零部件	língbùjiàn	25	美国友邦	Měiguó Yǒubāng	
领先	lǐngxiān	33	保险有限	Bǎoxiǎn Yǒuxiàn	
领域	lǐngyù	21	公司	Gōngsī	31
溜之大吉	liū zhī dà jí	30	门道	méndao	26
流量	liúliàng	29	门槛	ménkǎn	31
流失	liúshī	32	秘诀	mìjué	30
流速	liúsù	29	秘密	mìmì	34
流通	liútōng	36	密集	mìjí	22
龙头	lóngtóu	33	勉强	miǎnqiǎng	37
漏税	lòushuì	25	面临	miànlín	30
陆续	lùxù	28	面貌	miànmào	40
屡禁不止	lǚ jìn bù zhǐ	38	民事	mínshì	34
乱套	luàntào	25	民营	mínyíng	38

敏锐	mǐnruì	36		排除	páichú	35
名副其实	míng fù qí shí	21		排放	páifàng	32
明代	Míngdài	28		徘徊	páihuái	37
命运	mìngyùn	40		派遣	pàiqiǎn	24
模块	mókuài	33		攀升	pānshēng	23
摩擦	mócā	34		庞大	pángdà	29
陌生	mòshēng	38		抛售	pāoshòu	30
谋求	móuqiú	40		培训	péixùn	22
目标	mùbiāo	40		培育	péiyù	29
				赔付	péi fù	31
N				配置	pèizhì	30
				蓬勃	péngbó	32
耐克公司	Nàikè Gōngsī	25		膨胀	péngzhàng	28
内陆	nèilù	21		批准	pī zhǔn	26
内销	nèixiāo	25		披露	pīlù	30
内行	nèiháng	26		偏	piān	27
内需	nèixū	26		偏见	piānjiàn	39
能耗	nénghào	25		偏远	piānyuǎn	38
能量	néngliàng	29		篇章	piānzhāng	37
能手	néngshǒu	36		拼搏	pīnbó	30
逆差	nìchā	23		频繁	pínfán	36
逆转	nìzhuǎn	40		频频	pínpín	29
鸟笼	niǎolóng	32		聘用	pìnyòng	24
牛鼻子	niúbízi	40		平常	píngcháng	27
牛气	niúqi	30		平衡	pínghéng	23
牛市	niúshì	30		平台	píngtái	33
扭曲	niǔqū	35		迫近	pòjìn	32
农田	nóngtián	36		浦东	Pǔ Dōng	39
农作物	nóngzuòwù	37				
				Q		
O						
				期待	qīdài	22
欧元	ōuyuán	29		期货	qīhuò	28
				期权	qīquán	30
P				齐全	qíquán	28
拍卖	pāimài	39				

岐视	qíshì	35	取证	qǔzhèng	27
岂	qǐ	25	权威	quánwēi	27
起步	qǐbù	23	权益	quányì	27
起锚	qǐmáo	31	缺乏	quēfá	27
恰恰	qiàqià	35	确定	quèdìng	35
千家万户	qiān jiā wàn hù	31	群体	qúntǐ	26
牵	qiān	40	群雄争霸	qúnxióng zhēng bà	39
谦虚	qiānxū	23			
前列	qiánliè	31	**R**		
前所未有	qián suǒ wèi yǒu	29	燃气热水器	ránqì rèshuǐqì	27
前途	qiántú	24	扰乱	rǎoluàn	31
潜力	qiánlì	22	人才济济	réncái jǐjǐ	33
强化	qiánghuà	25	人格	réngé	27
强加	qiángjiā	34	人类	rénlèi	29
强劲	qiángjìng	29	人身	rénshēn	27
抢滩登陆	qiǎngtān dēnglù	39	人士	rénshì	24
敲锣打鼓	qiāo luó dǎ gǔ	27	人为	rénwéi	35
切分	qiēfēn	26	忍气吞声	rěn qì tūn shēng	27
切实	qièshí	38	认定	rèndìng	32
钦佩	qīnpèi	27	认证	rènzhèng	32
亲密	qīnmì	22	任意	rènyì	35
青春	qīngchūn	37	日本三洋	Rìběn Sānyáng	
青睐	qīnglài	34	电器	Diànqì	38
倾销	qīngxiāo	35	日趋	rìqū	32
倾斜	qīngxié	24	日新月异	rì xīn yuè yì	23
清代	Qīngdài	28	融资	róngzī	28
情报	qíngbào	22	软件	ruǎnjiàn	22
情绪	qíngxù	32	瑞士	Ruìshì	34
情有独钟	qíng yǒu dú zhōng	25			
穷光蛋	qióngguāngdàn	30	**S**		
秋千	qiūqiān	32	森林	sēnlín	32
趋同	qūtóng	37	杀菌	shājūn	32
取长补短	qǔ cháng bǔ duǎn	21	擅自	shànzì	25
取缔	qǔdì	24	伤残	shāngcán	31

《商标国际注册马德里协定》	Shāngbiāo Guójì Zhùcè Mǎdélǐ Xiédìng	34
上马	shàngmǎ	24
设计	shèjì	22
设施	shèshī	28
设想	shèxiǎng	23
设置	shèzhì	26
涉外	shèwài	38
申诉	shēnsù	35
伸缩	shēnsuō	35
深指(深圳证券交易所指数)	Shēnzhǐ(Shēnzhèn Zhèngquàn Jiāoyìsuǒ Zhǐshù)	30
深信不疑	shēn xìn bù yí	29
审理	shěnlǐ	34
审判庭	shěnpàn tíng	34
审批	shěnpī	26
升格	shēnggé	28
升极	shēngjí	23
升温	shēngwēn	31
生存	shēngcún	32
生态	shēngtài	32
生物	shēngwù	37
省会	shěnghuì	21
圣地	shèngdì	33
圣克拉拉谷	Shèngkèlālā Gǔ	33
胜诉	shèngsù	34
剩余	shèngyú	37
失控	shīkòng	25
失业	shīyè	31
诗人	shīrén	32
施工	shīgōng	24
实力	shílì	30
实体	shítǐ	22
实业	shíyè	33
拾遗补缺	shí yí bǔ quē	37
《世界版权日内瓦公约》	Shìjiè Bǎnquán Rìnèiwǎ Gōngyuē	34
世贸组织(世界贸易组织)	Shìmào Zǔzhī (Shìjiè Màoyì Zǔzhī)	23
市场准入	shìchǎng zhǔn rù	23
势必	shìbì	40
事务	shìwù	21
事物	shìwù	37
试验	shìyàn	39
适度	shìdù	29
誓不罢休	shì bù bà xiū	27
收购(购)	Shōugòu(gòu)	40
收集	shōují	23
收缴	shōujiǎo	34
收盘	shōupán	30
首屈一指	shǒu qū yì zhǐ	39
寿	shòu	31
受益匪浅	shòuyì fěi qiǎn	24
受益人	shòuyìrén	31
熟练	shúliàn	24
束缚	shùfù	21
衰退	shuāituì	21
甩	shuǎi	39
率先	shuàixiān	39
双向	shuāngxiàng	21
水稻	shuǐdào	22
水库	shuǐkù	24
水利	shuǐlì	24
水泥	shuǐní	22
水灾	shuǐzāi	31

水准	shuǐzhǔn	39	调节	tiáojié	28
顺应	shùnyìng	36	调试	tiáoshì	22
说法	shuōfǎ	27	挑战	tiǎozhàn	23
司法	sīfǎ	34	挑子	tiāozi	31
司空见惯	sīkōng jiàn guàn	40	条例	tiáolì	38
私营	sīyíng	38	贴近	tiējìn	40
肆意	sìyì	32	停止	tíngzhǐ	34
搜身	sōushēn	27	通货	tōnghuò	28
素质	sùzhì	24	通用汽车	Tōngyòng Qìchē	
塑料	sùliào	32	公司	Gōngsī	40
随心所欲	suí xīn suǒ yù	35	同义语	tóngyìyǔ	37
随意性	suíyìxìng	22	偷税	tōushuì	25
随着	suízhe	31	投保人	tóubǎorén	31
缩小	suōxiǎo	23	投标	tóubiāo	24
所得税	suǒdéshuì	38	投机	tóujī	29
所有	suǒyǒu	28	透明度	tòumíngdù	23
			突破	tūpò	33
T			推车	tuīchē	26
			推动	tuīdòng	32
台账	táizhàng	25	推广	tuīguǎng	39
态势	tàishì	28	推进	tuījìn	28
贪（图）	tān(tú)	27	推算	tuīsuàn	35
摊派	tānpài	38	托辞	tuōcí	27
昙花一现	tánhuā yí xiàn	37	托福	tuōfú	36
弹性	tánxìng	35	脱离	tuōlí	35
探索	tànsuǒ	39	妥善	tuǒshàn	27
探讨	tàntǎo	22			
套牢	tàoláo	30	**W**		
套现	tàoxiàn	31			
特征	tèzhēng	34	外向型	wàixiàngxíng	37
体系	tǐxì	31	外销	wàixiāo	25
体制	tǐzhì	35	外行	wàiháng	26
剃头	tìtóu	31	完整	wánzhěng	35
天赐良机	tiān cì liángjī	37	玩儿命	wánrmìng	30
天方夜谭	Tiānfāng yè tán	33	玩意儿	wányìr	33

挽回	wǎnhuí	27
晚会	wǎnhuì	27
万宝路	Wànbǎolù	34
万客隆	Wànkèlóng	26
旺盛	wàngshèng	26
威胁	wēixié	24
微电子	wēidiànzǐ	33
违背	wéibèi	25
违反	wéifǎn	31
围湖造田	wéi hú zào tián	36
唯独	wéidú	33
唯利是图	wéi lì shì tú	38
尾气	wěiqì	32
委靡不振	wěimí bú zhèn	33
卫星	wèixīng	23
未来	wèilái	21
温饱	wēnbǎo	36
闻名遐迩	wénmíng xiá'ěr	39
稳健	wěnjiàn	28
稳妥	wěntuǒ	28
问世	wènshì	33
窝囊气	wōnangqì	27
沃尔玛	Wò'ěrmǎ	26
乌拉圭回合	Wūlāguī Huíhé	35
乌鲁木齐	Wūlǔmùqí	39
污染	wūrǎn	32
污水	wūshuǐ	32
无情	wúqíng	37
无视	wúshì	35
无所作为	wú suǒ zuòwéi	29
无限	wúxiàn	29
无形	wúxíng	34
无休无止	wú xiū wú zhǐ	38
无庸讳言	wúyōng huìyán	35
梧桐	wútóng	39
武断	wǔduàn	35
武器	wǔqì	27
物质	wùzhì	38
物资	wùzī	32
误导	wùdǎo	31

X

吸纳	xīnà	29
吸收	xīshōu	26
稀里糊涂	xīlihútú	31
稀有	xīyǒu	39
席卷	xíjuǎn	32
洗钱	xǐqián	31
喜怒哀乐	xǐ nù āi lè	30
狭隘	xiá'ài	40
狭小	xiáxiǎo	37
下降	xiàjiàng	24
下探	xià tàn	30
先机	xiānjī	33
先期	xiānqī	22
鲜明	xiānmíng	34
闲散	xiánsǎn	37
嫌	xián	30
现实	xiànshí	34
现状	xiànzhuàng	21
限度	xiàndù	25
陷入	xiànrù	29
美慕不已	xiànmù bùyǐ	21
乡	xiāng	36
相称	xiāngchèn	21
相关	xiāngguān	35
相继	xiāngjì	39
相中	xiāngzhòng	28

向导	xiàngdǎo	33
削额	xuē é	31
削弱	xuēruò	25
消除	xiāochú	22
消毒	xiāodú	32
销毁	xiāohuǐ	34
小打小闹	xiǎo dǎ xiǎo nào	37
小康	xiǎokāng	36
效法	xiàofǎ	25
效率	xiàolǜ	23
协调	xiétiáo	34
邪	xié	30
携带	xiédài	33
心惊胆战	xīn jīng dǎn zhàn	30
新奇	xīnqí	33
新闻	xīnwén	27
新兴	xīnxīng	33
兴衰	xīngshuāi	37
兴许	xīngxǔ	28
行政	xíngzhèng	34
形式主义	xíngshì zhǔyì	38
形态	xíngtài	26
杏仁	xìngrén	36
性急	xìngjí	28
雄辩	xióngbiàn	34
熊市	xióngshì	30
熊样儿	xióng yàngr	30
休闲	xiūxián	39
许可证	xǔkězhèng	22
许诺	xǔnuò	31
宣判	xuānpàn	34
悬而未决	xuán ér wèi jué	27
学府	xuéfǔ	33
学科	xuékē	32

雪崩	xuěbēng	30
血缘	xuèyuán	37
寻求	xúnqiú	27
巡礼	xúnlǐ	28
循序渐进	xúnxù jiànjìn	23
迅猛	xùnměng	32

Y

亚太经济 合作组织	Yà-Tài Jīngjì Hézuò Zǔzhī	40
严厉	yánlì	25
言过其实	yán guò qí shí	33
沿边（境）	yán biān(jìng)	21
沿海	yánhǎi	21
沿江	yánjiāng	21
衍生	yǎnshēng	29
洋葱头	yángcōngtóu	30
养老	yǎnglǎo	31
要素	yàosù	40
耀眼	yàoyǎn	32
也罢	yěbà	39
野生	yěshēng	32
野味	yěwèi	32
业绩	yèjì	34
业态	yètài	26
业种	yèzhǒng	26
一举两得	yì jǔ liǎng dé	36
一揽子	yìlǎnzi	40
一荣俱荣， 一损俱损	yì róng jù róng, yì sǔn jù sǔn	37
一如既往	yì rú jì wǎng	38
一条龙	yìtiáolóng	36
一望无际	yí wàng wú jì	36
一味	yíwèi	30

一言难尽	yì yán nán jìn	31	拥护	yōnghù	25
一知半解	yì zhī bàn jiě	38	拥有	yōngyǒu	22
依靠	yīkào	23	涌现	yǒngxiàn	36
依托	yītuō	39	用武之地	yòngwǔ zhī dì	24
仪表	yíbiǎo	32	优化	yōuhuà	30
仪器	yíqì	32	优秀	yōuxiù	24
移动	yídòng	33	游览	yóulǎn	39
遗传	yíchuán	36	游戏	yóuxì	29
疑虑	yílǜ	21	有待	yǒudài	31
异常	yìcháng	29	有利可图	yǒu lì kě tú	38
异军突起	yì jūn tū qǐ	37	有目共睹	yǒu mù gòng dǔ	34
意味着	yìwèizhe	21	有缘	yǒuyuán	28
意愿	yìyuàn	22	诱骗	yòupiàn	31
意志	yìzhì	34	于是	yúshì	39
因故	yīngù	25	《与贸易有关	Yǔ Màoyì Yǒuguān	
因果	yīnguǒ	35	的知识产权	de Zhīshi Chǎnquán	
银号	yínhào	28	协定》	Xiédìng	34
引导	yǐndǎo	21	郁金香	yùjīnxiāng	30
引进	yǐnjìn	21	预料	yùliào	33
引力	yǐnlì	30	预言	yùyán	40
引擎	yǐnqíng	23	预言家	yùyánjiā	30
引人瞩目	yǐn rén zhǔmù	32	预约	yùyuē	26
隐患	yǐnhuàn	24	元件	yuánjiàn	25
印证	yìnzhèng	40	原告	yuángào	34
应诉	yìngsù	35	原始	yuánshǐ	36
应用	yìngyòng	32	源源不断	yuányuán bú duàn	29
应运而生	yìng yùn ér shēng	37	愿闻其详	yuàn wén qí xiáng	23
英雄	yīngxióng	27	云雀	yúnquè	32
迎接	yíngjiē	21	运转	yùnzhuǎn	29
盈余	yíngyú	28			
营造	yíngzào	25	**Z**		
硬功夫	yìng gōngfu	38			
硬件	yìngjiàn	22	杂货	záhuò	26
硬通货	yìngtōnghuò	29	杂交	zájiāo	22
			灾难	zāinàn	29

再生产	zàishēngchǎn	38	制止	zhìzhǐ	34
在意	zàiyì	35	治理	zhìlǐ	32
暂时	zànshí	40	致富	zhìfù	28
赞不绝口	zàn bù jué kǒu	26	致命一击	zhìmìng yì jī	30
赞誉	zànyù	28	秩序	zhìxù	25
遭	zāo	35	智慧	zhìhuì	22
噪音	zàoyīn	32	智力	zhìlì	33
增值	zēngzhí	40	智能	zhìnéng	24
债券	zhàiquàn	30	中关村	zhōngguāncūn	33
崭新	zhǎnxīn	23	中国科学院	Zhōngguó Kēxuéyuàn	33
占据	zhànjù	24			
障碍	zhàng'ài	35	中国证券	Zhōngguó Zhèngquàn	
招标	zhāobiāo	24	监督管理	Jiāndū Guǎnlǐ	
招揽	zhāolǎn	31	委员会	Wěiyuánhuì	30
朝阳	zhāoyáng	32	中介	zhōngjiè	28
召唤	zhàohuàn	40	中经指数	Zhōngjīng Zhǐshù	
照排	zhàopái	33	(中国《经济	(Zhōngguó《Jīngjì	
真相	zhēnxiàng	35	日报》指数)	Rìbào》Zhǐshù)	30
振兴	zhènxīng	32	忠告	zhōnggào	30
震荡	zhèndàng	29	终极	zhōngjí	38
镇	zhèn	36	终究	zhōngjiū	35
正当	zhèngdàng	24	中毒	zhòngdú	27
正视	zhèngshì	35	种植	zhòngzhí	36
证券	zhèngquàn	28	重心	zhòngxīn	24
支撑	zhīchēng	33	周边	zhōubiān	32
支柱	zhīzhù	23	骤	zhòu	37
执法	zhífǎ	27	逐步	zhúbù	22
指导	zhǐdǎo	24	主导	zhǔdǎo	29
指控	zhǐkòng	35	主题	zhǔtí	27
指数	zhǐshù	30	主宰	zhǔzǎi	37
至上	zhìshàng	23	助理	zhùlǐ	38
制裁	zhìcái	34	注入	zhùrù	28
制定	zhìdìng	23	著作	zhùzuò	34
制冷	zhìlěng	32	抓住	zhuāzhù	23

专业户	zhuānyèhù	27	自然人	zìránrén	30
转包	zhuǎnbāo	24	自信心	zìxìnxīn	29
转变	zhuǎnbiàn	21	自行	zìxíng	26
转产	zhuǎnchǎn	37	自由港	zìyóugǎng	39
转让	zhuǎnràng	22	自由化	zìyóuhuà	23
转型	zhuǎnxíng	35	总部	zǒngbù	38
庄家	zhuāngjiā	30	走马观花	zǒu mǎ guān huā	38
庄园	zhuāngyuán	36	走势	zǒushì	30
装配	zhuāngpèi	25	走私	zǒusī	25
装置	zhuāngzhì	33	租赁	zūlìn	26
壮观	zhuàngguān	28	阻碍	zǔ'ài	21
追加	zhuījiā	23	阻挡	zǔdǎng	40
追求	zhuīqiú	36	祖宗	zǔzong	36
追溯	zhuīsù	25	钻	zuān	25
姿态	zītài	21	尊严	zūnyán	27
姿深	zīshēn	31	作坊	zuōfang	37
自给自足	zìjǐ zìzú	36	左右逢源	zuǒ yòu féng yuán	37
自豪	zìháo	28	作为	zuòwéi	39
自律	zìlǜ	29			